Feuding Friends

European University Studies
Europäische Hochschulschriften
Publications Universitaires Européennes

Series XXXI
Political Science

Reihe XXXI Série XXXI
Politikwissenschaft
Sciences politiques

Vol./Bd. 496

PETER LANG
Frankfurt am Main · Berlin · Bern · Bruxelles · New York · Oxford · Wien

Eric Frey

Feuding Friends

U.S.-European Trade Relations in the Clinton Era 1992–2000

PETER LANG
Europäischer Verlag der Wissenschaften

Bibliographic Information published by Die Deutsche Bibliothek
Die Deutsche Bibliothek lists this publication in the Deutsche Nationalbibliografie; detailed bibliographic data is available in the internet at <http://dnb.ddb.de>.

Gedruckt mit Unterstützung des Bundesministeriums
für Bildung, Wissenschaft und Kultur in Wien.

ISSN 0721-3654
ISBN 3-631-51817-X
US-ISBN 0-8204-6527-5

www.peterlang.de

TABLE OF CONTENTS

INTRODUCTION

Transatlantic trade conflicts are older than the United States: British trade policy toward the 13 colonies was one of the main triggers of the American revolution of 1776. For the next 150 years, U.S.-European trade relations were dominated by high tariffs, conflicts and sometimes even military campaigns, such as in the War of 1812. Since World War II, the picture has changed: The U.S. and the European nations cooperated closely to create a multilateral trade regime under the General Agreement of Tariffs and Trade (GATT). Between 1945 and 1995, GATT members cut and sometimes even eliminated tariffs, reduced non-tariff trade barriers and facilitated in other ways the exchange of goods and services. The result was an explosive growth in transatlantic trade that became a pillar of post-war prosperity. In the 1970s, a general slowdown in growth caused an increase in protectionist pressures, particularly in the U.S., and both sides began to show growing irritations about the trade policies and practices across the Atlantic. The proliferation of regional trade agreements (RTAs) in the 1980s and 1990s, such as the European trading privileges for some developing countries and the North American Free Trade Agreement (NAFTA), also raised concern about a fraying of the multilateral trade system. Still, seven years of frequently tortuous negotiations culminated in the Uruguay Round Agreement of 1994, the most ambitious trade agreement to date. It established the World Trade Organization that provided the international trading system with a firm legal and institutional framework.

The launch of the WTO in 1995 was expected to herald a new era of more consensual trade relations. Instead, the Clinton administration and the European Commission under presidents Jacques Santer and Romano Prodi became entangled in a series of increasingly bitter trade disputes, ranging from U.S. secondary sanctions over Cuba and Iran to bananas, hormone-treated beef, aircraft, export subsidies and steel. As economic interests replaced security as the main glue in transatlantic relations in the post-Cold War era, trade increasingly became a drag on the partnership. The WTO was not used as an impartial arbitrator, but rather as a battleground and sometimes even as a weapon against the other side. International newspapers wrote about potential and real "trade wars", while U.S. and EU leaders approached their semi-annual summits with a long list of complaints. The peak of acrimony was the WTO conference in Seattle, where the breakdown in transatlantic cooperation was a key factor for the failure of the summit. Relations improved early in the administration of President George W. Bush, but his decision in 2002 to impose high tariffs on steel imports from the EU put the transatlantic partners once again on a collision course.

Is the increase in trade conflicts fortuitous, or is it proof of a larger trend in the transatlantic relationship? Has the disappearance of the Soviet threat eliminated the overriding common interest of self-defense between the U.S. and the Europeans allowing special interest groups on both sides to dominate the agenda? Are larger economic trends and a growing concern for non-economic issues such as the environment, labor standards and food safety in industrialized countries detrimental to free trade? Are the anti-globalization protesters, who dominate the headlines at international meetings since the Seattle summit, right that trade liberalization has gone too far? Or are the various disputes just minor irritants in an overwhelmingly friendly and cooperative relationship?

In this study, I will explain the trends in transatlantic trade relations since the early 1990s by showing the interplay between economic interest, domestic politics and international security in the transatlantic relationship during the Clinton administration. I will first present different models for explaining trade policy, followed by a look at the history and the policy-process of transatlantic trade, and conclude with my own model for the dynamics of transatlantic trade.

I will argue that trade conflicts are rarely driven by national economic interest, but usually by domestic political pressures. Because of their limited nature, the conflicts can be resolved through the overriding interest of both U.S. European leaders to keep the transatlantic partnership in the political, security and economic sphere alive. Whether trade issues result in cooperation, evolve into controlled conflicts or escalate into trade wars depends on the nature of the issue and the interaction between domestic and international decision-making processes. Surprisingly, there is an inverse relationship between the importance and breadth of a trade issue and the intensity of conflict: Major issues with significant economic and political interest are relatively quickly resolved, while small issues tend to result in bitter and prolonged confrontations.

The reasons lie in the nature of the transatlantic partnership. Long-standing political allies like the U.S. and the EU enjoy a predominantly cooperative relationship with a wide range of mutual interests. However, there exist a certain number of conflicting interests and positions of which both sides feel strongly. When disputes erupt, the two sides are caught in a typical prisoner's dilemma: While both sides might have an overarching interest to settle the dispute, the dynamics of the conflict may call for a fight even though it damages the interests of both sides. The pursuit of trade conflicts – often regardless of their actual significance – often becomes a winning domestic strategy, while premature concessions can cause a government to lose political capital or even the next election. The more a conflict escalates, the stronger the interest grows on both sides to achieve a favorable, even victorious outcome.

In narrow issues, the international cost of escalation is deemed to be lower, though the political cost of such a conflict may eventually rise high enough to force the leadership on both sides to intervene and reach a face-saving compromise. Just as the long-term stability of a marriage relies on the ability of the partners to work out their problems, the main determinant for the transatlantic trade relationship is the efficiency of the transatlantic damage-control mechanisms.

In chapters 3-5, I apply these two hypotheses – the inverse relationship between breadth of an issue and intensity of conflict, and the key role of damage-control mechanisms – to the transatlantic trade relationship in the Clinton era. These hypotheses will help to explain why the U.S. and the EU went all the way in a trade war on bananas and beef, found it so difficult to resolve the conflict over trade with such marginal trading partners as Cuba, Iran and Libya, and yet were still able to reach agreements in key strategic areas such as telecommunications and financial services. I will show that damage-control mechanisms set in quickly when big issues were involved, while small issues were allowed to smolder and escalate. The interplay between domestic benefits and international costs also casts a different light on the role of the WTO and its dispute-settlement body. By clarifying the rules of trade disputes, they limit the risks of pursuing these conflicts and actually create incentives for escalation.

Chapter 6 will deal with the reasons for the collapse of the Seattle conference in December 1999 and the subsequent more successful launch of the Doha Round in 2001. In chapter 7, I will draw some conclusions for the future of transatlantic trade relations from the domestic, international and institutional arenas.

As U.S. and EU leaders found out, the cost of escalation can never be precisely calculated. There is an atmospheric and emotional side to relationships, both personal and political, that can be affected by parochial disputes. As the trade fights of the 1990s turned out to be costlier than originally thought, controlling these disputes became one more challenge of transatlantic policy for the Bush administration. My conclusions are generally optimistic. Given the enormous stakes of the industrialized countries in smooth trade relations and further trade liberalizations, self-correcting mechanisms to keep disputes from running out of control exist. Whether these mechanisms succeed, however, depends primarily on the leadership skills in Washington and Brussels.

CHAPTER 1: FOUNDATIONS - THEORY, HISTORY AND POLICY PROCESS

1.1. Theories of Foreign Trade

There are few areas of public policy that can be subjected to such a wide range of explanatory theories and models as foreign trade relations. Trade is a key element of international relations as a consequence of a domestic policy process. While it is a profoundly economic activity, and therefore one of the core areas of economic theory, it is also the result of the political process and a subject for political scientists. Finally, the actual making of trade policy also provides ample material for studies in organizational behavior. All these faculties and approaches offer partial explanations of the decision-making in the area of foreign trade. None of them can by themselves offer a comprehensive explanatory model, keeping trade policy and trade relations unpredictable and inherently unstable.

There are several different ways to classify theories of trade policy:

- Economic and political models
- Liberal and nationalist (mercantilist) theories, applied both to trade theory and international relations[1]
- International-system theory, domestic politics, institutional theory, market perspective (economic and political markets)[2]

Because of the diversity of writing on trade policy, none of these classifications cover all approaches. The upcoming section will group the current literature in following ways: economics, international relations, domestic politics and finally the relatively young but expanding school of domestic-international studies.

1.1.1 The Economics Perspective

Since the dawn of time, the exchange of goods and services across political borders has been one of the driving forces of economic development. Private traders made a living from overcoming physical and political trade barriers, and were handsomely rewarded by consumers buying their goods at premium. The state, however, often took a different view on trade. In the 18th century, the theory of mercantilism did not regard the maximization of trade volume, but rather the maximization of exports and the maintenance of a trade surplus as the main goal of trade policy. The objective of trade was an accumulation of foreign reserves, i.e. gold, that was regarded as a boost to state power. A trade

---

[1] Gilpin 1987, pp. 172-183.

[2] Gibson 2000, p. 11-20.

surplus by one country automatically meant that another country must have a trade deficit. Mercantilism therefore resulted in trade policies based on rivalry and mutually exclusive benefits – trade as a zero-sum game.[3]

Adam Smith and David Ricardo, the two fathers of modern economics, bridged the gap between the private and state perspectives on trade. While Adam Smith described the advantages of trade in terms of absolute advantage (a country will export a product if it can produce it more efficiently than another country), while Ricardo made the compelling but counter-intuitive argument that countries will benefit from trade even if one is more efficient in every category. By importing those goods where the absolute advantage is smallest, the superior country is permitted to use an even larger share of its resources for its best product. The same hierarchical division of labor is used in hospitals, where doctors leave measuring blood pressure to nurses even if they can do it better. Their time is too valuable for such simple tasks.

Ever since Ricardo developed his theory of comparative advantage in the early 19th century, the benefits of free trade have been at the core of most economists' beliefs. From the point of view of a radical free trader, the best trade policy is none at all. In contrast, most of government trade policy, as well as the public perception of trade, is still based on mercantilist thought. Even in international trade agreements, tariffs are still the norm and market access is treated as a special concession to other trading partners.[4] In practice, trade policy is all too often not directed at boosting trade relations, but at restricting them.

Comparative advantage was refined in the 1930s by Eli Heckscher and Bertil Ohlin, who explained its existence in terms of availability of different factors like land, labor or capital. Paul Samuelson and Wolfgang Stolper used the Heckscher-Ohlin theorem to describe the distributional effects of foreign trade: If trade barriers are lowered, the owners of abundant factors will gain while the owners of scarce factors will lose. The uneven gains of trade liberalization call for compensation schemes, where winners will buy off the losers to permit a policy action that is beneficial to all. Most importantly, pure free traders believed that a country would be better off without import barriers, even if its trading partners did not permit the same kind of market access as they themselves allowed. The main advantage of trade is not – as mercantilists would argue - export and job creation, but the opportunity to buy cheaper and better imports. Classic trade theory also assumed that in the long run, current account balances would tend to balance as persistent current accounts deficits are unsustainable and will trigger some adjustment mechanism – devaluation, economic retrenchment or both. Developing countries might run a deficit, but

[3] For a discussion of mercantilism, see Gilpin 2001.
[4] See Krugman 1991 and Charnovitz 2001.

will switch into balance or surplus once a certain level of development is reached. This hypothesis has been thrown into doubt due to the experience of the U.S. since the 1980s, where massive and persistent current account deficits were financed through capital inflows over several decades. Still, the future of the U.S. trade position and its future exchange rates remain highly disputed issues within economics.[5]

The dogma of free trade – that everybody benefits from foreign trade - has been under fire since its start. Building on the views of mercantilists, whole generations of political thinkers, business leaders and economists have argued in favor of protectionist measures. The concept of infant-industry protection, popularized by Alexander Hamilton in the U.S. and advanced by Friedrich List in Germany, turned both the United States and Germany into major industrial powers in the late 19th century that hid behind protectionist walls. After 1945, many Latin American countries adopted policies of import-substitution, while East Asian countries like Japan and South Korea successfully pursued an export-led growth strategy that kept parts of it domestic industries protected behind non-tariff barriers.

The arguments for protectionism seemed to gain new force when a series of highly respected economists began to challenge more the assumption of classic trade theory. They focused on imperfect competition in many markets, the economies of scale and high barriers of entry in many modern industries such as semiconductors and on the possibility to change a country's comparative advantage through the choice of the right policies. Thus, new trade theory, as the school became known, suggested that certain protectionist or at least interventionist measures (usually referred to as "managed trade") could improve a country's overall welfare. Strategic trade theory became increasingly popular in the 1980s and has since developed a growing body of literature presenting examples where countries have turned themselves into market leaders in the most valuable of industries.6 In recent years, experts have focused on the value of retainable industries7 where market leadership is not so easily challenged, and the spillover effects from strategic industries.8 According to the latter model, countries will choose to subsidize a certain industry if it provides positive externalities, such as technological spin-offs, that can both be consumed and internalized, i.e. prevented from flowing out of the country.

[5] See, for example, "Wanted: $2 billion a day," *Economist*, February 14, 2001.
[6] Tyson 1992.
[7] Gomory/Baumol 2000.
[8] Busch 1999.

1.1.2. The International Relations Perspective

The exchange of goods and services is one of the most important aspects of international relations, and trade is a major objective of political and military power. Throughout history, the creation of stable trading regions was a major rational for the creation of empire. Trading powers that lacked the military muscle to defend its ships and stations were hard to sustain. This applies to the Phoenicians as much as to the Venetian and the Dutch empire. However, powerful empires that controlled large territories were often not very interested in foreign trade. By incorporating trade policy into a grand strategy, Britain was the first world power that found the right balance between trading power and military might. For 19th century Britain, the dominance of the sea-lanes was the economic backbone of the empire that in turn helped finance the military expeditions needed to keep free trade flowing.

The connection between free trade and global strategy became even more pronounced in U.S. post-war policy. After seeing how the collapse of free trade contributed to economic misery and political radicalism in the 1930s, the Roosevelt administration made free trade a cornerstone of its new international order. Keeping as much of the world open for trade as possible was one of the reasons for containing the Soviet Union and maintaining its expensive international engagement. Since expanding trade was seen as a key factor for creating growth and prosperity, it also became a weapon in the Cold War. For several decades, the United States made disproportional concessions in trade negotiations and opened its markets to the exports of its allies without insisting on symmetry – all in the name of maintaining a strong Western alliance keeping the Soviet Union at bay.

The collapse of the Soviet Union and the end of the Cold War profoundly altered the international environment. International relations experts, however, strongly differ on the effect of these changes on the international trade regime. Scholars from the Realist school have been far more pessimistic on the prospects of maintaining free trade in the post-Cold-War era than representatives of the liberal school.

Realists that focus on balance of power theory[9] argue that the global economic regime of the post-war era was primarily a result of the Cold War. The need for military protection by the U.S. made European countries also accept American economic leadership, and the U.S. engagement for an open economy was foremost motivated by security concerns. "Since the end of the Cold War, all the political elements that have supported an open global economy have considerably weakened," warned Robert Gilpin, the leading

[9] The best presentation remains Waltz 1979.

Realist among U.S. political economists.[10] According to this view, new international challenges such as the threat of global terrorism will revive the fortunes of economic cooperation and trade liberalization, whereas extended periods of international peace will result in growing economic conflict and protectionism.

A more radical school regards trade policy generally as an extension of foreign policy. Going back to the mercantilist theories of the 17th and 18th century, these thinkers see countries and economic blocks caught in "a global struggle for market share and technological supremacy,"[11] where one country's gain is the other country's loss. Just as countries need to build up alliances to succeed in international politics, trade blocs become essential for economic security. While economic nationalism of this kind is a fringe phenomenon, the idea of "geo-economics" garnered support among some highly respected economists and in the highest circles in the 1990s, including the Clinton administration.[12] A leftist, Marxist variation of this theme is the belief that international trading rules are inherently stacked in favor of the more politically powerful nations. Just as Ricardo's theory of comparative advantage and its application in the 19th century free trade regime served mostly British commercial and political interests,[13] the current rules of GATT and the WTO, (such as the protection of intellectual property) are heavily tilted toward U.S. and European interests.[14]

A different starting point for Realist and liberal theories of trade is the hegemonic stability theory that links the distribution of global power to the rise and decline of free trade.[15] According to hegemonic theory, a dominant power in the international system is needed to establish and maintain an international regime of economic cooperation, including monetary stability and trade. Free trade is seen as a public good that will be underprovided in an anarchical system. Only a hegemon with an overwhelming stake in the global welfare and the means to punish free riders can keep national protectionism at bay. When hegemony fades, as it did with the decline of British power before and World War I, free trade finds itself on the defensive.

Realists and liberals differ, however, on the consequences of a declining hegemony. While realists expect international order to vanish, the liberals focus on the institutions and values that keep international cooperation alive. Regime

---

[10] Gilpin 2000, p. 13.

[11] Ibid., p. 29.

[12] These include Prestowitz 1991, Garten 1992, Thurow 1992. For a good criticism of this literature, see Krugman 1996, pp. 69-84.

[13] Lovett 1999, p.117.

[14] Interview with Dani Rodrik, Professor of Economics, Harvard University, on February 21, 2001 in Vienna.

[15] See for example Kindleberger 1970, Keohane/Nye 1977, and Krasner 1976.

theorists argue the institutions established under hegemony will survive the decline of the hegemon and continue to fulfill their function. [16] Other theorists concentrated on value-based preferences that can maintain both political and economic cooperation, including a free trade regime.[17]

1.1.3 The Domestic Politics Perspective

Trade policy is important for domestic constituencies who try to influence the policy process. Since the seminal work of E.E. Schattschneider on the Smoot-Hawley tariff, political scientists have dissected the way domestic interest groups try to shape trade policy in to serve their own interests.[18] The analysis of interest group influence often tends to explain an increase in protectionism, as small producer cartels (or "distributional coalitions") hijack the policy-process against the interests of the larger public.[19] In other instances, however, it can also provide a framework to explain periods of trade liberalization in which export-oriented industries gain economically and politically the upper hand over import-competing sectors, as seen in Western Europe in the second half of the 19th century and again after 1945.[20] Furthermore, the use of trade sanctions is often better explained as a function of domestic politics than an international grand strategy – the persistence of the boycott against Cuba is a case in point.

Trade policy can also be seen as a function of political leadership. If it is true that domestic interest groups will push for protectionist measures to further their particular interest against the wider national welfare, it requires strong leadership to overcome this form of particularism. A popular president whose party has a majority in Congress should have a better chance to resist calls for trade barriers and push through liberalization than an embattled chief executive facing a hostile Congress.[21]

Trade policy can have an immediate effect on business prospects and employment in clearly defined sectors and economic areas. As such bread-and-butter issues often play a prominent role in democratic elections, the electoral cycle does have an impact on trade negotiations. Accordingly, the year before a U.S. presidential election is usually not conducive for earnest trade negotiations, and a weak chief executive faced with a hostile Congress is often unable to

---

[16] See Keohane 1980, Ruggie 1993 and Connybeare 1987.

[17] Moravcsik 1997.

[18] Schattschneider 1934.

[19] Mancur Olson developed this argument based on the game-theoretical analysis of political action first in his book *The Logic of Collective Action* and applied it to trade policy and other areas of economic policy-making in his later work (Olson 1982).

[20] Charles Kindleberger has dedicated much of his extensive work to the struggle between these economic actors in various stages of history. See, for example, Kindleberger 1975.

[21] Destler 1995.

deliver. In the EU, the room for maneuver of the trade commissioner can depend on the proximity of national elections in major EU countries like Germany or France. Meanwhile, promoting exports and bashing unfair foreign competition are frequently effective in election campaigns. These themes are more likely to be stressed when a government is about to face its electorate or has other reasons to shore up its popularity.

Ideology and party politics also play a role, with sometimes surprising reversals. In the U.S. the traditionally protectionist Republicans became the advocates of free trade, while the free-trade Democrats are today increasingly protectionist. Within both parties, there remains a vocal minority as well as a pragmatic center that will shift its position depending on the issue and political expediency.[22] A representative's position on trade policy depends more on the specific economic interests of his or her constituencies and on the interests of campaign finance donors than on party affiliation. A Republican from a steel-producing region might espouse a free-trade philosophy, and yet still fight for protection from steel imports. In the EU, the fault line on trade policy runs mostly between the more liberal north and the protectionist south. Even so, countries with strong free-trade credentials can be outright protectionist if specific domestic interests are affected.

A more complex approach to explain certain outcomes in trade policy is to combine economic interests of certain sectors and general economic conditions with the dynamics of domestic politics. These models suggest that sectors with a large dependence on exports and international operations will use their political weight to push for trade liberalization, and that a favorable economic environment will help their cause.[23] Economists have tried to establish models linking economic data such as growth and unemployment, exchange rates and trade balances to the choice of trade policy, but have not always succeeded in explaining and predicting the outcome. Countries in economic dire straits are frequently able to resist the demand for protection, while protectionism can be seen on the rise in some countries even in good economic times.[24]

Finally, organizational factors and bureaucratic politics also affect trade policy. Trade is by definition a multi-faceted issue at the dividing line between foreign and domestic policy, in which various players interact: In the U.S., the legislative and the executive branch, a whole range of departments and agencies, and thousands of business lobbies and other special interest groups; in the EU, the Commission and the Council, the member governments and dozens of domestic constituencies in the 15 member countries. While no specific

---

[22] Shoch 2001 provides the latest analysis of the interaction between party politics and trade policy.

[23] Baldwin 1985, Milner 1988.

[24] Schott 1998 makes this argument when analyzing the failure of the Clinton administration to regain fast-track authority in 1997 and 1998.

bureaucratic model of trade policy exists, professional observers are usually aware of these factors.

1.1.4. The Domestic-International Perspective

The past two decades have seen a growth in literature looking at the interplay between domestic and international factors. In his 1988 influential essay, David Putnam coined the term "two-level game" to describe the way domestic constraints affect international bargaining.[25] This idea has been particularly useful to explain foreign trade negotiations in which the negotiating government must take both the international partner and his domestic constituencies into account – and sometimes even the constituencies of the foreign government. Putnam's argument that bigger domestic constraints can actually strengthen the hand in international bargaining seems to be particularly true for trade talks – France would have hardly been as successful in defending the high level of agricultural subsidies without the strength and assertiveness of its farm lobby, highly visible through demonstrations and blockades whenever its interests appear at risk. Subsequent research has also focused on the question how governments in international conflicts can signal their willingness to escalate the dispute by creating for themselves "audience costs" – making public commitments that would be politically expensive to break,[26] and side-payments that buy off domestic opponents to an international deal.[27]

A slightly different approach is that of George Tsebelis with his "Nested Games" originally developed for comparative politics. He takes a game-theoretical look at the cohesion of coalitions and assumes that these coalitions are embedded, or "nested", in a higher-order network, that sometimes makes a seemingly irrational decision look rational.[28] This comparative policy approach also has some value for domestic-international interactions. For example, Martha Gibson applied Tsebelis' theory to U.S. trade policy as a way to explain why legislators who generally support free trade sometimes opted for protectionist policies.[29] Also, governments involved in international trade talks find themselves in multiple roles, or nested games, as they simultaneously have to keep in mind both the chances of subsequent ratification of any deal and its impact on their own electoral prospects.

---

[25] Putnam 1988.

[26] Fearson 1994.

[27] Mayer 1992. For an overview of domestic-international interaction, see Joe D. Hagan, "Domestic Political Explanations in the Analysis of Foreign Policy," in Haney/Hey/Neack 1995, pp. 118-143.

[28] Tsebelis 1990.

[29] Gibson 2000.

1.2. A Short History of U.S.-European Trade Relations 1789-1992

In its first one hundred years, U.S. trade policy strongly focused on Europe.[30] The United States was a marginal player in global trade and exports consisted mostly of agricultural products sold to European markets, while its fledgling industry constantly worried about the overwhelming, mostly British competition. The consequences were massive tensions between agricultural interests in the south and industrial interests in the north, contributing to the Civil War of the 1860s. Due to the victory of the North and driven by the Republican Party, U.S. trade policy became increasingly protectionist. The biggest break in this pattern came under Democratic President Woodrow Wilson, but the tariff reductions of his presidency were soon overwhelmed by the breakdown of international trade in World War I. The war turned the United States into an unchallenged world economic, though the U.S. was not ready to take on any global responsibility. In the inter-war period, a Republican-dominated congress and Republican presidents pushed up tariff rates again, culminating in the record-breaking Smoot-Hawley tariff of 1930. The blatant protectionism of the United States triggered a wave of retaliation and the collapse of the global trade volume, a major factor that turned the recession of 1929 into the Great Depression.

The U.S. underwent the biggest shift in its trade policy President Franklin D. Roosevelt and his Secretary of State Cordell Hull, the most ardent advocate of liberal trade in Washington at the time. The Reciprocal Trade Agreements Act (RTAA) of 1934 gave for the first time the president the power to negotiate reciprocal tariff reductions with various trading partners. As the Roosevelt Administration took advantage of the RTAA, U.S. tariff levels gradually fell in the 1930s. The continued economic and political crises prevented a significant increase in global trade until another world war brought normal commercial trade to a standstill.

The end of World War II opened a whole new chapter in U.S.-European trade relations. The U.S. was now committed to establishing a global free trade regime, but ran into difficulties on two fronts: Britain's adamant defense of imperial privileges for its colonies, and the weakness of the European economies that made quick trade liberalization impossible. Starting in the 1940s, the U.S. adopted a dual-track strategy: It opened its own market to European and Japanese exports as a form of support, and through the Marshall Plan and subsequent aid programs, it encouraged trade liberalization among the European countries, such as the European Payments Union. Efforts to establish an International Trade Organization (ITO), that would play the same role in trade as the International Monetary Fund in exchange-rate policy, failed amid

[30] For a good survey of U.S. trade history, see Cohen et al. 1996, pp. 25-54.

strong opposition in the U.S. Congress to the compromises made in the Havana Charter in the fall of 1947. However, the General Agreement of Tariffs and Trade (GATT), adopted in the U.S. by presidential decree, created a multilateral framework for subsequent trade negotiations. While tariff barriers remained high in many sectors, they were gradually reduced in a series of trade rounds. The U.S. continued to oppose the British Imperial Preference System as a violation of the most favored nation (MFN) principle. Still, it accepted the creation of an equally discriminatory customs union by six European countries in the Treaty of Rome. The European Community (EC),[31] the predecessor of the European Union (EU), did not violate GATT guidelines because the new common external tariff did not exceed the average tariff of the six member states.[32] U.S. exporters benefited from rapid economic growth in Europe and the generally liberal trade policies, and the rising prosperity of its European allies furthered U.S. strategic interests.

The U.S. had more problems with the Common Agricultural Policy (CAP) adopted by the EC in the early 1960s. The system of price supports kept U.S. products out of Europe and turned less efficient European farmers into fierce competitors in world markets. While the Dillon and Kennedy Rounds of multilateral trade negotiations succeeded in dramatic cuts in industrial tariffs, the U.S. failed in its efforts to open up the EC agricultural markets or at least gain guaranteed access for U.S. good at then-existing levels. The "Chicken War" of 1962, triggered by an increase in EC tariffs on frozen poultry, was one of many transatlantic skirmishes involving agricultural products.[33]

And yet, even outside the agricultural sector, transatlantic trade tensions rose in the 1970s. The trade balance shifted in favor of the Europeans as its industry expanded and the dollar became increasingly overvalued. The decision by President Richard Nixon to break up the Bretton Woods regime of fixed

[31] The different names of the European integration project create as many problems as its changing nature. The European Community (EC), which started in January 1958, embraced three different communities: The European Coal and Steel Community (ECSC) that existed since 1951, the European Economic Community (EEC) and the European Atomic Energy Community (Euratom). Until the 1970s, EC and EEC were used interchangeably. The Treaty of the European Union (TEU), also known as the Maastricht Treaty, established the European Union in November 1993, which subsumed but did not replace the EC or its components. The EC is the first pillar of the EU, the Common Security and Defense Policy (CSFP) the second pillar and judicial and police cooperation the third pillar. It is still legitimate to refer to the EC when discussing trade policy, because trade belongs to the first pillar. But in line with increasingly common usage, I will use EU for any policies and events after November 1993, even if they belong to the realm of the EC, and refer to EU in every general discussion. Fortunately, the change in name coincides nearly with the conclusion of the Uruguay Round negotiations in December 1993. See Dinan 1999, p. 2.

[32] Neal/Barbezat, chapter 3.

[33] Ibid. p. 209f.

exchange rates was a logical step, though it took away a system that had provided financial stability for several decades. The global economic downturn after the first oil shock of 1973/4 added to the trade tensions, even though both parties found themselves increasingly united in their concern about Japanese trade practices and Japanese competition. The Tokyo Round managed to tackle the mushroomed non-tariff barriers, but the U.S. and the EC were often feuding parties in the GATT dispute settlement process. The two trade powers filed more complaints against each other in these tribunals than were filed by any third party.[34] A constant irritant was the steel industry, where new low-cost competitors from developing countries and the attempts by national governments to keep its domestic producers alive in the face of declining competitiveness, led to a persistent global glut. Starting in the 1960s, Washington pressured Europeans to voluntarily restrict exports to the U.S. or claiming unfair trading practices, it repeatedly imposed unilateral tariffs on European steel products.

The 1980s saw a major dispute over the issue of Soviet trade, as the Reagan administration tried to stop European companies from delivering components for a gas pipeline to the Soviet Union by extending its domestic export restrictions to U.S. overseas subsidiaries and foreign companies working with U.S. licenses. The U.S. did backed down after a major outcry by European governments and business, but the question of Eastern trade remained a point of contention until the appearance of Mikhail Gorbachev led to a thaw in U.S.-Soviet relations. In the 1990s, the U.S. and the EU squared off repeatedly over the principle question of whether sanctions or closer economic ties were the better way of dealing with hostile regimes.

The biggest trade dispute of the 1980s involved the European Airbus Industrie consortium that used state aid and loan guarantees from Germany, France and Britain to become a major competitor to the U.S. aircraft giants Boeing and McDonnell Douglas. The development of Airbus Industrie goes back to the late 1960s, though Airbus did not became a transatlantic trade issue until Eastern Airlines agreed to buy twenty-three A300s in 1978 on extremely generous terms. Thus, the U.S. put aircraft on the agenda of the Tokyo Round, leasing to the signing of the Agreement on Trade in Civil Aircraft in 1979. This agreement focused primarily on export subsidies and left plenty of room for governments to help finance the development and construction of new aircraft. As Airbus Industrie expanded its range of aircraft and introduced a whole family of airplanes in the 1980s, the U.S. aircraft industry and government became increasingly concerned. When Germany proposed to compensate Deutsche Aerospace for exchange rate losses due to the decline in the dollar rate, the U.S. sharply increased its pressure. The subsequent negotiations

[34] Ibid., p. 206.

resulted in the 1992 Large Civil Aircraft (LCA) Accord, which put a cap on every form of state subsidy and created a regime to settle future disputes. Dispute continued grumbling in the U.S. over Airbus Industrie and tensions over the restructuring of the civil aircraft industry both in the U.S. and Europe, the accord kept the peace on that front for most of the 1990s.

The LCA agreement has become one of the most closely studied trade accords in recent years. In an industry that perfectly fit the notions of new trade theory, the agreement averted a trade war that could have seriously disrupted transatlantic relations at a critical historical juncture. Among the explanations why both sides accepted a compromise over the level of subsidies, Steven McGuire focuses on role of GATT and the mutual dependence of U.S. and European companies on each other's markets that made an all-out conflict a risky proposition. On the other hand, Marc Busch argues that the Europeans wanted a cap on subsidies because they realized that the economic benefits of supporting the development of new aircraft were externalities that flowed to other countries just as much as to the financers.[35]

The European project to complete a single market by the end of 1992 – the Single European Act (SEA) of 1985 - raised U.S. concerns in the late 1980s about an approaching "Fortress Europe" that would turn inward and close itself off to foreign products. While the harmonization required under the SEA triggered a number of trade disputes, the nightmare scenario of a protectionist Europe never materialized.[36] Heavy corporate investment in preparation of the single market raised the feeble European growth rates in the late 1980s and created new exporting opportunities for U.S. producers. Starting in 1986, the EC and U.S. were pursuing the most ambitious agenda of trade liberalization to date under the Uruguay Round that was intended to strengthen the GATT dispute mechanisms, eliminate non-tariff barriers and bring services, intellectual property and other new trade issues under the umbrella of GATT. By December 1990, the target date for the completion of the round, the talks had all but broken down over the issue of agricultural subsidies. This again pitted the U.S. against the EC, highlighting the continued potential for conflict in the transatlantic trade relationship.

Despite these high-profile disagreements, consensus and mutually beneficial cooperation continued to dominate transatlantic trade. If the EU is taken as a whole, US-EU trade remained the single largest global exchange of goods and services in the world, even when the U.S. boosted trade with East Asian countries and encouraged regional integration through the North American Free Trade Area (NAFTA). A growing volume of transatlantic direct investment by multinational corporations made the business community generally averse to

---

[35] McGuire 1997, and Busch 1999, chapter 3, "The Aircraft Rivalry," pp, 32-61.
[36] Hanson 1998.

trade conflicts. Unlike the U.S. trade relationship with Japan and newly industrialized countries (NICs), transatlantic economic integration and trade are not subject to criticism by any significant constituency either in the U.S. or in Europe. Due to the importance of the NATO alliance, government leaders often leaned on their trade negotiators to quickly solve individual disputes before they poisoned the general atmosphere between the allies.

U.S.-European trade has formed the backbone of the multilateral trade system since World War II, just as trade has been a cornerstone of the larger transatlantic relationship. This pattern has not changed over the past few decades. At the beginning of the new century, the U.S. remains by far the largest trading partner for the EU-15, and only Canada surpasses the EU-15 in terms of U.S. trade volume.[37] Trade between the world's two largest economic powers kept up with the overall growth in world trade in the 1990s, exceeding global economic growth. Their trade constitutes around 4 percent of global trade and accounts for about 20 percent of total trade volume on both sides of the Atlantic. These ratios have not changed much over the past decade, as transatlantic trade has appeared to settle into a state of "mature stability".[38] Even though the bilateral trade balance, including merchandise and services, shifted from a near balance in 1990 to a substantial surplus of $47 billion for the EU (U.S. imports from the EU totaled $302 billion, exports only $255 billion in 2000), the transatlantic relationship remains the most balanced element of the U.S. current account balance. Compared to its volume, there is little conflict in transatlantic trade. The areas of dispute involve at most 5 percent of total trade, according to some estimates less than 4 percent.[39]

As part of the process of globalization, the focus of transatlantic economic cooperation shifted from trade to investment. From 1995 to 1999, U.S. foreign direct investment flows into the EU tripled from 24 to 75 billion Euro, while EU FDI in the USA increased eight-fold from 25 to 197 billion Euro. In 1999, U.S. companies had direct investments of 399 billion Euro in the EU, and EU

---

[37] Trade rankings are easily distorted by the fact that the EU consists of individual countries, which primarily trade among each other, but act as a single unit in international trade. Intra-EU trade is often, but not always excluded from trade statistics. In a regional comparison, the U.S. conducts most of its merchandise trade with Asia ($684 billion in total exports and imports in 2000), followed by Western Europe ($430 billion), North America (i.e. Canada: $417 billion) and Latin America ($386 billion). In a country ranking, Canada, followed by Mexico ($252 billion) and Japan ($216 billion) are well ahead of any EU country. But the EU-15 together contributes with $392 billion more to U.S. trade than either Japan or Mexico. For the EU, the U.S. is by far the largest trading partner with $389 billion in total exports and imports, followed by Japan ($128 billion) and Switzerland ($112 billion). But the volume of intra-EU trade of $1,392 (exports only) billion dwarfs all other trade activities. Source: WTO World Trade Report 2001, Tables III.17 and III.39

[38] Hufbauer/Neumann 2002

[39] Ibid. and TABD 2001, p. 2

companies 597 billion Euro in the U.S.[40] Sales by U.S. subsidiaries in the EU and by European subsidiaries in the U.S. are today significantly larger than the annual trade volume.[41] These corporate investments have given rise to a strong constituency desiring closer economic ties and smoother trade relations.

1.3. The Making of Domestic and International Policy within the United States and the European Union

The U.S. Trade Representative (USTR) and the EU foreign trade commissioner normally conduct trade negotiations between the U.S. and the EU. These two officials are the top trade officials for their respective side, though they act in very different political and bureaucratic environment.

1.3.1. The United States

The most salient phenomenon in U.S. trade policy is the complex relationship between the United States Congress and the executive branch. Historically, foreign trade was under congressional authority, a right that is even enshrined in the first article of the U.S. constitution. "The Congress shall have Power...to regulate Commerce with foreign Nations, and among the several States, and with the Indian Tribes…" [42] As seen in the previous section, Congress took advantage of this right to push up tariffs to ever higher levels, culminating in the Smoot-Hawley tariff act of 1930. The pernicious effect of this blatant act of protectionism resulted in a dramatic shift of trade authority to the executive branch, that was at first not visible. The RTAA gave the Roosevelt administration the right to negotiate and enact reciprocal trade reductions without formal approval from Congress. This authorization was limited to three years, but was almost automatically renewed in subsequent years. After 1945, the act was amended to allow further tariff cuts, and trade policy in the post-war period was effectively run from the White House and the State Department, that took charge of trade negotiations. "Congress legislated itself out of the business from making product-specific trade law," notes the political scientist I.M. Destler who interpreted this move as a way for the parliamentarians to protect themselves from trade-related domestic pressures.[43]

---

[40] European Union website *http://europa/eu/int/comm/external_relations/us/intro/index.htm*

[41] The ratio of sales of manufacturing goods by U.S. subsidiaries in the EU to total EU manufacturing imports from the U.S. was 3.75 in 1998. See Navaretti/Haaland/Venables 2002.

[42] Article I, Section 8 of the United States Constitution. *www.house.gov/Constitution/ Constitution.html*

[43] Destler 1995, p. 13.

But Congress never renounced its principle right to influence trade policy. The Havana Charter of 1947 that called for the establishment of the International Trade Organization (ITO) was never put to ratification before Congress because both the Truman and the Eisenhower administrations knew that they could not get the necessary votes. A coalition of protectionists, unilateralists and free traders unhappy about the compromises in the charter prevented the establishment of a multilateral trade institution similar to that of the International Monetary Fund. The administration found a stopgap solution by joining the General Agreement of Trade and Tariffs (GATT) via a presidential directive that helped make GATT into a quasi trade organization.

Trade stopped being a domestic issue in the first post-war years because the U.S. had such an overwhelming economic advantage and a huge current account surplus. When this surplus began to shrink in the early 1960s, however, Congress returned to the stage. Concerned about the way the State Department put geopolitics ahead of domestic economic interests, Congress forced upon the Kennedy administration the establishment of the USTR. The trade representative was supposed to coordinate the various trade-related activities of different departments and reported directly to the president. Their mission was defined to act as "trade warriors": By opening up foreign markets, the USTR would fight both for global free trade and for U.S. economic interests.[44]

The administration's room for maneuver shrank further in the 1970s, as the U.S. began to build up persistent trade deficits and a growing number of industries felt threatened by Japanese competition. The Trade Reform Act of 1974 created the fast-track authority permitting the president to negotiate sweeping trade deals that could only be approved or rejected by Congress without amendment (though this crucial provision was limited in time and had to be renewed before another round of trade talks). Sections 201 and 301 of the act strengthened the instruments available to respond to injury through imports and unfair foreign trade practices.

Passed against the background of skyrocketing trade deficits, the 1988 Omnibus Trade and Competitiveness Act added the Super 301 and Special 301 provisions to U.S. trade law. These provisions forced the USTR to investigate foreign trade barriers and violations of intellectual property rights harmful to U.S. interests. If discriminatory practices were found and could not be removed through negotiations, the USTR was obliged to initiate retaliatory measures without prior recourse to the GATT.[45] Even though the bills usually left an escape clause to the administration, presidents found themselves under pressure to adopt tough trade measures to ward off even more protectionist or interventionist legislation in Congress. In 1997 and 1998, Congress refused to

---

[44] Dryden 1995.
[45] Hufbauer/Neumann 2002.

renew fast-track authority after it had lapsed at the end of 1993. The lack of fast-track authority inhibited the efforts to launch a new trade round at the WTO summit in Seattle in December 1999. The trade round was finally launched two year later in Doha, at which time Congress had not yet granted that right to Clinton's successor George W. Bush.

Congress itself is rarely united on trade issues. Several dozen committees and sub-committees in both chambers are engaged in the foreign trade agenda, and that often pursue very different goals. After decades of a general consensus, trade emerged as one of the most divisive political issues during the 1980s and particularly in the 1990s. Some of the hardest Congressional battles of recent years involved trade, foremost the narrow ratification of the North American Free Trade Area (NAFTA) in 1993.[46]

Even within the executive branch, trade policy is the result of a complex interplay of various departments and agencies. The State Department, particularly through the often-influential Under Secretary for Economic, Business and Agricultural Affairs, continues to play a pivotal role. The Commerce Department is in charge of export promotion, the Department of Agriculture plays a key role in farm trade, the Treasury Department sets exchange-rate policy, Labor and Energy departments and Environmental Protection Agency are all in involved in specific trade-related issues. When trade is seen as affecting the overall economic picture, the National Economic Council, the Council of Economic Advisors, the Office of Management and Budget (OMB) might also seek an active role. Finally, trade issues such as export controls for high-technology products and general trade sanctions against countries are a prime concern for national security, bringing the Defense Department and the National Security Council into the picture. As a result, companies asking for help from Washington on a trade issue often cite the State Department, Treasury Department and Defense Department as "problem agencies" because they are more concerned with larger international issues than the commercial interests of one U.S. firm or even a sector.[47]

All these different players tend to challenge the authority of the USTR on trade issues; his or her influence primarily depends on his or her relationship with the president. In the Clinton White House, Mickey Kantor, the USTR from 1993 to 1997, was Clinton's campaign chairman in the 1992 election and had a particularly close relationship with the president. His successor Charlene Barshefsky had far less access to Clinton and it was seen by some observers to undermine her effectiveness. Her "tough" approach in trade disputes was

[46] See, for example, Shoch 2001.
[47] Shaffer 2001, p. 103.

perceived as a way to establish her credentials and thus strengthen her position within the executive branch.[48]

The influence of the private sector on U.S. trade policy is one of the most closely studied and most controversial aspects of the American system. Unlike other countries, the U.S. actually encourages companies to raise their voice and give input into the policy process. Under Section 301 of the Trade Act of 1974, the USTR is obliged to respond to petitions of private firms by investigating foreign trade barriers and sometimes taking action against them. When the USTR files a complaint at the WTO, it relies on the information provided by U.S. companies and sometimes even the legal briefs which their lawyers prepare.[49] USTR negotiators working on specific areas sometimes come from that very industry, and will return there after their stint in government.[50] A large share of the more than 4000 trade and professional associations[51] in the U.S., effectively lobby groups, are concerned with foreign trade policy and ask for help to promote exports, inform and complain about trade barriers and unfair trade practices, and sometimes openly calling for protection from imports. The affinity between commercial interests and trade negotiators let Sylvia Ostry, a former Canadian trade negotiator and research fellow at the University of Toronto, conclude, "America doesn't have a trade policy. It has clients."[52]

Lobby groups also press their local congressman and senators, who in turn put pressure on the administration. The private sector can also be a force for trade liberalization: whenever an industry asks for relief from cheap imports, there are downstream producers who will lose out if prices go up. The main impetus for the creation of the Transatlantic Business Dialogue (TABD) came from U.S. industry.[53] Some of the largest multinational corporations, who depend on the bulk of their earnings from foreign business, are on the frontline to defend free trade and globalization.

1.3.2. The European Union

On the European side, the picture appears more structured, but is perhaps even more complex. The first problem is one of terminology: the EU is not a country, and the European Commission is not a government. Yet in foreign trade and other economic areas, the Commission acts like a government and is legally and politically the bilateral partner for the U.S. Member state

---

[48] See "Objection", *Economist*, January 23, 1999.
[49] Ibid.
[50] Interview with Hugo Paemen, EU ambassador to the U.S. from 1993 to 1999, on April 10, 2002 in Washington, D.C.
[51] Baumgartner/Leech 1998, p. 109.
[52] "At daggers drawn," *Economist*, May 6th, 1999.
[53] Kerremans 2000.

government acting like domestic constituents; it is therefore fair to use the terms "domestic politics" and "domestic interests" for intra-EU pressures and decision-making.

The Treaty of Rome of 1957 established the Common Commercial Policy (CCP) that gave the Commission the exclusive competence for external trade relations.[54] In addition, the treaty also gave the European Council, with qualified majority voting, the right to set the direction of trade policy, approve Commission proposals to implement the CCP and open negotiations with third countries. Article 113 of the Treaty of Rome (later Article 133 of the Treaty of the European Communities) also called for the creation of a "special committee appointed by the Council to assist the Commission". This so-called 133 Committee has at some times interfered with EU trade policy, while at other times stood aside and let the Commission set the tone. Article 300 of TEC (that granted the Commission the right to conclude international treaties), however, was amended in the Maastricht Treaty to include a larger role for the European Parliament, though limited.

The balance of power between the Commission and the Council in trade policy remains as much a political as a legal question. When the Commission tried to extend its trade authority to the "new trade issues" in services and intellectual property, the European Court of Justice (ECJ) ruled against it in 1994.[55] The Amsterdam treaty reaffirmed this restriction of the Commission's authority, and it was not until the Treaty of Nice of 2000 that a more workable solution was found. As these new issues have gained in importance in WTO cases and international trade talks, the Commission has been increasingly forced to negotiate jointly with member states. Politically, it has proven to be impossible to conclude a major international trade agreement against the objections of one of the large member states, i.e. France. Even if EU integration proceeds, this restriction is unlikely to change.

Since country positions are also the result of a domestic policy process, the EU find itself in international trade talks often in a so-called three-level game: when staking out a position, it has to take into account the interaction of negotiations occurring at the domestic level, the European Council level, and the international level.[56] The complex interrelationship led traditionally to a more cautious and defensive trade policies in Brussels. For decades, the commission's main goal was to protect vulnerable domestic sectors and react to U.S. trade initiatives.[57]

---

[54] Dinan 1999, pp. 483-488.

[55] Advisory Opinion 1/94 by the ECJ on November 15, 1994. See Hilf 1995.

[56] Patterson 1997, among others, uses the term "three-level game" in describing CAP reform.

[57] Shaffer 2001, p. 106.

Within the Commission, the responsibility for trade negotiations has also been diffuse at times. With the fourth enlargement of the EU in 1995 of Austria, Sweden und Finland, the number of commissioners reached the unwieldy number of 20. Commission president Jacques Santer split the Directorate-General (DG) 1, traditionally in charge of all external relations, and spread the trade portfolio among three commissioners, leaving Leon Brittan only in charge of the WTO and relations with North America, the Far East, Australia and New Zealand. Other commissioners were in charge of relations with Central and Eastern Europe and the majority of developing countries. Under Santer's successor Romano Prodi, the system was streamlined with Pascal Lamy now fully in charge of all trade relations. Trade issues split, however, in the areas of the commissioners for agriculture, competition, internal market, development and humanitarian aid, enlargement, and external relations.

Despite these limitations, the EU trade commissioner is generally seen as carrying more political weight than the USTR, who is only a high-level civil servant.[58] He has a vote in the European Commission, the highest executive body in the EU. Coordination within the 20-member commission and the relatively small civil service is easier than in the U.S. government: unless one or more member states take a strong position on a certain issue, the Council is an easier partner than the unpredictable U.S. Congress. In the final leg of international negotiations, the EU trade commissioner can reassure himself of the domestic backing by one or two phone calls. The reaction of Congress can never be predicted.

Whereas national governments are closely involved in the EU trade policy process, private companies play a far more limited role than in the U.S.[59] The Commission has traditionally discouraged such lobbying efforts, and most trade associations are still fragmented along national lines. Change came in the mid-1990s in response to the Uruguay Round Agreement and the growing pressure from U.S. market-opening strategies. In 1995, the EU enacted the Trade Barrier Regulation (TBR), the European answer to Section 301. It permits individual companies to petition the Commission to initiate a WTO complaint.[60] In February 1996, trade commissioner Leon Brittan launched a new Market Access Strategy intended to focus EU trade policy on opening foreign markets. This adoption of a U.S. model marked a clear departure from the "more prudent, protectionist, inward-looking, reactive trade policy of the past."[61] A new Market Access Unit was set up to interact with European business interests and find out more about their trade problems. Ironically, the first major market-

[58] Interview with Hugo Paemen, EU ambassador to the U.S. from 1993 to 1999, on April 10, 2002 in Washington, D.C.
[59] Ibid.
[60] Shaffer 2001, pp. 110-111.
[61] Ibid. p. 107.

opening move by the trade commissioner, the complaint against U.S. export subsidies in 1997, had little support in European industry. In the following years, the EU became better in challenging other country's trade practices at the WTO, particularly those of the U.S.

1.3.3. International Agreements and Institutions

Since the establishment of the GATT in 1947, international institutions have played an increasingly important role in transatlantic trade policy. The U.S. and the West European countries were founding members of the GATT that was originally a stop-gap measure to be replaced by the ITO. When the ITO failed in the U.S. Congress, the GATT developed its institutional features. In its first decades, it was mostly a negotiating forum for the settlement of trade disputes and trade liberalization agreements. Gradually, it built up its secretariat and through its dispute-settlement panels it developed quasi-legal powers as an interpreter of trade agreements. The increasing institutionalization of GATT made its shortcomings more visible, particularly its lack of enforcement powers, and this led to the creation of the WTO in the Uruguay Round Agreement. With a staff of just over 500 and an annual budget of $90 million,[62] the Geneva-based WTO remains a midget among international institutions and strongly depends on the personnel of its member states, particularly the U.S. and the European countries, to fulfill its functions of administering trade agreements, monitoring national policies, preparing new negotiations and handling disputes. An increasing share of trade-related activities in the Washington and Brussels are geared toward the WTO.

In addition, the U.S. and the EU have built up administrative structures for the regional trade agreements they have signed, such as NAFTA and the various preferential deals of the EU with candidate and developing countries. These regional commitments were sometimes seen as diverting political attention and capital away from the multilateral institutions,[63] with the exception of the European Union (that is a trade bloc) and perhaps the NAFTA secretariat, there are no institutions of which to speak.

With the end of the Cold War, the U.S. and the EU also tried to strengthen the institutional framework of the transatlantic economic partnership. In the Transatlantic Declaration of 1990 that came during the collapse of Communism, the U.S. for the first time acknowledged the EU as a major transatlantic player and agreed to semi-annual (twice a year) summits involving the U.S. president and the EU leadership. On a policy level, the Transatlantic Declaration was left vague. The 1995 New Transatlantic Agenda (NTA) included a much more

---

[62] WTO website *www.wto.org*

[63] See Gordon 2001.

concrete Joint Action Plan and gave rise to the Transatlantic Business Dialogue (TABD), the Transatlantic Consumer Dialogue (TACD) and the Transatlantic Labor Dialogue (TALD), designed to strengthen a transatlantic civic society. The plan for a more ambitious New Transatlantic Marketplace (NTM) was killed by France in 1998 and was substituted by the looser framework of the Transatlantic Economic Partnership (TEP).[64]

All these declarations, forums and institutions are primarily a reaffirmation of existing lines of communications and cooperation between the U.S. and Europe and do not rival the existing security institutions like NATO. But unlike the era before 1990, U.S. economic policy toward Europe is fully focused on the EU. They have helped coordinating and centralizing the intra-EU decision-making process and raised the international stature of the Commission. The TABD and other transatlantic business associations like the European-American Business Council (EABC) have tried to build up a transnational lobby in favor of free trade that could counter the protectionist interests at home. Whereas these chief executives know each other well and are often closely connected through mutual investments and trade, they have not become a joint political force to with which to reckon. If internationally oriented businesses want to affect transatlantic trade policy, they still have to work through their national structures, where they are more often than not overpowered by parochial pressure groups asking for protection. Transatlantic trade policy is still predominantly a matter of intergovernmental relations.[65]

[64] For more on this topic, see chapter 4, section 4.4.
[65] Pollack/Shaffer 2001 (3).

CHAPTER 2: EXPLAINING TRANSATLANTIC TRADE RELATIONS IN THE CLINTON ERA

Transatlantic trade relations are the product of international and domestic factors, as well as political and economic considerations. They are mostly consensual, but sometimes testy. Since the 1960s, a number of trade issues had the potential to trigger trade disputes or even a trade war between the U.S. and the EC. Overwhelming commercial interests on both sides and the desire for harmony among international allies usually led to a quick conflict resolution or prevented irresolvable conflicts from spilling into other areas.

The period since 1990 saw two major trends affecting the relationship: the end of the Cold War, that deprived the Atlantic alliance of its strongest common purpose, and globalization, that resulted in a strong growth both in the volume of trade and foreign direct investment (FDI) between the U.S. and Europe. The institutional environment also changed with the creation of World Trade Organization (WTO) from the Uruguay Round Agreement. On the bilateral level, the U.S. and the EU established a series of new transatlantic forums for dialogue and cooperation; on the multilateral level, they signed single-sector agreements on telecommunications, information technology and financial services. Starting in the mid-1990s, the number of parochial trade disputes increased dramatically and led toward the end of the Clinton administration to a stalemate in trade relations that at times threaten to poison the overall political partnership. Some of the disputes festered for months and years, but were resolved during the Clinton presidency: U.S. sanctions against Cuba, Iran and Libya, EU restrictions for noisy U.S. aircraft, EU Airbus subsidies, and the struggle over EU data privacy rules on the Internet. Others were not, such as EU restrictions on genetically-modified organisms and the EU challenge to U.S. export subsidies, both of which remained potentially explosive. The EU banana regime and its ban for U.S. hormone-treated beef even triggered sanctions. In 1999, the U.S. and the EU were so far apart on key trade issues that they could not arrive at a common agenda for another trade round, the declared goal of both sides. The fiasco of Seattle was a disappointing finale to a decade that could have advanced the cause of free trade farther than any earlier period.

The following section will test to what extent the theoretical approaches to foreign trade that were described in chapter 2 can explain the general state of transatlantic trade relations and the increase in trade disputes during the 1990s.

2.1. Applying Theories of Trade to Transatlantic Trade Policy

2.1.1. The Economics Perspective

Transatlantic trade today comes quite close to the classical economic ideal of a mutually beneficial free exchange of good and services. Unlike north-south trade, the main attraction of north-north trade is not so much the principle of comparative advantage but the dynamics of intra-industry trade, where similar products are exchanged and tend to create more competition among suppliers and more diversity of consumer choice. This factor makes transatlantic trade liberalization politically much easier to digest than trade between countries at different economic stages. New competition might hurt single companies, but due to the lack of strong comparative advantages, neither the U.S. nor the EU is in danger of losing complete industries and the jobs it provides. When a sector is opened up, it is not determined before hand which side is likely to gain the larger market shares. This helps to explain, for example, why the U.S. trade unions were rarely opposed to transatlantic free trade. The massive direct investment flows between the U.S. and the EU are another sign of the broad symmetry of transatlantic trade relations.

Classic trade theory would therefore suggest relatively frictionless trade relations between the U.S. and the EU. What about modern trade theory that identifies cases where free trade does not result in an optimal outcome for both sides? In particular, strategic trade theory suggests that some high-technology sectors with oligopolistic structures would be the most likely area of a competitive trade relationship with a high propensity for tensions.[66] In reality, however, there have been few transatlantic conflicts in the area of high technology, and those have usually been quickly resolved. The largest conflict potential still exists in the aircraft business through the rivalry of Boeing and Airbus. But even here, the U.S. and the EU reached a truce in 1992 that a decade later was still holding.[67] The main trade disputes at the turn of the century have involved mostly agricultural products and had absolutely no strategic value.

Trade disputes are often seen as part of a conscious strategy of unilateral trade liberalization. By threatening with sanctions, countries challenge trade barriers of their partners and if they succeed, help to open up markets for its own businesses and those of other countries. U.S. policy makers claim that their cherished practice of managed trade, particularly the anti-dumping and countervailing measures and the 301 provisions of the U.S. trade bills, is indispensable in a world full of protectionism and is needed to keep free trade

[66] Tyson 1992.
[67] McGuire 1997.

flowing. This argument, however, is regarded by U.S. trading partners as a self-serving excuse to pander to domestic interest groups. There is little evidence that any of the U.S. trade measures against the EU in the 1990s were part of a conscious trade-liberalization strategy. Even if they work, these measures "only pick at the edges of existing barriers",[68] while the main demolition work was done by multilateral and regional trade agreements. Usually, they hurt the cause of free trade.

Let us now turn to some economic variables that might affect the course of trade relations and trade policy. The most obvious ones are trade and current account balances. Without doubt, the persistent U.S. trade deficits since the 1970s have contributed to trade tensions with some major U.S. partners, particularly with Japan. Given the high priority of the U.S.-Japanese trade balance for several U.S. administrations, it is surprising how little effect the various measures to stem the flow of imports from and boost exports actually had on the trade deficit and persisted through several cycles of trade protection, proving to be much more dependent on growth differentials between the two countries. In contrast, the U.S. external trade position has played a very small role in transatlantic trade relations, which have been roughly in balance throughout the past decades. The U.S. current account deficit with the EU widened in the late 1990s, mostly due to the appreciation of the Dollar against D-Mark and Euro, but this gap never compared to the much larger deficits with Japan and China. It would be difficult to make a case that the state of transatlantic trade relations depends on the trade or current account balance.[69]

Another variable that could affect trade policy is economic growth: trade tensions are more likely to erupt during recessions than expansions because a shrinking output intensifies the fight over jobs and market shares. This was probably true in the 1930s, but not in the past decade. The most intensive disputes erupted neither the recession in the early 1990s nor in 2001, but during the boom years of 1998 and 1999. The only issue directly related to the economic cycle was steel. But even there, politics played a larger role than economics, for economic welfare of a nation is much better served through lower steel prices from foreign sources than through protection.

To summarize, neither economic theories of trade nor economic variables offer a satisfactory explanation for the ups and downs in transatlantic trade relations. While they can help to explain the move toward trade liberalization in the first half of the 1990s, they shed little light on the subsequent increase in trade disputes.

---

[68] Hufbauer/Neumann 2002

[69] See Calleo 2001.

2.1.2. The International Relations Perspective

As discussed previously, balance-of-power theorists attribute the rise in transatlantic trade tensions to the end of the Cold War of which loosened the strategic need for the Atlantic partners to maintain a united front against a common enemy. Harmony in the transatlantic relationship remained desirable, but was no longer a question of life and death. This allowed both sides to show fewer restraints in trade disputes.[70]

The Realist approach might help to explain foreign-policy disputes between the U.S. and the European powers, but it is of limited use in the economic realm. The last years of the Cold War actually saw some of the nastiest trade fights among the industrialized countries: the fight over European subsidies for Airbus escalated in the 1980s and was only resolved in 1992; the US sanctions against European companies delivering gas pipes to the Soviet Union; and the fight over car imports and semiconductors brought the US and Japan several times to the brink of all-out trade war. The collapse of the Soviet Union in 1991 coincided with an easing of trade tensions, culminating in the 1993 completion of the Uruguay round. Meanwhile, the strength and health of the transatlantic alliance remained a key U.S. interest under the presidency of George Bush Sr. and Bill Clinton, as the U.S. needed the support of its allies for the Gulf War, the NATO intervention on the Balkans and NATO's Eastern enlargements.[71]

Did perhaps the emergence of a more unified and stronger Europe exacerbate transatlantic tensions, as some political economists predicted?[72] Although the creation of the European single market caused some concern among U.S. academics and policy-makers in the 1980s that feared the building of a "Fortress Europe" and were concerned about discriminatory measures against U.S. business interests, these tensions eased with the conclusion of the Uruguay Round. The Clinton administration wholeheartedly supported European integration, including the launch of the Euro. While some trade disputes can be traced back to the dynamics of European integration, including the banana issue, they were hardly an expression of a new bipolar economic rivalry.

Hegemonic stability theory suggests that the decline of a global hegemon would also result in a decline in free trade. This explanation gained some credence in the 1980s, when the U.S. seemed in a phase of inevitable longer-term decline through "imperial overstretch"[73]; rising military spending, sluggish economic growth and a skyrocketing current account deficit. This picture

[70] A good example is Walt 1998.

[71] For a good evaluation of the validity of Realist theory for transatlantic post-Cold War relations, see Duffield 2001.

[72] See for example Bergsten 1999.

[73] This is Paul Kennedy's main argument in Kennedy 1989.

changed completely in the 1990s as the end of the Cold War permitted the U.S. to cut back on defense spending without fearing a weakening of its global military position. Strong economic performance and a huge inflow of foreign capital also eased the worries about the U.S. current account deficit. The creation of the WTO in 1995 could be seen as an expression of hegemonic multilateralism in the tradition of Bretton Woods- the strengthening of the international free trade regime in line with U.S. priorities. Yet just when U.S. global economic and political dominance seemed at its height in late 1999, the Clinton administration proved unable to launch another trade round in Seattle. Meanwhile, institutional approaches to international relations such as regime theory may help explain the continuation of trade liberalization after the end of the Cold War, but not the increase in transatlantic trade disputes within the institutions designed to make relations work more smoothly.

Transatlantic economic relations are also imbedded in the global economic triad that includes Japan and increasingly China as well as other emerging markets in East Asia. Trilateral relationships between equally strong powers are usually more volatile than bilateral relationships because there is no stable equilibrium: in every bilateral conflict, the third player can effectively decide the outcome by choosing sides.[74] One would expect this triad dynamics to play an important role in transatlantic trade issues. Surprisingly, this has never been the case. Japan never got involved in U.S.-European diplomacy and did not spend much effort to gain the support of either the U.S. or the EU in its squabbles with the other partner. While Japan is part of the Quad, an informal governing council for GATT and WTO negotiations, it usually kept to the sidelines. Despite the importance of Japan, China and the Tiger countries for international trade flows, they are all minor players in multilateral trade diplomacy.

In totality, the theories of international relations do not offer a good framework to explain post-Cold-War transatlantic trade relations. Liberals have little to say about the increase in tensions, while the Realists cannot explain why overall trade relations remained so strong.

2.1.3. The Domestic Politics Perspective

Some of the most plausible explanations for the rise in transatlantic trade tensions can be found in the domestic arena both in the U.S. and the EU and should therefore be easily explained by theories of the domestic policy process. With producer cartels and special interest groups hurt by foreign competition,

---

[74] Krugman 1986 applies this concept in his oligopolistic trade theory. George Orwell (1992) gives a nice illustration of the pernicious dynamics of a trilateral global order in his novel *Nineteen Eighty-Four*.

domestic politics will always be a source of protectionist pressures. Their influence on a nation's trade policy depends on the fragmentation of the policy process, public opinion and the quality of political leadership. In the 1990s, all three factors suggested growing protectionism in the U.S., and to a lesser extent in Europe. The 1990s saw a growing "privatization" of policy-making in Washington, as legislators became increasingly beholden to local interests and campaign donors.[75] The debate over the NAFTA ratification 1993 mobilized the opponents of free trade in Congress put a large part of Clinton's own Democratic Party into the protectionist camp and made Americans more aware of the drawbacks of free trade.[76] In addition, the Clinton administration suffered a decline in its authority, first through the Republican victory in the Congressional mid-term elections in 1994, and later through a series of scandals that peaked in the unsuccessful impeachment in early 1999 because of his untruthful denial of an affair with White House intern Monica Lewinsky.

In the EU, the balance between public trade policy and special business interests did not shift the way it did in the U.S. Yet the whole project of European integration suffered a crisis of confidence in the wake of the Maastricht Treaty, and the European Commission saw its authority dwindle compared to the member states under the feeble leadership of its president Jacques Santer. Several health scares reduced public trust in the EU institutions and contributed to transatlantic trade tensions. Perhaps not accidentally, the resignation of the commission in 1999 coincided with the peak of transatlantic trade tensions.

It would be hard to make a case, however, that internal politics were the sole determinant in transatlantic trade relations. Both in Washington and in Brussels, the executive branches maintained broad control over trade policy and were able to advance the overall goal of free trade against special interests. One can point to individual cases were narrow lobbies caused major tensions, such as the role of Chiquita chairman Carl Lindner in the banana dispute (see chapter 5) or some U.S. airlines in the fight over hush kits (chapter 4). Their influence was offset by the keen interest of some of the largest U.S. and European corporations in a smooth and expanding trade relationship. Moreover, trade with Europe never ranked high on the list of priorities for Congressional leaders and public interest groups, who were usually more concern about Japan, South Korea, Mexico and other developing countries. Positions taken or successes achieved in the transatlantic trade relationship did not have much effect on the electoral prospects of the president and his party. It is also interesting to note

[75] Jonquières 2001 sees the U.S. campaign finance system as a one of the main sources of trade tensions.
[76] Shoch 2001.

that most of the recent studies about the domestic political forces behind U.S. trade policy hardly mention trade with the Europe at all.[77]

2.1.4. The Domestic-International Perspective

The best explanations for the trend in transatlantic trade relations and trade policies can be found at the crossroads of domestic and international factors. The most widely used model for this interaction are Putnam's "two-level games" and as one trade expert states, transatlantic trade policies offer "a prime test case for observing two-level games played by intergovernmental elites representing political entities" that are increasingly fragmented, difficult to lead and demonstrate a very different kind of rationality than what is usually called the national interest.[78] While some developing countries may still draw short-term benefits from keeping its markets protected, for advanced industrialized countries, mutual trade liberalization and even a complete removal of all trade barriers is clearly a win-win strategy.[79] This even applies to export subsidies and other forms of state aid that are often described as a positive and even necessary element of competitiveness. International trade agreements call for the elimination of such corporate welfare, reflecting a global consensus on the question. If the U.S. and the EU still pursue protectionist policies, they do so because of concern for domestic political pressures.

But Putnam's model of "two-level games" also has limitations: its main purpose is to show how domestic constraints affect international bargaining tactics and bargaining outcomes.[80] His approach assumes that governments: i) act rationally, and ii) actually pursues conflicting national goals in the negotiations. Their goal is therefore to make the largest possible gains with the fewest number of concessions. Most trade economists would question this scenario: a country actually benefits itself if it makes concessions in form of the removal of trade barriers. From the point of view of national welfare, every bargaining outcome short of a reduction or even elimination of trade barriers is collectively sub-optimal.[81] Trade negotiations, and particularly the pursuit of

---

[77] See for example Destler 1995, Gibson 2000, Shoch 2001, or Burtless et al. 1998.

[78] Peterson 2001, p. 46.

[79] A recent study predicts that in a world of free trade, the EU would boost its exports to the U.S. by $44 billion annually, and the U.S. its exports to the EU by $48 billion. See Drusilla K. Brown, Alan V. Deardoff and Robert M. Stern. 2001. "CGE Modeling and Analysis of Multilateral and Regional Negotiating Options" Discussion Paper 468, University of Michigan: School of Public Policy. Quoted in Hufbauer/Neumann 2002.

[80] Putnam 1988.

[81] There might be other aspects of national interest, such as protection of the environment of consumer protection. Contrary to the criticism of globalization opponents,, current trade agreements actually go quite far to accommodate such interests. They draw the line where the non-trade concern is misused as a trade barrier.

trade disputes, are therefore exercise in collective economic irrationality. They become rational only in a specific context of domestic politics.[82]

Even there, rationality must sometimes be questioned as domestic players can find themselves torn between different trade objectives. Industries might want protection from foreign competitors but also market access to foreign markets and no protection for their inputs. Legislators want to be seen as champions of their local businesses, but support the general principle of free trade, particularly in the transatlantic arena. Government leaders want to win elections by appealing to popular issues while maintaining domestic coalitions for legislative projects, but also avoid conflict with the international partners and pursue policies that a conducive to economic growth.

Such conflicting goals based on different rationalities are best captured in Tsebelis's "nested games" model, which illuminates the unpredictable outcome of trade politics.[83] The following analysis will use this model and Gibson's application to U.S. trade policy as a starting point to illustrate the dynamics of transatlantic trade policies.

2.2. The Hypothesis of the Inverse Relationship

2.2.1. Narrow and Broad Issues

Transatlantic trade relations can best be defined as a struggle between domestic and international pressures on the policy-making authorities both in the U.S. and the EU. From any given status quo, domestic forces will push toward protection and conflict, international concerns toward liberalization and cooperation. Given the extensive commonality of interests between the U.S. and Europe, cooperation is usually the dominant strategy. The vast majority of voters, parties, interest groups and companies on both sides of the Atlantic are interested in smooth and constructive transatlantic relations. This applies to economics and business, but even more so to diplomacy and security.

Because these interests are so universal and so diffuse, there is no strong transatlantic lobby that regards the state of transatlantic relations its primary goal. Even the CEOs of the multinational corporations that are members of the Transatlantic Business Dialogue rarely think of transatlantic issues when they return to their corporate headquarters; their lobby activities are usually directed at other issues. This leaves plenty of room for specific domestic interests, who

[82] The irrationality of trade conflicts was reflected in a series of press headlines in the 1990s, particularly when it came to the fight over bananas. See "Going Bananas", *Economist*, May 6, 1999.

[83] Tsebelis 1990, which is applied to U.S. trade politics in Gibson 2000. Gibson, however, does not discuss transatlantic trade issues, which do not quite fit into her explanatory framework.

are either opposed to a further trade liberalization or are willing to risk a conflict in their fight for additional market access. The narrower the specific issue, the more attention is given to the voices of special interest groups. Transatlantic cooperation is therefore easier to achieve on broader, weightier issues, even if they involve deep-seated disagreements, where conflict is more likely on narrower and smaller issues. There is an inverse relationship between the breadth of an issue and the intensity of conflict, and this can be shown throughout the trade policy issues during the Clinton era.

To illustrate this hypothesis, I have identified in the following table (1.1) separate trade issues that played a role during the Clinton era. They include trade agreements, trade disputes and some related economic issues with a direct impact on bilateral trade. Several of them continued into the early years of the Bush Jr. administration, some remained still unresolved at the time of publication.

Table 1.1
Transatlantic Trade issues during the Clinton Presidency

Issues (Bold: years of highest intensity)	**Dates**
Uruguay Round Agreement	1992-1994, **1993**
IT Agreement	1995-1996, **1996**
Telecom Agreement	1995-1997, **1997**
Mutual Recognition Agreement	1995-1997, **1997**
Boeing-MDD Merger	1996-1997, **1997**
Helms-Burton Act	1995-1998, **1996-1997**
Financial Services Agreement	1995-1997, **1997**
Iran-Libya Sanctions Act	1996-1998, **1997-1998**
Macroeconomics	1998-1999, **1998**
EU Banana Import Regime	1995-2001, **1998-1999**
Data Privacy	1995-2000, **1998-1999**
Beef	1996- , **1999**
Steel	1998- , **1999, 2002**
Launch of New Trade Round	1996-2001, **1999**
Genetically modified (GM) Foods	1997- , **1999**
Aircraft Noise	1998-2001, **1999-2000**
Export Subsidies (FSC)	1997-, **2000, 2002**
Airbus A380	1997-, **2000**
Gluten	1998-2001, **2001**
Music Homestyle Copyright Law	1999-2002, **2001-2002**

One can see that the number of trade issues increased toward the end of the decade. Their nature also changed as all trade agreements of the Clinton era were completed by 1997 and the following years saw mostly failed agreements or conflicts.

Analysts have tried various ways to classify such trade issues.[84] Some of these issues represent traditional market access conflicts (steel and some agricultural products); others involve the use of industrial policy (aircraft industry and export subsidies). Some are rooted in foreign policy concerns (Helms-Burton and Iran-Libya Sanctions Acts), while others are rooted in new ideological questions such as food safety and consumer protection (hormone-treated beef, GMO, aircraft noise and data privacy). Some are idiosyncratic and unlikely to be repeated, others are rooted in domestic-structural causes, and some can be characterized as endemic.

My own criteria for classification is whether an issue took the form of cooperation or conflict, and whether the conflict was contained, resolved without any concrete negative consequences, or led to retaliation and other forms of counter-measures detrimental to trade. This leads me to three categories:

Cooperation in trade means that the negotiations result in trade liberalization, removing trade barriers and facilitating trade.

In a *controlled conflict* the conflict resolution results neither in any liberalization nor in higher trade barriers. The pursuit of the conflict might cause political tensions and exert a political cost by preoccupying policy-makers, but it does not have any concrete negative consequences.

In a *trade war* one side or both sides erect higher trade barriers as a means to punish the other side or induce a change in behavior. These punitive trade barriers can come about through unilateral action or the WTO dispute-settlement body authorizes them. In both cases, they inflict short-term costs on both sides. If they achieve their objective to remove the other's trade barriers, they ultimately have a positive effect on the trade relationship; if they trigger retaliation and escalation, they will be detrimental also in the medium term. While such actions in recent years were far removed from the all-out trade wars or militarized conflicts of earlier centuries, they fit the definition of a limited war.

---

84 For different categorizations of transatlantic trade disputes see Kerremans 2000 and Hufbauer/Neumann 2002. None of these categorizations create perfect matches. There are several issues that fit several categories.

In the next table, the 20 trade issues are divided among the following three categories.

Table 1.2
Character of Transatlantic Trade Issues during the Clinton Presidency

Cooperation
Uruguay Round Agreement
IT Agreement

Mutual Recognition Agreement
Telecom Agreement
Financial Services Agreement

Controlled Conflicts
Helms-Burton
Iran-Libya
Boeing-MDD
Aircraft Noise
Airbus 380
Data Privacy
Macroeconomics
Steel/Anti-Dumping
New Trade Round
GMO
Music Copyright

Trade Wars
Gluten
Bananas
Beef
Export Subsidies

Even within the categories, there is a difference in degree of cooperation and conflict. In the next table, a ranking of the issues is created based on the degree of cooperation and on breadth, including both the variety of interests and their approximate financial value. This is not a statistical exercise, as any attempt to attach an exact numerical quantification to either category would only create a false appearance of precision (estimates about the volume and value of trade are usually guesswork and the degree of cooperation can only be measured subjectively). The rankings are not arbitrary, though they are admittedly open to discussion. Even with these caveats, the chart below should serve to illustrate the hypothesis of the inverse relationship: the areas where transatlantic relations are most contested are the economically least significant.

Table 1.3

Correlation between Breadth and Cooperation in Transatlantic Trade Issues during the Clinton Presidency

Issue	Breadth	Cooperation
Uruguay Round Agreement	20	19
New Trade Round	19	13
Financial Services	18	16
Telecom Agreement	17	18
IT Agreement	16	20
Mutual Recognition Agreement	15	17
Macroeconomics	14	15
Data Privacy	13	11
Airbus A380	12	12
Boeing-MDD Merger	11	8
Steel	10	9
GMO	9	10
ILSA	8	7
Aircraft Noise	7	5
FSC	6	4
Helms-Burton	5	6
Beef	4	2
Banana	3	1
Gluten	2	3
Homestyle Copyright Law	1	14

Source: Own Estimates

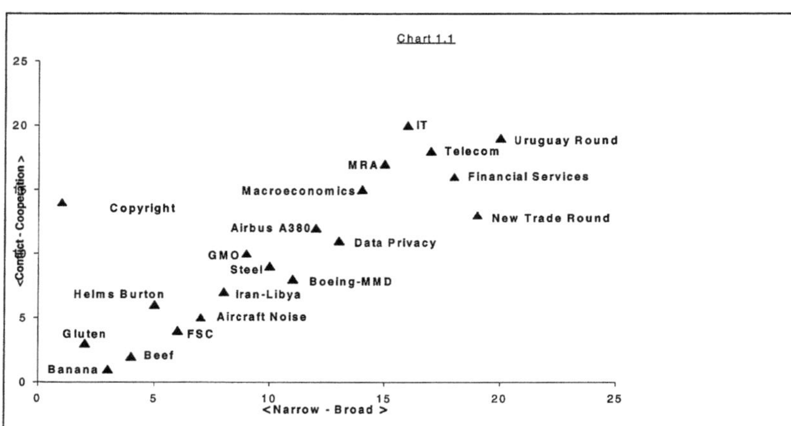

Just as the U.S. and the EU agreed on the opening up of the huge information technology, telecommunications and financial services markets, they became involved in petty fights over bananas, beef and hush kits. As we will see in chapter 4, there were large commercial interests at stake in these agreements, and there was plenty of scope for conflict. Due to the size and breadth of interests, U.S. and EU negotiators made significant efforts to reach viable compromises. On narrow issues, they did not.

2.2.2. The Cost of Escalation

However, it makes only limited sense to look at these issues in isolation as they have an impact on the larger transatlantic relationship. In a second step, I will discuss how the decision to pursue a strategy of cooperation or of conflict in single trade disputes can have costs and benefits that go well beyond the specific issues.

Long-standing political allies like the U.S. and the EU enjoy a predominantly cooperative relationship with a wide range of mutual interests. However, there exist a certain number of conflicting interests and positions of which both sides feel strongly. When disputes erupt, the two sides are caught in a traditional model of international conflict, described by Thomas Schelling as a mixed-motive game.[85] While both sides might have an overarching interest to settle the dispute, the dynamics of conflict might call for a fight even though it damages the interests of both sides.

Beside the economic relationship, the strongest common interest in the transatlantic relationship is security. The EU and the U.S. need each other as partners for global economic and political governance and security cooperation. From this larger political perspective, trade disputes are solely an irritant, of which divert the attention of policy-makers and can hinder cooperation in other, more important areas. They should therefore not be pursued but quickly settled, even on somewhat unfavorable terms.

At the same time, the domestic political climate in either the U.S. or the EU can sometimes be conducive for the pursuit of a conflict. Neither side is caught in a nationalistic spiral like India and Pakistan, where domestic pressures call for the escalation of conflict all the way to military action. But anti-Americanism is occasionally popular in European politics, and Congressional leaders like it if the White House is tough on the EU. This means that the pursuit of trade conflicts – often regardless of their actual significance – becomes a winning domestic strategy. Governments might choose such a strategy sometimes to politically "sell" a compromise on other more important

[85] Schelling 1980, p. 89.

areas.[86] Premature concessions can cause a government to lose political capital or even the next election. The longer the conflict goes on and the more it escalates, the stronger the interest grows on both sides to achieve a favorable, even victorious outcome.

This hypothesis offers another explanation why transatlantic conflicts usually involve narrow issues: the international cost of escalation is deemed to be lower when the stakes are smaller, the opportunity to score domestic points through an aggressive posture at the expense of the Atlantic partnership, possibly through a strategy of tit-for-tat retaliation.

This assumption that the pursuit of such minor conflicts is relatively benign remains only correct if they remain relatively self-contained and do not spill over into other policy areas. This is, however, rarely the case. The nature of trade retaliation calls for counter-action on other products and even completely unrelated trade issues. If unrestrained, this can lead to a retaliatory spiral. As past experience has shown, single trade disputes also negatively affect the ability to cooperate on other trade issues and eventually damage the overall political relationship. While the dynamics of the conflict calls for further escalation, the political cost will eventually rise so high that leaders on both sides will intervene and reach a face-saving compromise. Even with a favorable outcome for one side, the actual economic gain from winning a trade dispute is usually quite small. Usually, both sides would have been better off if the conflict had never started.

One can argue that the U.S. and the EU are caught in a typical prisoner's dilemma: in a single encounter, the individual logic calls for defection, while the collective logic suggests cooperation. What makes transatlantic trade disputes unique is that they yield both relatively small gains and small costs, even as the conflict escalates. The total political and sometimes even economic damage of a drawn-out conflict can actually become quite significant. The fight over the Helms-Burton Act, bananas and beef preoccupied U.S. and European leaders for several years, diverting their time and energy away from other, more important issues. As discussed in chapter 6, the trade disputes were also a cause for the failure to launch a new trade round during the Clinton presidency.

Societies, countries and even individuals have found solutions to the prisoner's dilemma: repeated games and mutually agreed rules or the intervention of a higher authority help to raise the cost of defection and make cooperation a dominant strategy. In a close relationship, such as a marriage, a political coalition or an international alliance, the cost of defection is particularly high. This has not stopped spouses from squabbling, coalition

[86] This was widely seen as the most plausible explanation for the decision by the Bush Jr. administration in 2002 to impose broad steel tariffs. It was fighting for every vote in Congress to gain Trade Promotion Authority (TPA).

partners from fighting and allies from getting into nasty disputes. Whether the marriage is patched up or ends in divorce depends less on the nature of the conflicts than on the ability of the partners to control and settle them. The same, I will argue, is true for the transatlantic partners. The main determinant for the transatlantic trade relationship is the efficiency of the transatlantic mechanisms of damage control.

In the following chapters, I will apply these two hypotheses – the inverse relationship between breadth of an issue and intensity of conflict, and the key role of damage-control mechanisms – to the transatlantic trade relationship in the Clinton era. This will help explain why the U.S. and the EU went all the way towards a trade war on bananas and beef, found it so difficult to resolve the conflict over trade with such marginal trading partners as Cuba, Iran and Libya, and yet were still able to make reach agreements in key strategic areas such as telecommunications and financial services. I will show that damage-control mechanisms set in quickly when big issues were involved, while small issues were allowed to smolder and escalate. The interplay between domestic benefits and international costs also puts a different light on the role of the WTO and its dispute-settlement body. By clarifying the rules of trade disputes, they limit the risks of pursuing these conflicts and create incentives for escalation.

As U.S. and EU leaders learned, the cost of escalation can never be precisely calculated. There is an atmospheric and emotional side to relationships, both personal and political that can be affected by parochial disputes. As the trade fights of the 1990s turned out to be costlier than originally fought, controlling these disputes became one of the main challenges of the transatlantic partnership toward the end of the old century and remains so in the new one.

CHAPTER 3: COOPERATION

The 1990s were a decade of nearly unprecedented progress in transatlantic trade relations. Despite U.S. misgivings about the effect from the creation of the single market in the EC and European worries about the more combative rhetoric of the newly elected Clinton administration, the two sides broke the impasse in the Uruguay Round trade negotiations and paved the way to the most ambitious multilateral trade agreement in history. Subsequent multilateral negotiations liberalized the markets for information technology, telecommunications and financial services. Spurred by political and economic motives, the U.S. and the EU improved the institutional framework for governmental negotiations and private contacts through the Action Plan of the New Transatlantic Agenda (NTA) in 1995 and the Transatlantic Economic Partnership (TEP) in 1998.

3.1 Trade Issues at the Start of the Clinton Administration

When William Jefferson Clinton entered the White House in January 1993, U.S. trade policy, as all of economic policy, appeared at a crossroads. The radical free-market course of the first Reagan Administration lost its direction in the late 1980s. The rising budget and trade deficits – the "twin deficits" – were increasingly seen as heavy burdens on the U.S. economy. Reagan's successor George Bush Sr. tried to deal with both problems by raising taxes, breaking his "read my lips" promise of his acceptance speech at the 1988 Republican Convention, and by adopting an increasingly combative attitude toward America's trade partners, particularly Japan. The Bush Sr. administration continued to favor minimal government interference in any economic activity, including foreign trade. He opposed the Super 301 provision of the 1988 Omnibus Trade act that forced upon the administration investigation of and eventual retaliation against foreign trade barriers to U.S. exports. While the Bush Administration seized upon the Super 301 mechanism to negotiate the Structural Impediments Initiative (SSI) with Japan, it let it lapse in 1990.

As the U.S. economy pulled out of the 1990/91 recession only sluggishly, unease about slow economic growth, the decline in real wages and reduced job prospects for average Americans became intertwined with the general worry about a long-term decline in U.S. competitiveness. Harvard historian Paul Kennedy's 1989 bestseller *The Rise and Fall of the Great Powers* captured a wider public's imagination: as before Spain or Britain, the United States was a great power that had overextended itself and was now paying the price in form of economic decline. Mercantilist Japan and a unified European Community would beat the U.S. in the high-technology game, while the movement of manufacturing plants to low-wage developing countries would cost thousands of American workers their job. [87] Opinion polls showed that a majority of Americans did not see the country on the right track. The quick U.S. victory over Iraq in the Gulf War, while temporarily boosting President Bush's popularity ratings, actually exacerbated his dilemma: America had the best military in the world, but was unable to turn its military strength into economic benefits.

Amid this economic discomfort, foreign trade became an easy scapegoat. It became increasingly popular to blame competition from abroad for America's economic troubles. Moreover, the end of the Cold War paved the way for a whole series of books suggesting that economic conflict would take the place of military conflict in the 21st century. Lester Thurow's *Head to Head*, Jeffrey Garten's *A Cold Peace*, *Trading Places* by Clyde Prestowitz, *The Silent War* by Ira Magaziner and Mark Patinkin, and *Who's Bashing Whom* by Laura Tyson[88] all made a similar point: the international economy was no longer about mutually beneficial exchange, but about competition. To survive in this game, the U.S. had to change its internal and external policies.

The economic unease, combined with a clumsy handling of economic decision-making, made Bush highly vulnerable in the in 1992 presidential elections in which two rivals challenged his economic record from different sides. Both Democratic nominee Bill Clinton and the independent candidate Ross Perot attacked Bush on the budget deficit, rising unemployment, and the failing health care system. On trade policy, however, the two candidates parted ways. While Perot rejected the agreement to create the North American Free Trade Area (NAFTA) with Canada and Mexico and demanded protectionist barriers to defend American workers against allegedly unfair trading nations like Japan, Clinton took a much more differentiated view.

Going against the rising tide of protectionist feeling within his Democratic Party, Clinton repeatedly endorsed the principles of free trade. Even so, he called for tougher approach toward Japan and more activist domestic policies, both to retrain American workers and help businesses compete. "The issue is not whether we should support free trade or open markets," said Clinton, "Of course we should. The real question is whether or not we will have a national economic strategy to make sure we reap its benefits."[89] It was a balancing act, combining general adherence to open trade principles with a harder tactical approach.[90] His proposals for a partnership with high-tech industry garnered him the support of such Silicon Valley heavyweights like John Sculley, head of Apple Computers, and John Young from Hewlett-Packard. A defining moment

[87] Kennedy 1988.
[88] Thurow 1992, Garten 1992, Prestowitz 1988, Magaziner 1989, and Tyson 1992. An insightful survey of this literature can be found in Krugman 1996, p. 71.
[89] Bush, Clinton Differ on Government's Role" Washington Post, October 8, 1992..
[90] Dryden 1995, p. 383

came in October 1992, when Clinton endorsed the NAFTA agreement that had just been initiated by the leaders of the three countries, calling only for some mild additional measures to improve worker retraining and strengthen environmental standards. This helped him to create distance from the trade unions, underlining his image as a political centrist.

But there was another side to Clinton's trade position, a side that unsettled America's trading partners and free-trade advocates like Columbia economist Jagdish Bhagwati.[91] Clinton wholeheartedly embraced the notion that world trade is about competition. "Now the United States is like a big corporation in the world economy," he told a Silicon Valley audience.[92] While the focus of "Clintonomics" was on domestic moves to strengthen the country's educational, job-training and research and development policies, his support of "strategic trade" never seemed to far removed from the dreaded specter of "managed trade".[93] The new administration's bible on trade policy was Laura Tyson's just published book *Who's Bashing Whom: Trade Conflict in High-Technology Industries*, where the new chair of the Council of Economic Advisors laid out a "cautiously activist agenda" to expand American access to global markets and to counter aggressively violations of the multilateral trading regime like the European Airbus subsidies. She warned that, "All to often ... the costs of inaction for American economic welfare are unacceptably high."[94] She also supported a renewal of Super 301 that Clinton did renew by an executive order in 1994. Tyson's book was a far cry from outright protectionism, but justified an industrial policy and some tough measures in trade.

Tyson's activism did not go unchallenged in the Clinton camp. The top economic team included people like Lloyd Bentsen, the treasury secretary, and Robert Rubin, investment banker turned national economic advisor who combined moderate views on budget policy with a strong skepticism of any form of industrial policy. As his USTR, Clinton chose his influential campaign manager Mickey Kantor, a tough lawyer with little experience and few preconceived notions on trade.

The Commerce Department, meanwhile, took up the mercantilist mantra, defining its mission as a fight for export markets against foreign rivals. Commerce Secretary Ron Brown adopted the European and Japanese model of joint government-industry trade mission to drum up exports and led a series of corporate delegations to Asia, Latin America, the former Soviet Union and even Africa.[95] Jeffrey Garten, who became his undersecretary for international trade, orchestrated a political push to open European procurement markets like power

[91] Hobart Rowen, "Trading Theory for Results", Washington Post, April 22, 1993.
[92] Krugman 1996, p. 114.
[93] Clinton's Trade Stance Can't Yet Be Defined." Washington Post, November 29, 1992.
[94] Tyson 1992, p. 13.
[95] "Devoted to Mission till the End", Washington Post, April 4, 1996.

generation for U.S. business.[96] U.S. ambassadors in foreign countries were told to shift their attention from political to commercial issues in order to help the prospects of U.S. companies.

With the Cold War over, U.S. policy makers were believed to consider using their vast national security infrastructure for commercial objectives, such as gaining industrial and technological secrets from European companies. The prospect of CIA commercial espionage aroused serious anger in Europe and triggered serious transatlantic tensions during the Clinton years. In 1995, France expelled five Americans – four of them CIA officers operating as diplomats in the U.S. embassy – as they were caught bribing French officials for information about France's bargaining position in global trade talks. In 1997, Germany expelled another U.S. diplomat accused of trying to steal secrets related to high-technology projects.[97] In 2000, a European Parliament report suggested that the U.S. and Britain used the global Echolon system of electronic surveillance to gain access to trade secrets[98] - of which both governments denied.

Trade diplomacy throughout the Clinton presidency was marked by ambivalence. On one hand, Washington stepped up its attacks on Japanese trade practices and adopted increasingly a result-oriented approach to negotiations, i.e. insisting on certain market shares for U.S. companies in Japan rather than just a general change in business practices. Tensions increased in 1994, when the Japanese refused to accept U.S. demands to set numerical targets for a wide range of products. A year later, Washington came close to impose punitive tariffs on Japanese luxury cars over the question of better access for U.S. car manufacturers to the Japanese markets. U.S. also challenged China over the protection of software and intellectual property, reaching an agreement the day that punitive sanctions were to take effect.[99] Kantor and U.S. secretary of commerce Ron Brown took on the role of advocates for specific U.S. business interests rather than of general principles.[100] To many observers, the Clinton people looked like managed traders with a protectionist slant and some felt that the United States today appears more protectionist than at any other time since the 1920s and early 1930s.[101]

However, most of the actions by the Clinton administration were only rhetorical. While making big demands and threatening repeatedly sanctions, the government ultimately settled for relatively modest outcomes. This pragmatic approach also reflected the divergent interest of U.S. industry. One of the first

[96] "U.S. Pushes Europeans on Markets," Washington Post, Mach 10, 1995

[97] "Bonn Exples U.S. Official for Spying," Washington Post, March 9, 1997.

[98] "Report to EU Says U.S. and U.K. Spied on Allies," International Herald Tribune, February 24, 2000.

[99] Kaplan 1996 p. 162-164.

[100] Dryden 1995 p. 393.

[101] Kaplan 1996 p. 165.

and surprising decisions by the Clinton White House in the realm of trade policy was to refuse punitive tariffs on South Korean computer chips amid strong resistance by domestic computer makers.[102] In a speech at the American University in Washington, where his great model John F. Kennedy had once given one of his major foreign-policy addresses, Clinton laid out his trade philosophy: "The truth of our age is this, and must be this: open and competitive commerce will enrich us as a nation," he said, but added, "We must enforce our trade laws and our agreements with all the tools and energy at our disposal." Clinton's main focus was not on foreign trade diplomacy, but rather on measures to strengthen domestic productivity through investment in education and research and development.

Clinton came down firmly on the side of free trade when he fought a hard battle, mostly against his own party, for the ratification of NAFTA in Congress. To respond to the critics of the free trade pact, Clinton had negotiated some mild side agreements on environmental and labor standards with Mexican government, though this did not placate the opponents to the deal. While the majority of the business community fought hard for NAFTA, a coalition of labor unions, environmental groups, various business interests and political leaders from far-right Pat Buchanan to civil rights leaders Jesse Jackson opposed the agreement. The debate over NAFTA, that in reality was just one small regional liberalization accord,[103] became a defining moment for U.S. economic policy in the 1990s. It was the first major encounter between proponents and opponents of globalization, between the winners and losers of dramatic economic changes in the late 20th century.[104]

The Congressional vote in favor of NAFTA in November 1993 was one of the biggest domestic achievements of Clinton's troubled first year in office, but it alienated his union supporters and large parts of the Democratic Party. After NAFTA, the majority of Democrats found themselves repeatedly on the side of protectionism, while it defined Clinton early on as a free trader. His administration did not waste any time to carry the momentum of the NAFTA victory over the stalled GATT negotiations.

3.2 The Road to the Uruguay Round Agreement

The Uruguay Round of multilateral trade negotiations (MTN) was launched at the GATT conference of Punta del Este, Uruguay in September 1986. It was the result mostly of pressure by the U.S. government that had pushed for new trade talks since November 1982, when the EC stubbornly refused open

[102] "Administration doesn't have a Trade Policy," Washington Post, March 21, 1993.
[103] Kaplan 1996, p. 387.
[104] Cohen 1996, p. 238/9.

negotiations on agriculture and services at the GATT ministerial conference in Geneva.[105] In the following years, the U.S. interest for a new trade round continued to grow. Washington wanted to make sure that the completion of the single market in the EC, targeted for completion by the Single European Act (SEA) for the end of 1992, would not undermine the multilateral global trade framework. In light of the skyrocketing U.S. trade deficit, the Reagan administration was also eager to push its own trade agenda in multilateral talks, primarily a reduction of agricultural subsidies in the EC and Japan and the liberalization of trade in services in which the U.S. economy had its strongest advantages. The Europeans were far less enthusiastic. They were worried about U.S. pressure to reform the expensive, distorting, and politically deeply entrenched Common Agricultural Policy (CAP) and would have preferred to focus on intra-European process of liberalization through the single market. With protectionist pressures in the U.S. Congress rising, EC leaders finally relented in 1986.

European resistance to a deal on farm subsidies continued to slow the negotiations. The original deadline of the end –of 1990 passed without an agreement. Negotiations broke down in December amid French and Japanese resistance to the proposed reduction in agricultural subsidies.

When GATT director general Alfred Dunkel revived the talks in 1991, the new deadline became June 1993, when the Congressional fast-track authority was bound to expire.[106]Throughout 1991, Dunkel struggled the break the stalemate in the trade negotiations. In December, he proposed a compromise that was criticized by the EC and received little support from the U.S.[107] The EU agricultural policy remained the key hurdle to agreement. U.S. negotiators were adamant to change the European practice of subsidies and protection, and not only because of the interest of its own farmers. Better access to the EC market was also a major demand for developing countries that were eager for something in return before agreeing to the trade liberalization measures pursued by the U.S.

EC leaders made some progress in the reform of the CAP by agreeing in May 1992 to the proposals of agricultural commissioner Ray McSherry that shifted nontransparent consumer subsidies to more transparent taxpayer subsidies via a direct compensation program for farmers. Although the McSherry reform was not directly tied to the GATT talks, it opened a door to further EC concessions. A reduction in cereal prices reduced the need for export subsidies, the most troublesome aspect of CAP for Europe's trading partners.[108]

---

[105] Schott 2000, p. 5.
[106] This deadline was later extended to December 15, 1993.
[107] Kaplan 1996 p. 125.
[108] "U.S. to Hit Europe with Stiff Tariffs," Washington Post, November 6, 1992.

Hopes that EC leaders would try to reach an agreement with the Bush administration before the November 1992 elections did not materialize. By fall, the GATT talks had not only stalled completely as the EC waited for the results of the presidential elections, but a new trade dispute over EC oilseed subsidies was looming. Earlier in the year, two GATT panels had ruled that these subsidies unfairly deprived the U.S. of the benefits of a 30-year-old agreement to cut European oilseeds tariffs to zero. The EC's refusal to cut the subsidies added to the U.S. anger over its allies.

Only days after losing the presidential elections, President Bush announced it would slap punitive tariffs 200 percent on $300 million worth of agricultural products. Hardest hit would be French white wine exports to the U.S. While the oilseed dispute was not directly related to the GATT talks, the move was widely seen as an effort to raise the stakes in the larger multilateral negotiations. The oilseed dispute moved the center of conflict from the transatlantic to the intra-European arena. In late November 1992, U.S. and EC negotiators reached an agreement in Washington in which the Europeans accepted significant cuts oilseed subsidies as well as other agricultural support measures.[109] As the only member country, France rejected the so-called Blair House agreement and threatened to invoke the national security clause to veto the deal in the Council of Ministers. The split within the EC also thwarted the last-minute efforts by Bush's trade representative Carla Hills to complete the Uruguay round before leaving office.[110] Hopes for a quick deal dimmed further when Kantor expressed reservations about key elements of the preliminary agreements, including the proposed new rules for settling trade disputes. As the June deadline for completing the round looked increasingly unrealistic, the White House asked Congress for another six-month extension of fast-track authority until mid-December.

In February 1993, Kantor stepped up the pressure on Brussels when he announced retaliatory measures against EC procurement rules that were seen as favoring European telecommunications and electrical equipment manufacturers. But Washington pulled back from its threat shortly before its self-imposed deadline as both sides pledged to work towards a resolution of the conflict within the GATT talks. Introducing another potential dispute in the talks, the U.S. stepped up the pressure on European countries, and particularly France, to open up audiovisual trade by eliminating television quotas for U.S. movies and limiting subsidies for the domestic film industry.[111] The chances of a trade deal improved in July after a late-night negotiating session at the G-7 summit in Tokyo resulted in unexpected progress with the Japanese government agreeing

[109] "France Calls Trade Pact Inadmissible," Washington Post, November 22, 1992.
[110] "At GATT Talks, Motion is Tabled," Washington Post, January 29, 1993.
[111] "U.S., EC Try to Revive Trade Talks," Washington Post, March 30, 1993.

to compromise on some sensitive issues.[112] But it was again the issue of agricultural subsidies that caused the momentum to slow. The new conservative French government of Edouard Balladur took an exceedingly hard line on the issue by rejecting the 1992 subsidy agreement as unacceptable for French farmers.

As trade talks went into the final round in December Balladur realized that he had committed himself politically to modifying the 1992 agreement. If the U.S. did not compromise on this issue, the GATT accord was dead.[113] When in the wee hours of December 15, agreement was finally reached between the U.S. and the (newly named) EU, the scorecard looked rather better for the Europeans (particularly the French) than for the Americans. The U.S. achieved its overall goal to make agriculture for the first time part of the GATT framework, but the actual concessions from the EU fell short of the 1992 agreement. France also got its way in keeping audiovisual trade out of GATT. U.S. demands on the liberalization of financial services and stock brokerage were also postponed to a later round. The same was true for the German demands to revise the 1992 aircraft agreement. To the disappointment of Europeans and other trading partners the U.S. was allowed to keep its anti-dumping laws, including the controversial Section 301 provision.[114]

Overall, the U.S. made more concessions than the EU. Like in a game of "chicken", where two drivers approach each other on a road to see who will swerve first, France got its way by relinquishing the initiative. With the biggest stake in a further liberalization of global trade, the U.S. accepted a less than perfect agreement that left key issues for later negotiations. Clinton followed the example of all U.S. governments since 1945 to forgo some short-term national economic interests to the benefit of global prosperity. This was particularly urgent because as in 1993 the world economy had not yet pulled out of recession; a trade deal was seen as a key factor for economic recovery. This calculation was accurate: large sectors in the U.S. economy benefited from the liberalization of the Uruguay Round and its follow-up agreements, as well as from the subsequent years of strong global growth. The biggest loser of the Uruguay round may have been the developing countries, who gained very little market access in the area where they are strong, mostly agriculture and textiles, but had to open up some sensitive sectors and accept strict new rules on intellectual property and services.

Ministers from 124 countries and the EU met in April 1994 in the Moroccan town of Marrakesh to sign the new trade agreements. Its main features were the

---

[112] "G-7 Ministers Breathe New Life into World Trade Talks," Washington Post, July 8, 1993.

[113] Kaplan 1996, p. 127

[114] "Key Agreement Clears Way for Global Trade Pact," Washington Post, December, 13, 1992.

first-time inclusion of trade in services into the GATT framework through the General Agreement of Trade in Service (GATS), which also broadened the definition of trade to include sales of foreign subsidiaries in the host country and purchases of services by non-residents; the agreement on trade-related intellectual property rights (TRIPs) and trade-related investment measures (TRIMs), the clarification of anti-dumping rules, and a modest liberalization of agricultural trade. The countries defined permissible subsidies and anti-dumping measures in the Agreement on Subsidies and Countervailing Measures (ASCM), and set rules for the import regulations of agricultural products in the Sanitary and Phytosanitary Agreement (SPS). Finally, the countries made the biggest institutional change in the global trading regime since 1947: they agreed to a new Dispute-Settlement Understanding (DSU) and established the World Trade Organization (WTO) 45 years after U.S. Congress had rejected the creation of the International Trade Organization (ITO) and put its teeth into enforcement mechanisms. This had been a major demand from Washington, who had seen too many times trading partners ignore unfavorable GATT rulings.[115]

Under GATT, one country could block the establishment of a dispute-settlement panel or the adoption of its finding. The DSU created a stronger procedure for settling complaints against alleged violations of WTO rules: if consultations between the parties failed to reach agreement, the WTO would set up a panel of trade experts to investigate. The losing side could appeal the panel's finding, but the decision of the Appellate Body was binding. If the defendant country did not comply within a reasonable amount of time, the complainant country could negotiate financial compensation or ask the WTO for authorization to suspend trade concessions – i.e. impose punitive tariffs – commensurate to the damage inflicted on its trading interests. While this system did not limit a country's sovereignty - compliance could not be enforced – it created a cost for non-compliance.[116] The U.S. also won a commitment that issues left open in the Uruguay Round Agreement would be addressed in new trade negotiations that had to start before the end of 1999. This so-called "built-in agenda" for the next trade round consisted mostly of agriculture, services and a review of intellectual property rights.

Clinton's previous commitment to free trade could have turned the failure of the GATT talks into a big political setback. Clinton actually had the support of key Democrats on GATT, including house member Richard Gephardt, a major critic of NAFTA. Republicans were also in favor of the agreement, but wanted to deny the president a success. Ratification became tied up in political

---

[115] "Will the New World Trade Organization Work?" Washington Post, June 26, 1994.
[116] Charnovitz 2001, p. 792-794.

maneuvering of the mid-term election year.[117] The White House did not introduce the bill until September, and Republicans succeeded to postpone the vote until after the election, where they hoped to score gains against the Democrats. After the Republican upset victory, Clinton tried to push the vote through before the old Congress sojourned. In the end, the president had to agree to a "trigger mechanism" that would allow Congress to vote to withdraw from the WTO if it ruled consistently against U.S. interests.[118]

The vote in the House in November 1994 was 288 to 146, far wider than the narrow NAFTA vote a year earlier. Critics charged that most representatives had not even bothered to study the thousands of highly detailed and technical points in the agreement.[119] Even so, 89 Democrats voted against their president on such a crucial issue. It was only after the clear senate vote (76 to 24) on December 1 that most of the other countries sent the agreement for ratification to their legislative bodies. On January 1, 1995, the WTO opened its doors in Geneva, marking the biggest institutional change in the management of the global economy since the 1940s.

3.3 The WTO hat trick: The liberalization of information technology, telecommunications and financial services

The twelve months from December 1996 to December 1997 brought three major multilateral trade agreements that helped to liberalize some of the most important economic sectors: information technology (IT), telecommunications and financial services. In these single-sector talks the U.S. and EU shared a strong interest in global liberalization and quickly succeeded in resolving disputes relating to specific product groups. Europeans worried about possible U.S. dominance in all three areas, but the intra-EU liberalization agenda made it easier for negotiators to open the markets to U.S. companies.

3.3.1. The Information Technology Agreement

Lobbyists from the U.S. technology industry had sought an elimination of all tariffs on all electronic goods in the Uruguay Round. At that time, however, the European industry was reluctant to lower its tariffs on semiconductors and other IT products.[120] The U.S. took up the issue in the WTO and began pressing for duty elimination on all IT products by the year 2000. As IT trade exploded in the following years, Canada, Japan and finally the EU came on board. At the

---

[117] Kaplan 1996, p. 130-132.

[118] "Congress to Cast Vote on Historic Trade Pact," Washington Post, November 28, 1994.

[119] Lovett 1999, p. 151.

[120] 1996 Annual Report of the President of the United States on the Trade Agreements Program. *www.ustr.gov/html/1997tpa_part4_1.html*

APEC summit in the Philippine capital Manila in November 1996, Clinton succeeded to persuade APEC leaders to endorse the initiative and called for its conclusion by the impending WTO Ministerial Conference in Singapore in December.[121]

For any agreement to become effective, 90 percent of global IT trade (estimated at $500 billion a year) had to be covered. The Quad countries – the U.S., the EU, Japan and Canada – alone had 60 percent of the world market. As the WTO members met in Singapore, 28 countries representing 83 percent of IT trade were in principle on board and several others signaled their desire to join. But April 1, 1997, 40 countries representing well over 90 percent of IT trade were part of the agreement. All countries had to commit themselves to the abolition of tariffs by January 1, 2000, thought some developing countries were granted the right to phase in the tariff cuts until 2004.

The final obstacles to achieve the breakthrough in Singapore were some complex disagreements between the U.S. and the EU over a variety of products and classifications. In a three-day bargaining session, U.S. deputy trade representative Charlene Barshefsky and EU trade commissioner Leon Brittan resolved these disputes and paved the way for the agreement. Both sides had plenty of bargaining chips – product groups that the other side wanted to keep out. The two sides reached a compromise the majority of the time towards liberalization. For example, when they agreed that the pact would cover both digital photocopiers, that the EU wanted excluded, and capacitors (electronic components which regulate the flow of electrical current), that the U.S. wanted excluded because it did not consider it an IT product.[122] France got its way on CD-ROMs containing music or movies that were classified as entertainment and therefore, left out of the agreement.

Generally, the IT agreement was seen as being more in the commercial interest of the U.S. than of the EU, who had reason to fear for some of its domestic manufacturers. But by 1996, the IT industry was widely accepted as a major engine of economic growth and productivity increases. EU negotiators took a decidedly non-mercantilist position: the gains from lower prices and better technology would outweigh any job losses due to increased exports from the U.S. and Asia. "The fact that this deal would increase our trade deficit is a matter of complete indifference to us," said EU negotiator Peter Carl.[123]

In the U.S. Congress, not everyone took such an enlightened approach. When Barshefsky presented the agreement to Congress in 1997, she came under strong pressure to withdraw the offer on capacitors in which European and

---

[121] "Clinton in Drive for IT Trade Pact," Financial Times, November 25, 1996.

[122] "U.S. and Europe Agree on Freeing Technology Trade," New York Times, December 12, 1996.

[123] "Trade Ministers Agree on Global High-Tech Accord," International Herald Tribune, December 12, 1996.

Japanese producers had technological and cost advantages. Because these components were widely used in the defense industry, lobbies used national-security arguments for protecting the industry against foreign competition. Barshefsky argued successfully that a retraction on that issue would unravel an agreement that overall was highly beneficial for the U.S. economy.[124] The ITA entered into force on July 1, 1997 with the first staged reduction in tariffs.

3.3.2. The Telecommunications Agreement

Talks on the global opening of the telecommunications markets (estimated in 1995 to be worth $600 billion) proved to be more difficult. Unlike IT, telecommunications did not involved trade in manufactured goods but the more complex area of services. They had traditionally been seen as a public utility served by a state-owned or tightly regulated monopoly combining post, telephone and telegraph (PTT) services. These monopolies generated plenty of revenues for the government, though they stifled technological and managerial innovation. The first country to introduce competition in that sector was the U.S., which broke up the AT&T monopoly in the early 1980s and succeeded both to reduce prices and accelerate the pace of technological progress. But in other parts of the world, attitudes changed much more slowly. Still, by the mid-1990s, most economists and many public officials had shifted "from seeing telecommunications liberalization as a threat to needed revenues to a necessary precondition to be competitive in the new global economy."[125]

Telecommunications was one of the agenda items in negotiations on the General Agreement on Trade in Services (GATS) of the Uruguay Round, but only a partial agreement was reached on a liberalization schedule. Thus, this issue was put into an Annex on Telecommunications. The Annex required WTO members to ensure non-discriminatory access to telecom services, but did not address the question of market access for telecom providers. Countries, however, agreed to pursue the matter further and conclude a telecommunications agreement by April 30, 1996.

The driving forces behind a complete liberalization of telecom markets continued to be the U.S., who had removed most regulatory barriers in the Telecommunications Act of 1996 that was enacted on February 8, 1996.[126] The EU was a few years behind in its liberalization efforts, and was therefore "the main foot dragger" in the Uruguay Round negotiations.[127] By 1996, the EU positions had fundamentally changed. With most of its 15 members committed to a complete liberalization of local, long-distance and international services by

---

[124] "US Senators Seek to Change IT Pact," Financial Times, February 19, 1997

[125] Senunas 1997, p. 11.

[126] Gelb 2001.

[127] Senunas 1997, p. 8

January 1, 1998, the EU could credibly argue in favor of global liberalization. Within the EU, only the group of poorer countries, Spain, Portugal, Ireland, and Greece would keep some of their markets closed beyond that date. Moreover, the new democracies in East-Central Europe were also on a path of radical liberalization. In Asia and most developing countries, however, the willingness to abolish the entrenched PTT monopolies was much weaker. Given the principle of non-discrimination under GATT, these countries could hope to benefit from the liberalization elsewhere while keeping their own markets closed. The U.S. and the EU differed on their approach toward this 'free rider" problem. While the EU was willing to accept a slower pace of liberalization from trading partners, the U.S. insisted on symmetry.

In February 1996, the U.S. presented an offer for full access to its own telecom markets, including local services, under the condition that a "critical mass" of countries would reciprocate.[128] At a meeting in Geneva just before the April 30 deadline, most of European and some Asian nations matched the U.S. offer, but the U.S. declared that 10 out of 52 countries were just not enough. "We are deeply concerned about a lack of critical mass at this stage," a U.S. trade negotiator said when his country walked out of the talks. The U.S. decision infuriated the EU negotiators. They recognized the shortcomings of the existing offers, but warned that the U.S., in the name of free-trade ideology, was holding out for too much.[129] Some viewed the real reason behind the walkout Motorola's successful resistance to a U.S. offer to open the American satellite telephone market to foreign competition. Motorola was a major investor in Iridium, the satellite phone company that subsequently failed because of a lack of demand.[130]

WTO members decided to postpone the deadline until February 15, 1997, and eventually the tougher U.S. position paid off. Over the following nine months, the U.S. put pressure on key developing countries to open up their telecom markets. In the EU, Spain, Italy and Portugal decided to move the date for the abolition of their state monopolies forward from the year 2000 to January 1, 1998, in line with the other EU members.[131] By February 15, 66 countries representing 90 percent of the global telecommunication markets worth about $600 billion had offered to do away with most restrictions on their telecom markets. The last remaining hurdles were Canada's and Japan's insistence to restrict foreign equity stakes in their dominant telecom operators,

[128] "U.S. Offers Full Access to Telecoms Market in Trade Talks," Financial Times, February 27, 1996.

[129] "U.S. Rebuff Imperils Communications Pact," International Herald Tribune, April 30, 1996.

[130] "Is the U.S. Souring on Free Trade?" New York Times, June 25, 1996.

[131] "68 Nations Agree to Widen Markets in Communications," New York Times, February 16, 1997.

affecting primarily U.S. business interests. EU trade commissioner Leon Brittan again urged the U.S. delegation to go for a compromise. The offers on the table "represented "a massive liberalization of the world telecom market that it would be crazy not to grab with both hands" he said.[132] With a stronger and more unified EU position, his voice carried more weight than a year before. After putting some adding on some face-savings restrictions against Japanese and Canadian companies doing business in the U.S., Washington agreed to a deal. On February 15, 1997, 68 nations endorsed the WTO Agreement on Basic Telecommunications Services, committing themselves to opening up their telecom markets to full competition by 2005.[133]

The telecommunications agreement consisted of three elements: companies from signatory countries gained access to all basic telecommunications markets; they gained the right to acquire and/or hold significant ownership or control of telecommunications services and facilities; and the participants agreed to establish common regulatory principles that defined and prohibited anti-competitive practices such as discrimination and non-transparency.[134] Based on the MFN principles, these results were extended to all WTO members, including non-signatory countries. The telecommunications agreement was the first great success of the GATS. Observers, however, argued that it came about through the forces of the market and technology that had made telecommunications cost a key determinant of competitiveness and thus helped to overcome the shortcomings of the GATS.[135]

Three years later, the issue of foreign ownership once again became a point of transatlantic tensions, though this time the roles were reversed. When Deutsche Telekom agreed to acquire U.S. mobile phone operator VoiceStream in July 2000, Senator Ernest Hollings from South Carolina tried to stop the $45 billion deal because the majority stake held by the German government in Deutsche Telekom. It required heavy lobbying by the Clinton administration to stop the Senate from passing legislation that would have prevented foreign government-owned companies from acquiring U.S. licenses. As the VoiceStream deal would reduce the government stake in Deutsche Telekom to 45%, as well as the possibility of European retaliation against U.S. companies investing in the EU, helped to defeat the bill.[136]

---

[132] "Telecoms Pact Waits for U.S. Verdict," Financial Times, February 14, 1997.
[133] Gelb 2001.
[134] Ibid.
[135] Senunas 1997, p. 16.
[136] "Battle of the Two Rons over Deutsche Telekom," Financial Times, September 5, 2000.

3.3.3. The Financial Services Agreement

The negotiations on a multilateral agreement on trade in financial services followed a similar pattern as the telecom talks. Financial services encompassed banking, insurance, securities and financial information and were widely seen as the most promising area of liberalization. Global domestic bank lending amounted to $38 trillion in the mid-1990s, global securities trading to $19.5 trillion, and worldwide insurance premiums to $2.1 trillion.[137] Yet, inefficiency and lack of competition in the financial sector was a major brake on economic growth in many countries. While capital controls had been lifted in most parts of the world, many developing countries kept tight restrictions on foreign ownership of financial firms.

With the world's most competitive companies the U.S., particularly in investment banking and securities trading had a strong commercial interest in liberalization. In 1995, the U.S. walked away from a near-complete accord because it entailed too little liberalization. The EU salvaged the talks by pushing through a stopgap agreement that was due to expire at the end of 1997. Talks were restarted in April 1997, giving the WTO members nine months to reach an agreement.

The Asian financial crisis, which began in Thailand in July 1997 but quickly spread all over the region, simultaneously boosted and hampered the talks. On one hand, the weakness of the Asian banking sectors was seen as a major cause of the crisis. But the often-destructive force of short-term capital flows made some countries wary of any further liberalization. Malaysia even went back to impose capital controls that it years before lifted.

The talks were threatened in November 1997 when Congress rebuffed the Clinton administration in its pursuit of a renewal of fast-track authority. The White House subsequently tried to demonstrate increasing toughness on trade issues. It was direct pressure from the U.S. and European banks, which wanted to get rid of restrictions on their foreign expansion plans, that kept Washington constructively engaged in the negotiations.[138]. The U.S. and the EU acted together to put pressure on key developing countries to agree to open their financial sectors. The ferocity of the Asian crisis made many of them more willing to embrace reform.

The final negotiations in December 1997 became a "cliffhanger."[139] U.S. lead negotiator, treasury secretary Robert Rubin, tried to get additional market access concessions from Malaysia and Japan that resisted most of the U.S. proposals. Critics from the U.S. Senate, primarily the influential

---

[137] 1999 USTR Annual Report, March 2000. *www.ustr/gov/wto/99ustrrpt/ustr99_finser.htm*

[138] Guy de Joncquières, "Vision of a Global Market," Financial Times, April 9, 1997.

[139] Guy de Joncquières, "Happy end to a Cliffhanger," Financial Times, December 14, 1997.

Republican Alfonse d'Amato, told Rubin that they would not accept a deal that denied U.S. its financial institutions access to most foreign markets. Picking up a suggestion by d'Amato, Rubin proposed to limit the agreement to three years. The EU rejected that approach; its council of ministers instructed Brittan not to accept anything but a permanent agreement. When the EU threatened to walk out of the talks if no agreement was reached by 2 am of the next day, the U.S. relented and agreed to the deal that was on the table.

On December 12, 1997, seventy WTO members signed the FSA, the first agreement to bring financial services permanently under the WTO's multilateral rules. Fifty-two countries guaranteed broad market access terms across all insurance sectors, another fourteen countries committed to open sub-sectors of their insurance markets. Fifty-nine countries committed to permit 100 percent foreign ownership of banking subsidiaries and branches; forty-four countries did the same for securities firm.

The deadline for ratification of these commitments was set for January 29, 1999. Most of these offers just reaffirmed the status quo, as many countries had moved toward a gradual liberalization in previous years. The FSA formalizes the status quo, enabling most of the key countries to bind their existing liberalization through an international agreement. Very little additional reform was agreed in the key banking sector, however.[140] With WTO members committed to start negotiation further liberalization of trade in service in 2000, the U.S. felt it could live with these modest results. Countries like Thailand, South Korea and Indonesia continued on the path of banking reform in the following years. This was only a beginning: experts estimated the potential global welfare gains from future financial reforms at $1.3 trillion.[141]

The "hat-trick"[142]of IT, telecom and financial services marked the high point of multilateral trade liberalization in the post Cold-War era. The three sectors contributed well several trillion dollars annually to global trade, and the opening of these sectors became an important element of the strong economic growth rates of the 1990s. Single-sector multilateral talks were a new strategy in the global trade regime, and potentially risky because they did not permit any trade-offs between unrelated issues. Even so, stellar growth rates in these industries and a general global consensus in favor of liberalization helped to remove the biggest obstacles. The U.S. and the EU shared similar interests on these issues, as both had committed themselves to internal liberalization even before the multilateral talks. Both sides understood that the general economic gains from liberalization in these key sectors would outweigh any loss of market share for domestic producers.

---

140 Dobson/Jacquet 1998.

141 Ibid.

142 "WTO Hopes for Hat-Trick," Financial Times, September 18, 1997.

In established industries with small or no growth rates this strategy was bound to fail. The single-issue talks on the liberalization of maritime trade never really came off the ground as the U.S. never made an offer to open its own shipping market. U.S. negotiators claimed the lack of serious offers from other countries, but it was generally suspected that the Clinton administration did not want to take on the entrenched interests in the shipping industry and labor union.[143] In IT, telecom and financial services, the transatlantic axis was the engine behind global liberalization and disagreements between the U.S. and the EU were mostly limited to tactical issues. While the EU was satisfied with deals that indicated the road toward liberalization, the U.S. wanted to push as far as possible and risked not to have a deal at all. In the telecom case, the U.S. tactics were fully vindicated. "I am glad we waited", said WTO director general Renato Ruggiero after the Feb. 1997 breakthrough.[144] Since the EU Commission was pushing itself an ambitious agenda of deregulation against the resistance of some member states, the tough U.S. stance actually served its own interests.

In financial services, EU warnings of an international financial backlash if the talks failed made the U.S. accept less than it originally wanted.[145] But again, the largest players in the U.S. banking industry were satisfied with what they received and embraced the accord. Against the background of fading support for Clintons' trade polices in the U.S. Congress and transatlantic disputes over U.S. sanctions against Cuba, Iran and Libya, the major industrialized nations demonstrated tremendous willpower and skill in the interest of free trade.

3.4. Towards a post-Cold War Transatlantic Partnership

3.4.1. Post-Cold War Beginnings

The decade after the end of the Cold War saw a flurry of initiatives to put the transatlantic relationship on a new footing. As the Cold War ended and the Warsaw Pact dissolved, Europeans were keen for renewed U.S. security commitments to its allies. Yet in the absence of a major external threat, ideas started to emerge that trade linkages would provide a stable basis for the continuation of the mutual security commitments.[146] The result was the Transatlantic Declaration, adopted in December 1990. It espoused principles of cooperation without calling for any specific measures. The only concrete result was the establishment of semi-annual U.S.-European summits, involving the

---

143 "US lets shipping trade talks gently sink," Financial Times, February 8, 1996.
144 "68 Nations Agree to Widen Markets in Communications," New York Times, February 16, 1997.
145 Guy de Joncquières, "Happy end to a Cliffhanger," Financial Times, December 14, 1997.
146 Kerremans 2000.

U.S. president, the president of the European Commission and the chief of government of the country holding the rotating six-month EU presidency. These summits were often seen as empty rituals with embarrassingly few results. Still, they created a forum for regular consultations and deadline pressure to solve bilateral disputes.

Until the end 1993, trade discussions were dominated by the difficult and very concrete negotiations over the Uruguay Round. Once agreement had been reached, however, the time was ripe for new ideas about the future of the transatlantic relationship. While the Clinton administration was looking for ways to strengthen its free-trade credentials and reach quick agreement on those issues left open in the Uruguay Round, Europeans were concerned about a U.S. turn toward regionalism in the wake of NAFTA. Frustrated with the slow progress in the Uruguay round, U.S. policy-makers were putting increasing efforts both into the extension of NAFTA toward Latin America, the Free Trade Area of the Americas (FTAA), and the creation of a free-trade zone in the Pacific region through the intensification of the Asia Pacific Economic Cooperation (APEC) forum. While Europe had for decades been the main driving force behind regional trade agreements, there were now fears of becoming the odd man out in a regionalized trading world.[147]

Both sides admitted that the growing volume of trade and investment across the Atlantic required new trade agreements and rules. After eight rounds of multilateral trade negotiations since 1947, average tariffs between the U.S. and EU had come down to 6.4 per cent (for U.S. products in the EU) and 3.2 per cent (for EU products in the U.S.), but had still not completely disappeared.[148] In addition, there remained a plethora of administrative and regulatory barriers that made transatlantic trade far more cumbersome than commercial exchange either within the U.S. or the EU. Removing these remaining hurdles, experts were convinced, could generate billions of dollars of additional economic growth on both sides of the Atlantic.

3.4.2. The Transatlantic Free Trade Area (TAFTA)

The opening call for new transatlantic initiatives came from Washington. Asked by Clinton to come up with some proposals for the Group of Seven summit in Naples in July 1994, Kantor developed an agenda called "Open Market 2000." Despite its name, it set no timetable but included ambitious goals for the liberalization of airline landing right, telecommunications markets and financial services. However, America's partners gave the plan a frosty reception, France rejected it outright and the EU Commission, whose

[147] Ibid.
[148] Blackwill/Archick 1998.

importance was obviously underestimated in Washington, complained that it had not been consulted at all. Other countries warned that the proposals could stir political resistance against the still pending ratification of the Uruguay Round agreements.[149]

The idea for a transatlantic free trade area (TAFTA) came also first from North America. Clyde Prestowitz, a prominent critic of U.S. trade policy, called for such an agreement as an answer to what he considered to be unfair Japanese and Asian trade practices.[150] In October 1994, Canada's trade minister Roy McClaren was the first political leader who proposed a trade pact linking the EU with NAFTA.[151] German foreign minister Klaus Kinkel in a speech in Chicago then took up the ball in April 1995 in which he presented the first comprehensive blueprint for TAFTA. Kinkel's speech reflected European concern that the U.S. would extend NAFTA further south, a goal endorsed at the 1994 Miami Summit of the Americas, and build a Free Trade Area of the Americas (FTAA) while moving East toward a Pacific Free Trade zone, all the while neglecting the transatlantic axis. Early support for the idea came among others ranging from British foreign secretary Malcolm Rifkind, to U.S. commerce secretary Ron Brown to EU Commission president Jacques Santer.[152] Criticism came from Asian leaders who feared to be left out of the next round of trade liberalization and from the director general of the newly founded World Trade Organization (WTO), Renato Ruggiero. He expressed worries that TAFTA would undermine the multilateral framework of the WTO and widen the gap between the haves and have-nots.

The TAFTA concept created a split between foreign policy and foreign trade officials both in the U.S. and the EU. Foreign ministers saw the potential for the overall strategic relationship through such an agreement and did concern themselves too much with the economic details. Trade experts immediately recognized the inherent conflict in TAFTA: to make it WTO compatible, the free trade privileges had to be either granted to all trading partners with Most Favored Nation (MFN) status or had to cover "substantially all trade," i.e. also sensitive areas like agriculture, textiles and audio-visual products, where the EU and the US remained at loggerheads. Like Kinkel and U.S. secretary of state Warren Christopher ignored this dilemma when he said in a speech in June 1995: "The long-term objective is the integration of the economies of North America and Europe, consistent with the principles of the WTO."[153]

---

[149] "Opportunity Lost: Clinton's Naples Reversal," Washington Post, July 16, 1994.
[150] Prestowitz/Gaster 1994
[151] Hindley 1999, p. 45
[152] "Trade Zone plan intrigues leaders on both sides of the Atlantic," Washington Post, May 28, 1995.
[153] Gordon 2001, p. 51.

Both U.S. secretary of commerce Ron Brown and EU trade commissioner Leon Brittan favored a more pragmatic building-block approach. Brown was particularly interested in engaging the private sector in the transatlantic relationship, both as an advisor and a lobby group for free trade. The EU Commission and some European business leaders were at first skeptical, fearing that a business forum would become just another talking shop without any concrete input into the decision-making process. In the end, Brown convinced the skeptics that the "Transatlantic Business Dialogue" would attract sufficient political attention to create added value to the large number of existing institutions.[154] In late April 1995, Brown and Brittan sent a joint letter of invitation for the TABD to more than hundred large European and American companies and trade associations, where they said:

> "The goal is to provide a means for U.S. and EU companies and organizations to develop an agenda of key issues that could be addressed by the European Commission and the U.S. Administration so as to improve and deepen the transatlantic business relationship....We believe that a direct business perspective could make a constructive contribution to defining our vision of the future shape and direction of that relationship."[155]

3.4.3. The New Transatlantic Agenda (NTA)

When Clinton, Santer and French President Jacques Chirac met in Washington in June 1995 to discuss a New Transatlantic Agenda (NTA) for the US-EU summit in December, they still faced the options of a lofty, vague declarations of principles similar to the 1990 document, an ambitious proposal for TAFTA, and a "building-bloc approach" consisting of the TABD, bilateral talks on regulatory issues and a show of support for a new WTO trade round. A High-Level Working Group was set up to arrive at answers to these choices. In the end, the pragmatists won out both in Washington and Brussels. At meetings of the EU Council of Ministers (General Affairs) and a sub-cabinet group in the U.S. capital, both sides endorsed the search for deeper transatlantic relations. While the EU emphasized regulatory issues, such as testing and certification, the U.S. side was mostly concerned in locking in EU support for trade liberalization in the WTO, including the pending IT and telecom negotiations.[156]

The NTA adopted by the EU-US Summit on December 3, 1995 in Madrid and the attached Action Plan covered a whole range of issues. It called for new

[154] Kerremans 2000.
[155] Ibid.
[156] Ibid.

communication channels between the two sides to discuss trade issues as well as actions against cross-border criminality, security, cultural and educational exchanges. Most importantly, the NTA opened the way for a new involvement for civil society. Beside the already launched TABD, it too provided for a dialogue for labor and environmental groups.

While the NTA gave a strong endorsement for further multilateral negotiations, it remained purposely vague on the issue of free trade. It commissioned a joint EU-US study on "reducing or eliminating" barriers to trade, but set no deadline. France insisted on the word "reducing" to avoid a commitment on the elimination of agricultural or audio-visual tariffs.[157]

The NTA and its spirit of cooperation helped to pave the way for the breakthroughs in the multilateral single-sector negotiations. Though to the disappointment of many, the drive toward NAFTA did not gain momentum. The German Federation of Industry (BDI) in 1996 gave a luke-warm endorsement of TAFTA, in which it mostly warned of trade diversion and possible retaliation by excluded countries.[158] In the U.S., the administration tried to keep trade issues out of the public debate ahead of the November 1996 presidential elections.[159] France continued to object to any transatlantic trade deal where the U.S. might exert pressure on agriculture and audio-visuals.[160]

3.4.4. The New Transatlantic Marketplace (NTM) and the Transatlantic Economic Partnership (TEP)

The prospects for new transatlantic initiatives did not improve after Clinton's reelection. The president encountered growing resistance against his trade agenda, including the renewal of fast-track authority, in the still Republican-dominated Congress. Jeffrey Garten, the Harvard professor and Under Secretary of Commerce in the administration's first term, called the trade policy a shambles in, "What was once a vigorous approach to commercial diplomacy has been eviscerated...And in Congress, the political foundation for a broad trade policy has crumbled."[161] The June 1997 G-7 summit in Denver, Colorado, was overshadowed by European anger over Clinton's triumphantalism, as the administration tried to present the U.S. economic system as a model for the whole world, and over U.S. hesitation to ratify the Kyoto accord on measures against climate change. Furthermore, the Helms-Burton and d'Amato bills plus the threatened veto of the EU Commission

[157] Ibid.
[158] Gordon 2001, p. 52.
[159] "Perils of a Transatlantic Alliance," Financial Times, October 14, 1996.
[160] Gordon 2001, p. 52.
[161] "Clinton Effort On Freer Trade Is Losing Steam," New York Times, June 9, 1997.

against the merger of U.S. aircraft giants Boeing and McDonnell Douglas contributed to the sour mood.

But the atmosphere of crisis gave rise to new ideas. Both academics and political leaders were again looking for ways to link security and trade issues in a constructive way: instead of letting trade disputes damage military cooperation in the Balkans and elsewhere, the transatlantic partners were told to turn their common security interests into a powerful engine to break up any impasse over trade.

Ellen Frost, the councilor to the U.S. Trade Representative from 1993 to 1995, proposed in a book that the creation of North Atlantic Economic Community (NATEC) should combine economic and strategic elements of cooperation. While she rejected TAFTA as a threat to the multilateral trade regime, she was also critical of the "current building-blocks approach" to the transatlantic partnership as "too limited, because it precludes broader linkages that can facilitate comprehensive breakthroughs."[162] Her stated goal was completely free transatlantic trade by 2010.

In Brussels, Trade Commissioner Brittan became increasingly concerned about the domestic weakness of President Clinton and his inability to get fast-track authority renewed by a Republic Congress. As the list of transatlantic trade disputes grew, Brittan feared that the U.S. would turn the WTO talks on agriculture and services that had to be started by December 1999 into a tribunal over the CAP. Brittan's solution was a new all-encompassing round of multilateral trade negotiations that would address a whole range of trade and trade-related issues, not just agriculture. "For the first time since the creation of the GATT…the Europeans would initiate such a round, the Millennium Round."[163] Britain believed a transatlantic initiative to bring industrial tariffs to zero, create free trade in services, accelerate of mutual recognition agreements, and achieving some progress on the sensitive issues like agriculture, audiovisual products, public procurement, shipping, and textiles, could pave the way to the new round.

At the annual meeting of the World Economic Forum of political and business leaders in January 1998, trade was again on top of the agenda for the assembled politicians, business leaders and academics. "The building block approach toward a transatlantic market place – first developed through the transatlantic business dialogue in 1995 – has shown its limitations…progress is painfully slow," wrote Lionel Barber in the Financial Times.[164] Washington agreed to explore these issues, but was quite unenthusiastic: USTR Charlene

---

[162] Frost 1997, p. 4.
[163] Kerremans 2000.
[164] "Europe's exhibits stir," Financial Times, February 3, 1998.

Barshefsky called the talks "very informal" and "very preliminary."[165] In a February 11, 1998 letter she listed five principles that the U.S. would insist upon for a NTM:

> First, any initiative must be in the interest of the United States. Second, it must be trade creating, not trade diverting. Third, it must enhance the global trading system and build a model for the future. Fourth, it must not prejudice the resumption in 1999 of global talks on the WTO built-in agenda, most notably in agriculture. And finally, it must in no way detract from our ability to enforce aggressively our existing agreements with the EU. If we can develop a proposal that adheres to all of these principles, we will then have a solid basis for moving forward.[166]

On March 11, 1998, the EU Commission approved Brittan's blueprint for a "New Transatlantic Marketplace," calling for intensified cooperation in four areas: technical barriers to trade, trade in services, the elimination of all industrial tariffs by 2010, and multilateral trade issues such as government procurement, investment and intellectual property. To forestall criticism from EU member states, the proposal excluded aviation, agriculture, fishing and audio-visual products. In his presentation, Brittan focused on the linkage between trade and politics:

> The New Transatlantic Marketplace is a specifically tailored package of measures to address the real barriers that exist in the EU/US trading relationship. It represents a huge leap forward for Europe's relationship with the US, bringing not only strong economic benefits for both business and consumers, but also a new political momentum to relations across the Atlantic.[167]

The French government immediately objected to the proposal, warning that such an ambitious bilateral initiative would undermine the move toward the next multilateral WTO round. Its main motive, however, was the worry that any US-EU trade initiative would soon focus on the two issues dearest to the French – the protection of its farmers and its movie industry[168]. Foreign minister Hubert Vedrine expressed his "deep disagreement on the substance of the initiative"

---

[165] "U.S. in talks with EU on easing trade curbs," Washington Post, February 4, 1998.
[166] Kerremans 2000.
[167] "European Commission Backs New Transatlantic Marketplace," PRNewswire, March 11, 1998.
[168] Gordon 2001, p. 61.

leaving no doubt about his government's determination to block the plan. French President Jacques Chirac dismissed the NTM as a "personal initiative by Sir Leon Brittan, who, all alone, went off to negotiate a free trade area between the U.S. and Europe without a mandate."[169] The French stance was mirrored by critical remarks in the U.S. Congress, where the chairman of the Senate Finance Committee William Roth and the Senate Finance Subcommittee on Trade Chuck Grassley objected to the exclusion of agriculture, fishery and other issues high on the U.S. agenda. France had good reason to fear that these issues could not be excluded forever once US-EU negotiations got under way.

In the face of France's objections, the EU Council took the NTM off the agenda for the impending EU-US summit set for May 18 in London. However, the council endorsed Brittan's proposal to launch the Millennium round and also accepted some of the elements of the NTM. In the following weeks, the Commission and the U.S. administration arrived at a new, more modest set of proposals covering mostly the elimination of regulatory issues.[170] The Transatlantic Economic Partnership (TEP) was officially unveiled at the London summit. According to Brittan, it "proposes a rolling agenda of cooperation and negotiation rather than a single, big-bang agreement" and had as its chief aim the launch of a new WTO round by the end of 1999.[171] While some observers regretted the vagueness of the TEP, they saw it as a more realistic vehicle for further trade talks than the more ambitious NTM. For a EU stance in trade policy matters to be improved by a French veto may be unprecedented. This is what happened, however.[172]

The main achievement of the London Summit was the compromise over the U.S. sanctions policy on Cuba, Iran and Libya, Europe's main condition for signing the TEP. With the disputes over sanctions mostly behind them, the partners were ready to tackle other less sensational, but equally thorny issues of transatlantic trade. In several meetings between U.S. and EU trade negotiators in the summer and fall of 1998, an Action Plan based on the TEP took shape. It included talks to "strengthen market access" for services, a framework for regulatory cooperation with a focus on harmonization of standards over mutual recognition, the opening of government procurement markets, and a new effort to reach global investment rules after the failure of the negotiations over the Multilateral Agreement on Investment (MAI).[173] Barshefsky, in testimony before the House Ways and Means Committee on July 28, 1998, reassured Congress that the TEP would not weaken the U.S. determination to fight against EU farm subsidies and regulatory barriers. Even though it was overshadowed

[169] Quoted in Pollack/Shaffer 2001, p. 53.
[170] "That awkward relationship," *Economist,* May 14, 1998.
[171] Brittan 1998.
[172] Hindley 1999, p. 60.
[173] Kerremans 2000.

by the impeachment procedures against Clinton and the U.S. bombing of Iraq, the US-EU Summit of December 18, 1998 endorsed the TEP Action Plan. Thus, TEP became more than just a gesture of good will between friends, but rather offered a blueprint for both multilateral and bilateral negotiations on a whole range of trade issues.

3.4.5 The Transatlantic Business Dialogue (TABD) and the Vision of a Transatlantic Civil Society

Parallel to the political process on the highest level, new institutions for non-governmental contacts helped to push the trade agenda forward. The Transatlantic Business Dialogue (TABD), a semi-annual meeting place for corporate executives and political leaders from the U.S. and the EU and the Transatlantic Policy Network (TPN), a loose forum for parliamentarians and opinion leaders, were set up in 1995, followed by the Transatlantic Dialogue for Sustainable Development in 1997 and the Transatlantic Labor Dialogue in 1998.[174] The least successful of these ventures was the labor dialogue, while the meetings of environmental and consumer-protection activists from the U.S. and the EU at least provided an interesting exchange of positions, strategies and information.[175]

In contrast, the TABD quickly developed into a highly visible lobby group for trade liberalization and dispute settlement during times of increasing transatlantic tensions. The TABD was less interested in lofty visions of free transatlantic trade than in the day-to-day technical obstacles that still hampered companies involved in U.S.-European trade. The first TABD meeting in Seville, Spain, in November 1995 resulted in seventy specific policy proposals, many of which were realized in subsequent agreements.[176] Policy-makers from the EU and the U.S., aware of the informed and highly interested audience, used the TABD meetings to make public progress and sometimes even announced a breakthrough on practical business issues. In Chicago in November 1996, Washington and Brussels announced a customs cooperation agreement designed both to simplify foreign trade transactions and combat fraud.[177] Subsequently, the Customs Cooperation and Mutual Administrative Assistance Agreement was signed in May 1997 at US-EU summit in The Hague. In April 1997, trade negotiators agreed on mutual recognition of veterinary tests (with the exception of poultry) in a Veterinary Equivalence Agreement.

---

[174] "The TEP of the Iceberg: How the New Transatlantic Marketplace became the New Transatlantic Economic Partnership," *Corporate Europe Observer*, Issue 2, October 1998.
[175] See Knauss/Trubek 2001 and Bignami/Charnovitz 2001.
[176] Blackwill/Archick 1998.
[177] "Drive to lessen transatlantic trade divisions," Financial Times, November 8, 1996.

The main achievement of the TABD was its contribution to the six Mutual Recognition Agreements (MRAs) signed on May 28, 1997 in Paris. For almost two years, agreement on a whole range of products had been held up over the issue of pharmaceuticals. The EU demanded mutual recognition of drug testing, while the U.S. wanted to keep its Food and Drug Administration (FDA) as the sole authority for drug approval "which cannot be overridden or overruled."[178] Europeans accused the FDA of purposefully keeping European health products out of the U.S. market. As negotiators missed the January 1997 deadline, business pressure increased. Executives complained about the huge costs of dual product testing and stepped up lobbying efforts both in Washington and Brussels. The breakthrough finally came through a back room deal in which unrelated issues were successfully linked. "The Europeans want access to our pharmaceutical industry, we want access to their telecommunications industry. We need an umbrella MRA to ensure that everything stays tied together," an unnamed U.S. Commerce Department official said.[179]

The final agreement covered $444 billion worth of two-way trade in telecommunications and IT equipment, pharmaceuticals, medical devices and recreational boats.[180] The compromise on pharmaceuticals fell short of unconditional mutual recognition that the FDA strongly opposed, but it called for standardized testing and a joint curriculum for training European and American inspectors on standards and certification.[181] "This is the first down-payment on plans to create a transatlantic market place," said Stuart Eizenstat, then U.S. undersecretary of state for economic affairs.[182] The breakthrough came just in time for political leaders to have an accomplishment at the 50th anniversary celebrations for the Marshall Plan in June, who were otherwise overshadowed by the transatlantic disputes on Cuba and Boeing. In a similar vein, U.S. and EU negotiators reached agreement on an Anti-Bribery Accord in November 1997 at the OECD in Paris.

In the subsequent years, the early momentum of the TABD faded as frustration over the growing number of trade disputes built up. Business leaders began to focus again on an institutional framework that could keep the overall relationship running more smoothly. At the TABD summit in Berlin in May 1999, business leaders called for an "early warning system" on trade disputes. President Clinton and the main EU leaders at their summit officially adopted the

---

178 "EU and US agree plan to cut red tape," Financial Times, May 28, 1997.

179 "The TEP of the Iceberg: How the New Transatlantic Marketplace became the New Transatlantic Economic Partnership," *Corporate Europe Observer*, Issue 2, October 1998.

180 "U.S. reaches long-awaited pact with EU on inspections," International Herald Tribune, May 29, 1997.

181 Foot-dragging by the FDA, however, slowed down the implementation of the MRA on pharmaceuticals, said Guy de Jonquières in a personal correspondence with the author.

182 "EU and US agree plan to cut red tape," Financial Times, May 28, 1997.

proposal in June 1999,[183] but its effectiveness has not yet been proven. Two years later, in the 2001 Mid Year Report, the TABD leaders admitted the limits of their pragmatic approach in the absence of political leadership.

> "The strategic framework that TABD has promoted since 1995 does not yet exist. Governments do not have strategies for the free flow of transatlantic trade, investment, capital and technology. Failure to develop such a framework has created an environment in which business' recommendations in support of trade growth are being held hostage to political tensions between our economic superpowers. This allows more attention to be paid to trade disputes than to trade facilitation, despite the fact that disputed areas amount to less than 4% of our economic partnership. Even at less then 4%, the disputes serve to disrupt business, dampen economic activity and deflect government focus from trade progress."[184]

3.4.6 Transgovernmental Cooperation

Another goal of the NTA and the TEP was the fostering of transatlantic intergovernmental cooperation below the level of chiefs of government. Here, the record was also mixed. The most extensive network of information exchange and cooperation was created in the field of competition policy, through the 1991 Competition Cooperation Agreement between the U.S. and the EU and the 1998 Positive Comity Agreement that was designed to restrict the extraterritorial use of anti-trust legislation in transatlantic cases. As a growing number of corporate mergers affect businesses in the U.S. and the EU, both the U.S. agencies – the Justice Department and the Federal Trade Commission – and the European Commission had to approve the deal. Statistically, the system was a success: Between 1991 and 1999, the competition authorities cooperated in 689 cases of mutual interest.[185] The two major cases of disagreement, however, were enough to turn competition policy into a transatlantic battlefield: the 1997 merger between Boeing and McDonnell Douglas, where the EU gave its approval only in the last minute (see chapter 4), and the EU veto against the merger of General Electric and Honeywell in 2001 that sparked even heavier criticism in the U.S. When interests and fundamental views collide, even the most intense exchange of information cannot avert a major conflict.

---

[183] "Clinton and EU move to head off trade disputes," Washington Post, June 22, 1999.
[184] TABD 2001, p. 2.
[185] Devuyst 2001, p. 127.

Other areas of transgovernmental exchange are even less developed. In the area of food and drug safety, the EU still lacks common institutions, while the powerful Food and Drug Administration (FDA) and the Occupational Safety and Health Administration (OSHA) refuse to engage in transatlantic cooperation. They define themselves as purely domestic institutions and are regard any international agreement as an infringement on their territorial authority. Despite the high level of interdependence on various governmental and non-governmental levels, transatlantic relations are still highly centrally managed.

CHAPTER 4: CONTROLLED CONFLICTS

Beginning in 1996, US-EU trade relations resembled a constant battlefield with threats and accusations flying across the Atlantic on a whole range of issues. From U.S. sanctions against European companies investing in Cuba, Iran and Libya over various aircraft issues and steel to macroeconomic policy and rules governing the Internet, the partners always appeared at each other's throat. But as this chapter will show, political leaders managed to contain and resolve most of these issues before any concrete action was taken. Damage control was facilitated by the fact that controversial new laws or regulations did not always take effect immediately and gave both sides one or several grace periods to sort things out. In cases with strict deadlines, such as the EU ruling on the Boeing-McDonnell merger, one side caved in order to avoid greater fallout. The disputes described below preoccupied government officials for months and even years, caused some bad blood between Washington and Brussels, though they did not necessarily cause any long-term damage.

4.1. Politically Motivated Sanctions

From February 1996 to April 1998, transatlantic relations were overshadowed by U.S. attempts to influence its allies' policy toward so-called problem countries through the use of secondary sanctions. While the undertaking was partly successful, European policy toward Cuba, Iraq and Libya changed under massive U.S. pressure and the costs to the transatlantic relationship were also considerable. The two main sources of the conflicts were: on one hand, disagreements over foreign policy in the post-Cold War era; on the other hand, political constellations both in the U.S. and the EU that encouraged both sides to take a tough stance in these disputes. In several instances, the two sides went to the brink of doing damage to each other and to the international institutions, particularly the WTO. Ultimately, the conflicts were resolved in a way that left nothing more than bruised egos and hard feelings behind.

4.1.1. The Helms-Burton Act

Cuba has split Americans and Europeans for decades. While the allies were united in their opposition to the Castro regime they viewed as an agent to Soviet power and a major threat to its allies in Latin America, Europeans tended to see Castro as a normal third-world dictatorship. Even though the economic embargo in place since the late 1950s was ineffective in toppling Castro and might have even helped to cement his rule, the political influence of the Cuban exile community in Florida and New Jersey prevented successive U.S. administrations from normalizing relations. The futility of the embargo was usually explained by massive Soviet support for Cuba, amounting to $6 billion a year in the 1980s. With the collapse of the Soviet Union, the U.S. was forced to reconsider its Cuba policy. The choice was either to loosen or even lift the embargo as with the disappearance of the Soviet Union, Castro was no longer as strategic threat to the U.S. and a policy of engagement might trigger democratic change on the island. Others suggested tat as with Castro's main ally dissolution, now was the time to step up the pressure to bring about a change in regime.

U.S. policy in the early 1990s was torn between these two conflicting goals. Florida legislators had long tried to close a loophole in the embargo that allowed foreign subsidiaries of U.S. companies to trade with Cuba that had risen from $292 million in 1980 to $705 million in 1990.[186] A bill sponsored by New Jersey Democrat Robert Torricelli combined this and other punitive measures, such as a ban on ships entering Cuban ports from loading and unloading freight in U.S. ports for 180 days, with incentives for closer contacts. U.S. president George Bush rejected the Cuban Democracy Act (CDA) because he feared that its extraterritorial reach would anger U.S. allies. However, democratic candidate Bill Clinton endorsed the CDA in hopes of gaining support in Florida. A month before the election, Bush changed his position and signed the bill. It did help him to win the state of Florida by a narrow margin, though he still lost the election.

Clinton's endorsement of the CDA reflected his attitude toward Cuban policy. Like in most other foreign policy areas, the governor of Arkansas did not hold any strong convictions, but focused mostly on electoral benefits. This opportunistic approach shaped the Cuba policy of the Clinton administration in its first years. There was a consensus in Clinton's foreign policy team that sanctions were ineffective; they all favored a normalization of relations. In one indicative move, Clinton stopped granting automatic asylum to Cuban refugees, putting them on par with other Caribbean people.[187] A 1993 memo by the assistant secretary of state for inter-American affairs Alexander Watson even compared the administration's approach to the German *Ostpolitik* and described its main purpose "to strengthen the civil society that has been so devastated by 30 years of dictatorship."[188] But the Clinton administration tried to keep as low a profile on Cuba, afraid of arousing the anger of the powerful domestic constituencies. The timidity of administration officials made the gap between U.S. and European approaches to Cuba appear much larger than they actually were.

---

186 Purcell 1999.

187 Haney, Patrick J. and Walt Vanderbush, "The Helms-Burton Act: Congress and Cuba Policy," in Carter 2001.

188 Richard A. Nuccio, "Cuba: A U.S. Perspective," in Haass 1999, p. 11.

EU member states and Canada did not like the CDA because it tried to impose U.S. law on non-U.S. based subsidiaries. Yet by barring U.S. companies from Cuba, the bill actually benefited European and Canadian companies trading with Cuba. For that reason, and in the expectation of an imminent change in the administration's policy, EU leaders decided to ignore the extraterritoriality of the CDA and not to mobilize against it.[189] The CDA hurt the Cuban economy by significantly raising its shipping costs and just as its sponsors had hoped, Castro reacted with a further liberalization of the economy that allowed the holdings of dollars and facilitated foreign direct investments. FDI increased dramatically between 1993 and 1996 and the number of foreign tourists visiting Cuba rose from 300,000 in 1990 to 1.171 million in 1997.[190] Following the Chinese example, he did not match his move toward a market economy with any political reforms.

The prospect of European, Canadian and Mexican companies investing in Cuba and sustaining the Castro regime angered Republicans in Congress. In the midterm elections in November 1994, they gained control of both chambers of Congress. When the archconservative senator from North Carolina, Jesse Helms returned as Chairman of the Foreign Relations Committee, he immediately began to work on legislation that would stop the U.S. allies from dealing with Cuba. In February 1995, he proposed the outline of the Cuban Liberty and Democratic Solidarity (Libertad) Act that later became known as the Helms-Burton Act. Its two most controversial clauses were specifically targeted at non-U.S. companies investing in Cuba. Some of these investments involved former U.S. property that were confiscated by Castro shortly after taking power, enabling U.S. nationals to bring lawsuits against foreign governments, companies and individuals who "traffic" in expropriated U.S. property under Title III. Title IV denied executives, directors, controlling shareholders, and owners of these companies and their immediate families the right to enter the U.S.

Clinton showed little sympathy for the bill, but never threatened an actual veto against it. In April 1996, he called Helms-Burton "unnecessary because of the existing CDA."[191] His tactic was to delay the passage of the bill long enough so it would never even reach his desk. Even though the House of Representatives passed the bill on September 21 with 294 to 130 votes, it got subsequently stuck in the Senate. A version of the bill without the controversial Titles III and IV passed in the Senate, bound to die in the Senate-House conference. Clinton's tactics seemed to have succeeded.

---

[189] Susan Kaufman Purcell, "Cuba," in Haass 1998, p. 47.

[190] Joaquin Roy, "Europe: Cuba, the U.S. Embargo, and the Helms-Burton Law," in Haass 1999, pp. 32-33.

[191] Haney/Vanderbush, in Carter 2001.

The picture changed completely through a military incident on February 24, 1996: the Cuban military shot down two civilian planes with Cuban exiles on board. They were part of an organization called "Brothers to the Rescue," that searched the coast for rafts with refugees and dropped pro-democracy leaflets over Cuba. Three U.S. citizens and one U.S. residents were killed. The outrage over this act left Clinton with no choice but to sign an even stricter version of Helms-Burton.

The shooting down of the planes was no accident. As the events leading up to it suggest, Castro was consciously looking to provoke both the U.S. and the EU. With quiet encouragement from Washington, the EU, led by the Socialist government in Spain, had intensified its contacts both with the Cuban regime and dissidents in 1995. The European offer was basically more trade and investment in exchange for political reforms. In February 1996, the vice president of the EU Commission, Manuel Marin, traveled to Havana in an unofficial visit, where he presented Castro with a whole range of demands and concessions. Castro rejected all of Marin's demands. The stirrings of domestic dissent, symbolized by the emergence of the opposition Concilio Cubano, worried him more than the embargo.[192] Just hours of Marin left, the Concilio leader who had met with the commissioner was arrested. A few days later, the two U.S. planes were shot down. The door towards a rapprochement with Cuba was shut.

In the following days, Clinton officials tried to defuse the most explosive elements of Helms-Burton. On Title III, he insisted on a presidential waiver that would allow the administration to delay any court action for six months. No such waiver was inserted in Title IV, however, and an additional Title I codified all existing U.S. embargo measures that in future could only be lifted by an act of Congress. On March 12, 1997, Clinton signed the Helms-Burton Act whose main provisions were set to go into effect on August 1st.

The reaction in Europe was immediate and strong. While most companies active in Cuba took a relatively relaxed attitude,[193] both governments and EU authorities condemned the move and threatened with retaliation. "We condemn in the strongest possible terms specific provisions of the bill which run the risk of putting non-American companies investing in Cuba on the wrong side of American justice," a EU spokesman said shortly before Clinton's signature.[194] The vehement reaction caught the Clinton administration off guard. Following Europe's acquiescence to the CDA, it had hoped that Europeans would recognize the bill as a concession to domestic politics and help the White House

---

[192] Nuccio in Haass 1999, p. 16.
[193] "Move may not deter many foreign investors," Financial Times, March 7, 1996.
[194] "Cuba trade bill to spur legal action," Financial Times, March 6, 1996.

to contain international fallout.[195] In the following months, "the US government made a considerable effort to convince the EU to find an elegant face-saving solution" and to present itself as the reasonable partner in a fight with the Republicans in Congress.[196]

But the EU did not play along. While Europeans were accustomed to U.S. extraterritorial legal practices in areas such as anti-trust policy, securities, insolvency and money laundering,[197] Helms-Burton was a step too far. EU leaders feared that by accommodating the bill, the gate would be opened for further for the U.S. attempts to impose its foreign policy views through secondary sanctions, particularly as they watched Congress working on the Iran-Libya Sanctions Bill (ILSA). Finally, there was the public opinion in Europe: Helms-Burton confirmed the widely held view of the U.S. as a bully and did more to unify the EU governments than any other issue. Responding to Helms-Burton brought Britain, France, Germany, Spain, and Italy together and became a test case for the EU's common foreign policy. "Seasoned observers say they have rarely witnessed greater solidarity, or stronger demands for immediate action among EU foreign ministers."[198] The European Parliament was particularly eager to pursue a tough course against the U.S.[199]

As retaliatory measures, the EU considered government procurement boycotts of U.S. companies and reintroducing visa requirements for U.S. citizens. Eventually, the EU focused on two strategies: preparing a list of companies that might sue for damages under Helms-Burton in order to prepare counter-suits, and filing a complaint at the WTO. EU governments exerted strong and public pressure on Clinton to grant all EU-based companies a waiver for Title III in order to deny U.S. citizens and U.S. companies the opportunity to sue. "If there is no waiver next week, member states will act to defend themselves, alone, together, or both," threatened Brittan's spokesman Peter Guilford ahead of the decision.[200] Instead of granting the blanket waiver desired by the Europeans, Clinton bought some time. On July 16, 1996 he confirmed Title III, but delayed its implementation for six months and called upon the EU to reach an agreement on a joint approach to Cuba. We "use the law not as a sledgehammer but as a lever to promote democracy in Cuba," said Clinton's Deputy National Security Advisor Sandy Berger.[201] The decision neither

---

[195] Purcell in Haass 1998, p. 49.
[196] Roy in Haass 1999, p. 37.
[197] "Cross-border dilemma," Financial Times, July 16, 1996.
[198] "EU united over US measures against Cuba," Financial Times, July 18, 1996.
[199] Erika Mann, "Der Handelskonflikt muss politisch gelöst werden," Handelsblatt, February 26, 1997.
[200] "Allies press U.S. to back down on Cuba Sanctions," International Herald Tribune, July 12, 1996.
[201] Clinton delays effect of Cuba Lawsuit Act," Washington Post, July 16, 1996.

satisfied the Republicans nor the Europeans but it helped to take the conflict out of the ongoing presidential race.

The task to settle the dispute was given to Stuart Eizenstat, Undersecretary of Commerce for Trade, who as former U.S. ambassador to the EU knew EU politics better than anyone else in Washington. On August 16, 1996, the turning point of the conflict, Clinton appointed him special envoy to the EU with the explicit mission to settle the spat over Cuba.[202] In the following five months, Eizenstat and Brittan actually managed to calm the waters. At the EU summit in Dublin in December 1996, the union adopted a "Common Position" officially linking expanded ties with Cuba to an improved human rights record. Although this statement only confirmed existing EU attitudes, it was designed to give Clinton 'sufficient cover to allow him to extend the waiver."[203] With the presidential election behind him, Clinton extended the waiver for European companies indefinitely in January 1997 after claiming a success for U.S. foreign policy.

But the issue was far from settled. On one hand, there was still Title IV, which Clinton could not waive. The State Department notified nine executives from the Canadian mining group Sherritt International, who had a major joint venture in Cuba, that they could not enter the U.S. This included two prominent British businessmen. Otherwise, there was hardly any action on Title IV, causing Senator Helms to complain that the administration was flouting the law.[204] Even more surprisingly, Clinton loosened some restrictions on Cuba on remittances from family members, humanitarian aid and food sales. In some ways, Clinton acted as if Helms-Burton never existed.[205]

This lack of action did not satisfy the Europeans. They focused on their complaint at the WTO where they hoped to once and for all settle the issue of secondary sanctions. Rather than serving as a neutral mediator, the WTO actually became a weapon in the dispute. U.S. officials were not about to let the WTO judge in a dispute that belonged in their view into the realm of foreign policy, not trade policy. The Clinton administration was less concerned about losing the case, than about the domestic fallout of such an outcome. Given the general unease of Republican politicians with supranational authorities, a negative ruling might trigger a movement to pull out of the WTO all together. Even if the worst-case scenario did not come to pass, the WTO was bound to suffer. If the U.S. just ignored the verdict, its authority would be damaged. And the EU's right to retaliate could only be symbolic, because it was impossible to put a financial value on the damage done by Helms-Burton.[206] The EU heard

202 "Eizenstat Named as Envoy to EU," Financial Times, August 16, 1996.
203"EU Policy puts strings on Cuba ties," Washington Post December 4, 1996.
204 "Helms in Anti-Cuba law probe," Financial Times, October 10, 1997.
205 Haney/Vanderbush in Carter 2001, p. 284.
206 Christopher Wall, "Cross-border dilemma," Financial Times, July 16, 1996.

plenty of warnings in early 1997 not to proceed with the WTO complaint, but the case had developed a momentum of its own. In February, the EU asked WTO director general Renato Ruggiero to name a three-person dispute-settling panel. The U.S., however, threatened to challenge the WTO's right to hear the case and veto Ruggiero's choice of panelists. "A dangerous game of brinkmanship" commented the Financial Times.[207]

Both sides were aware of the explosiveness, but did not know how to entangle themselves without losing face. On February 12, 1997, Brittan asked the WTO to postpone the nomination for a week, warning of "immeasurable damage" to the WTO, and appealed to the U.S. not to block the panel.[208] Washington decided not to block the formation of the panel, but still refused to participate. The WTO has "no competence" to rule on U.S. foreign policy, argued Eizenstat. But as former deputy USTR Julius Katz warned, "This runs a major risk of tearing down the WTO. If one country can say 'we're not even going to appear', that is a terrible precedent."[209] The panel, consisting of former GATT director Alfred Dunkel, a member from Singapore and from New Zealand, officially took up the case and was bound to arrive at a ruling in mid-August. On April 12, 1997, the EU was set to make its first submission to the panel. As it would have been difficult to drop the case after that, this became the "drop-dead date" for the dispute.

Standing at the brink of what amounted to "pressing a nuclear bottom" in trade relations, both sides were ready to pull back.[210] Brittan seemed well aware that he had boxed himself into a corner by going to the WTO. The draft accord he reached with Eizenstat on April 11, 1997, following 50 hours of almost non-stop negotiations, constituted a climb-down for the trade commissioner. The EU would suspend its complaint at the WTO and agree to measures against companies dealing in confiscated property in Cuba and elsewhere in the ongoing negotiations on a Multilateral Agreement on Investments (MAI). In exchange, Clinton would ask Congress to modify the Helms-Burton law so that the president could also waive Title IV measures. There was also some progress on the U.S. sanctions against companies investing in Iran and Libya, but no clear agreement.[211] The reaction to the compromise was muted on both sides of the Atlantic. Senator Helms complained that a verbal commitment by the EU to constrain investment in expropriated property was not enough, while EU member states such as France, Italy, Spain and Belgium complained that the accord would not give their companies sufficient legal protection.[212] Diplomats

---

207 "Cuban feud," Financial Times, February 3, 1997.
208 "A Stay in EU-US Trade Spat," International Herald Tribune, February 13, 1997.
209 "U.S. vows to boycott WTO Panel," Washington Post, February 21, 1997.
210 "Europe turns to WTO on US anti-Cuba law," Financial Times, February 2, 1997.
211 "Trade Clash on Cuba is Averted," Washington Post, April 12, 1997.
212 "Helms-Burton antagonists keep fingers crossed," Financial Times, April 13, 1997.

spoke about U.S. "blackmail" and threatened to veto the deal. Facing the prospect of damaging the WTO, the EU finally endorsed the agreement.[213] The WTO complaint, however, was not shelved but instead suspended for six months. Demanding a complete waiver on the d'Amato Act, the EU kept the threat of WTO action alive. The case was not revived, however, even though the deadline of Oct 15, 1997 passed without a settlement. Meanwhile, the Italian telecommunications group STET became the first European company to settle a U.S. claim to confiscated property. STET had taken Cuban telecom assets from the Mexican Domos group that once belonged to ITT. By paying somewhere between $25 and 30 million to the U.S. group, the Italians became exempt from Title IV measures. U.S. officials welcomed the move as prove that Helms-Burton was working, and EU officials were also relieved.[214] Even though other companies did not follow the example, Title IV was subsequently not enforced.[215]

4.1.2. The Iran-Libya Sanctions Act (ILSA)

An unspoken agreement worked quite well to defuse the Cuban spat, but not on the fight over Iran and Libya. Here, far more was at stake. Policy toward the Islamic regime in Tehran had divided the EU and the U.S. since the early 1980s. Following the humiliation of the Iranian hostage crisis, the U.S. pursued a policy of isolation and containment against Iran mostly through trade sanctions. Even after Iraq became the bigger enemy in the 1991 Gulf War, it was Iranian sponsorship of terrorism, its active opposition to the Arab-Israeli peace process, its efforts to develop weapons of mass destruction and its appalling human rights record that prevented any rapprochement. Europeans shared the U.S. concerns and were directly affected by Iran's misdeeds, such as the deadly Fatwah against British novelist Salman Rushdie but they did not believe that sanctions would help solve the problem. As British foreign secretary said in a speech in Washington on January 15, 1998: "We must respond to the dangers posed by Iran as well as the opportunities. But isolating Iran is not the right response."[216] Instead, the EU pursued a policy of "critical dialogue" with Tehran, in which it attempted to balance intensive commercial relations, including massive oil purchases, with public criticism of Iran's human rights record.

---

[213] "Bitterness over US-EU trade deal proves it a truce, not a settlement," International Herald Tribune, April 15, 1997.

[214] "Italy's STET to Pay ITT For Cuba Property," International Herald Tribune, July 25, 1997.

[215] "Phony War," *Economist*, October 16, 1997.

[216] Geoffrey Kemp, "The Challenge of Iran for U.S. and European Policy." In Haass 1999, p. 66.

In its first two years in office, the Clinton administration made some feeble attempts to win the Europeans over for a tougher policy on Iran, while U.S. oil companies through its foreign subsidiaries purchased large quantities of Iranian oil.[217] After the defeat in the mid-term elections, Clinton decided on a tougher line against Iran. The finalization of a major nuclear reactor deal between Russia and Iran in January 1995 and the agreement between Iran and the American oil group Conoco to develop the South Pars gas deal convinced U.S. officials that existing U.S. sanctions were ineffective. On April 30, 1995, Clinton announced in a speech to the World Jewish Congress that he would ban all U.S. trade with and investment in Iran. This move forced Conoco to pull out of the gas deal. Since Europeans refused to go along, Congressional leaders then began to draft legislation that would sanction foreign companies dealing with Iran. Sponsor of the legislation was Alfonse d'Amato, whose New York constituency included a large number of Jewish voters.[218]

A first draft would have penalized any company investing in or selling equipment to the Iranian energy sector. The Clinton administration at first opposed the bill out of concern for relations with the EU, but was less hostile toward a compromise version that restricted sanctions to investors in Iran. When the French oil group Total prepared to take Conoco's place in the South Pars gas deal, the d'Amato Bill gained momentum. Another factor was a terrorist bombing in June of 1996 outside a U.S. military base in Dharhan, Saudi-Arabia. U.S. officials strongly suspected the involvement of Iranian intelligence agencies, even though they had no proof at the time.[219] The crash of a TWA airliner off the coast of Long Island on July 17, 1996 was immediately thought to have been caused by a bomb and heightened the fear of radical Islamic terrorism (The cause of the crash later turned out to be a technical defect). Pressure from relatives of the victims of the Lockerbie bombing of 1988, in which the Libyan secret service was the key suspect, led to the inclusion of Libya in the bill.

On July 24, 1996, Congress passed a version of the Iran and Libya Sanctions Act (ILSA) that forced the president to take at least two of six possible sanctions against any company investing more than $40 million in the Iranian or Libyan energy industry (in the case of Iran, the trigger would drop to $20 million for countries not cooperating on terrorism). The sanctions were: 1) a ban on imports; 2) ban on U.S. government purchases; 3) ban on loans over $10 million from any financial institution in the U.S.; 4) ban against acting as primary dealer of US government bonds, an agent of the Federal Government or as a repository for Federal Government funds; 5) denial of Export-Import Bank

[217] Ibid. p. 54.
[218] Ibid, p. 54-55.
[219] Ibid., p. 58.

assistance; and 6) denial of licenses for exports of controlled technology to companies under sanction.[220] D'Amato described the motive for the bill with following words: "It's time to take real action against terrorism and the countries that sponsor it. Now the nations of the world will know they can trade with them or trade with us. They have to choose."

Clinton agreed to sign the Bill after the inclusion of two possible waivers: Section 4c applied to companies from countries that had shown sufficient commitment in the fight against terrorism; Section 9c offered a case-by-case waiver on national security grounds. He could also delay action for two consecutive 90-day periods.[221] While the EU had regarded Helms-Burton mostly as a nuisance, the d'Amato bill was a direct attack on its foreign and economic policy. French President Jacques Chirac, whose country had the biggest commercial interests in Iran, threatened retaliation as early as May of 1996. Several other EU countries including Italy, Spain, Belgium, Germany and Austria, were more affected by the Libyan sanctions, which originally had not been high on the list of U.S. priorities were now against the U.S. They helped, however, to forge a common European position on the bill.[222]

The EU immediately demanded a sec. 4c waiver for all member states and the U.S. refused to grant it. Even so, the EU decided to wait for concrete U.S. actions that could only be triggered by new investments. Thanks to Helms-Burton, the instruments for retaliation were already in place and the complaint about U.S. secondary sanctions at the WTO already filed.

In the spring of 1997, several events coincided to bring the U.S. and the EU closer together on its Iranian policy. When a German court found the Iranian government responsible for the assassination of Iranian Kurds in the Berlin restaurant Mykonos in 1992, the EU suspended its "critical dialogue" with Tehran and improved the chances for a sec. 4c waiver. Six weeks later, however, the moderate cleric Mohammed Khatami reformist candidate won a surprise victory in the Iranian presidential elections, raising hopes of a fundamental change in policy.

While U.S. experts quietly searched options for improving relations with Iran, the d'Amato bill faced its first test when Total moved ahead on the South Pars gas project. Washington warned its European partners "of a massive step backward" in transatlantic relations if the deal went through, but the French were unperturbed. Total shielded itself from any fallout by putting its small U.S. operations up for sale, while the EU threatened to reinstate the WTO complaint against Helms-Burton if sanctions were imposed.[223] On September 28th, Total

---

220 "Foreigners investing in Libya or in Iran face U.S. Sanctions," New York Times July 24, 1996.
221 "Clinton signs bill against investing in Iran or Libya," New York Times, August 6, 1996.
222 "Politics sets tone for trade barriers," Financial Times, July 25, 1996.
223 "Stay out of Iran, US Warns French Oil Group," Financial Times, September 8, 1997.

announced it had signed the $2 billion contract together with its partners, Petrobas of Malaysia and the Russian Gazprom group. The U.S. State Department opened an investigation to see whether the deal fell under the provisions of the ILSA.

The Total deal reopened the whole conflict over U.S. secondary sanctions. Clinton officials argued that even though U.S. and EU policies had converged, the high-profile Total deal would make it impossible to settle the dispute through a blanket waiver for all EU members. Brittan warned Washington that sanctions against a European company would force his hand to return to the WTO on Helms-Burton after the end of the six-month truce on October 16th.[224] This time, Washington blinked. On October 3, 1997, Clinton deferred action on any sanctions for six months and promised the EU a blanket waiver if it demonstrated sufficient support for U.S. actions against Iran.[225] The following months saw intensive negotiations to remove that issue from transatlantic relations once and for all. A group of U.S. senators sent a letter to Clinton demanding sanctions against Total warning that "a decision not to sanction will reveal the U.S. as a paper tiger."[226] Meanwhile, Brussels made it clear that it would not accept a 9c waiver based on national security, but only a full Section 4c waiver that would confirm EU cooperation on the fight against terrorism. Otherwise, the EU would take up the complaint against Helms-Burton at the WTO.

As the US-EU Summit in London approached in May 1998, both sides stepped up the pressure. In exchange for blanket waivers on Helms-Burton and d'Amato, Washington wanted the European to make far-reaching foreign-policy commitments. The EU insisted on guaranteed protection from current and any future secondary sanctions legislation. The agreement announced on May 18th, 1998 in London consisted of common "disciplines" on investments in expropriated properties that would be pursued in the MAI negotiations and common "principles" on trade sanctions on third parties. The U.S. and the EU committed themselves to, "not seek or propose, and will resist, the passage of new economic sanctions legislation based on foreign policy grounds which is designed to make economic operations of the other behave in a manner similar to that required of its own economic operators."[227] The EU promised to step up cooperation in combating terrorism and fighting the spread of weapons of mass-destruction. This included EU support for pressure on Russia to stop assisting Iran's ballistic-missile program. In exchange, Clinton granted a sec. 4c waiver on the d'Amato Bill and repeated his promise to seek Congressional approval

---

224 "EU and US talk tough in Total row," Financial Times, September 30, 1997.

225 "U.S. Defers sanctions on Iran Gas Deal," Washington Post, October 4, 1997.

226 "Senators ask sanctions over Iranian Gas deal," Washington Post, May 9, 1998.

227 Smis/van der Borght 1999, p. 231/232.

for a waiver of Title IV of Helms-Burton. With UN sanctions still in place against Libya, dealings with that country were not mentioned.[228]

The deal was "an armistice, not a peace treaty," one EU official noted, and some sensitive issues were left unresolved. While the EU saw all constraints on EU investments in the Iranian energy sector removed, Eizenstat in subsequent Congressional testimony insisted that the waiver would not be granted in case a European company would invest in an oil or gas pipeline across Iran.[229] The agreement affected only US-EU relations and did not forestall any secondary U.S. sanctions against other countries. None of the agreements were legally binding. They "constituted political commitments belonging to the domain of soft law rather that of hard law,"[230] and most of the promises were left unfulfilled. Congress never amended the Helms-Burton Act to include a Title IV waiver; the EU never signed an agreement about dealings with confiscated property.

The U.S. and the EU continued to pursue different policies toward Iran, even though Washington developed slightly warmer relations with the Khatami government in Tehran. Foreign investments in Cuba declined, contributing to an economic slowdown on the island, and the EU did not continue its earlier efforts to affect a change in Cuban human-rights record through economic incentives. The 1998 accord "avoids conflict over Helms-Burton but does nothing to advance the cause of a peaceful, democratic transition in Cuba.... [Both sides] address their own domestic political constituencies rather than Cuban realities."[231] Finally, the London summit put the issue of secondary sanctions to rest and helped create an image of unity. This was reinforced by the approval of the Transatlantic Economic Partnership (TEP) and its promise of further economic cooperation. Both U.S. and EU leaders presented the agreement as a success. Without making major concessions, an explosive dispute had been defused with mostly face-saving gestures. Rather then resolving the underlying issues, the U.S. and the EU decided to let the dispute just fizzle out.

Given the intensity of the dispute over two years, this outcome is surprising. However, it begins to make sense if one looks at the different factors driving the crisis. The underlying reasons were the differences of opinion between the U.S. and EU about the use of sanctions and particularly, the best strategy to deal with "difficult" states. U.S. experts and politicians tended to favor in many instances economic, political and military pressure, including economic sanctions as "a valuable tool for enforcing international norms and protecting our national

[228] "U.S. and EU make peace over Trade with Iran," International Herald Tribune, May 19, 1998.
[229] Smis/van der Borght 1999, p. 235.
[230] Ibid., p. 229.
[231] Nuccio in Haass 1999, p. 26.

interests."[232] Europeans, however, usually prefer engagement and do not subscribe to the U.S. view that "engagement would simply feed the regime's appetite for inappropriate or dangerous behavior."[233] Neither side has shown to be dogmatic about this question. The U.S. pursues a policy of commercial and political engagement with various dictatorship, most prominently China, while the EU imposed economic sanctions and political isolation on Slobodan Milosevic's Serbia and followed the U.S. lead on sanctions against Iraq. But in the case of Cuba and Iran there were profound disagreements that did not diminish over time. While the European governments saw Khatamis's election in Iran and the economic opening of Cuba as evidence that engagement was working, the U.S. used continued human-rights violation and other examples of irresponsible behavior as a justification for continued pressure.

Americans and Europeans could have just agreed to disagree, and that is exactly what happened in the early 1990s. After 1994, domestic pressures drove the conflict. The Republican majority in Congress was determined to impose its hawkish worldview on U.S. foreign policy and did not consider the fallout for the transatlantic relationship. Republicans like Jesse Helms, Alfonse d'Amato and Newt Gingrich not only accepted, but also even welcomed, the resulting discomfort and even embarrassment for the president. Forcing Clinton to vacillate between domestic pressure groups and international allies was good electoral politics. Domestic (or to be exact intra-European) factors also played a role in the EU. The dislike for the bullying tactics by the U.S. bound European leaders together and helped to paper over deep fissures in the European foreign policy. At the height of the dispute in 1997, there was nothing to gain either for the EU Commission or any governmental leader to recommend backing down. The political dynamics on both sides of the Atlantic suggested further escalation.

This escalation continued until the point when important national interests were seen to be at stake. This did not happen in the sphere of commercial interests as Cuban trade was too insignificant for the European Companies and the potential financial fallout of the Iran sanctions were limited as Total had little business in the U.S. Surprisingly the issue of the strategic relationship and particularly the cooperation in NATO never became a factor. Unlike the dispute over the Soviet pipeline deal in the 1980s, the Helms-Burton and d'Amato bills were always seen as a trade issue.

In that case, the dispute reached the crisis point when it moved to the WTO. Rather than serving as a neutral arbiter, the World Trade Organization actually had a stake in the fight. EU insistence to let the WTO mediate in a conflict that was only partially a trade issue and the U.S. refusal even to listen to what the

---

[232] Eizenstat 1997 also quoted in Haas 1997, p. 86.

[233] Ibid.

WTO dispute panel had to say threatened to destroy the organization shortly after its birth. At that point, a process of bilateral damage control set in that succeeded in neutralizing the political pressures from home. As the Josef Joffe put it, "...Europe and America threaten each other with economic warfare when negotiations stall. But threats are where the conflict usually stops because everyone is deadly afraid of destroying the global trading system."[234] Once Eizenstat and Brittan took control of the process, a deal was inevitable. Neither side cared much about the substance of the deal; they were just looking for the one outcome that the domestic constituencies could tolerate. The result was a series of face-saving compromises that did not serve any larger political or economic objective except putting the conflict to rest. This spectacle became an easy target for commentators lamenting the sad state of transatlantic affairs. It is fair to argue that the two conflicts over secondary sanctions constitute fine examples of successful diplomatic damage control.

4.1.3. The Havana Club Dispute

Just when the Clinton administration thought it had defused all transatlantic disputes over Cuba and Iran/Libya, Congress succeeded to create a new bone of contention. In 1998, the Bahama-based rum producer Barcadi, a formerly Cuban company that was expropriated by Castro, lobbied for legislation that would deny the French liquor company Pernod Ricard the U.S. trademark right for its rum "Havana Club" that it produced in a joint venture with CubaRum, a Cuban state company. Although the rum cannot be sold in the U.S. because of the embargo, the joint venture registered the trademark in the U.S. to prevent others from using it. The trademark "Havana Club" had belonged to a Cuban family, whose business was expropriated in 1960. The U.S. trademark lapsed in the 1970s because it was not re-registered. Still, Bacardi bought the U.S. rights from the family in 1995 and began producing its own "Havana Club" in the following year. Pernod Ricard sued Barcadi for trademark infringement. A hearing was scheduled for January 1999. Based on existing U.S. legislation, Pernod would have certainly won.[235] So Bacardi lobbied Congress to pass a law that would deny recognition of trademarks or trade names substantially similar to those used by Cuban companies expropriated by Castro, unless the original owner gave his consent.

Virtually unnoticed by the public and most legislators, the "Mack Amendment" in late 1998 slipped as Section 211 into the Omnibus

[234] Josef Joffe, "How America Does It," *Foreign Affairs*, 76/3: 25.

[235] Wayne S. Smith, "European Union – U.S. Understanding Fails to Resolve Dispute over Helms-Burton Act," Center for International Policy, March 1999. *http://www.us.net/cip/9903ipr.htm*

Appropriations Act of 1998. The law violated not only the 1931 Inter-American Trademarks Convention, but also the Trade-Related Intellectual Property Rights (TRIPS) Agreement of the WTO as it discriminated against foreign-rights holders with Cuban assets. Moreover, U.S. companies voiced concern that Cuba could use a similar tactics in regard to U.S. trademarks, launching for example a "Coca Cola Cubana."[236]

Based on Section 211, a New York court ruled against Pernod's claim in early 1999, and a U.S. appeal court upheld the ruling in February 2000. The EU raised the issue at several meetings with U.S. authorities and filed a complaint at the WTO. On June 30, 2000, it requested a dispute-settlement panel that issued its report on August 6, 2001. The panel ruled in favor of the EU on the specific case, but did not share the European position on two more general questions: it argued that trade names (company names that had not been registered as trade marks) were not covered by TRIPS disciplines, and that WTO members had freedom over the process for determining intellectual property rights ownership, as long as TRIPS procedural requirements were respected. Both the U.S. and the EU appealed. On February 2, 2002, the appellate body reversed the earlier decision on trade names, but upheld the latter ruling. The USTR took this decision as a signal that "in the absence of discrimination, a law along the lines of section 211 would be consistent with WTO rules, and therefore those trademark owners who currently enjoy protection under section 211 could continue to enjoy that protection."[237] At the following DSM meeting on February 18, 2002, the U.S. informed the DSM of its intentions to implement the recommendations and rulings, though they also advised that they would need "a reasonable period of time" to complete the necessary changes. Thus, the European Communities and the DSB granted the U.S. an extension until December 31, 2003. By December of that year, however, the U.S. was still not able to implement them and worked an agreement with the EC and the DSB to once again further the extension period until December 31, 2004. For its part, the U.S. does have legislative proposals pending in Congress that would, among other things, repeal section 211.[238] Given the difficulties of passing any legislation that can be seen favoring investors in Cuba, the conflict remains difficult to resolve and has the potential to result in a drawn-out legal battle and eventual EU retaliation

---

[236] "A Rum Affair", *Economist*, July 8, 1999

[237] EABC Abstracts, January4/02, *www.eabc.org/abstracts/abstracts/010402.htm*

[238] Status report by the United States to the WTO DSB on April 8, 2004.

4.2. The Aircraft Industry

As a textbook example for a product where strategic trade policy can succeed, and Europe's determination to do so, the aircraft industry remains the potential biggest source of transatlantic economic conflict. The bilateral U.S.-EC Agreement on large commercial aircraft (LCA) in 1992 defused the conflict on subsidies, and an uneasy truce held throughout most of the Clinton presidency.

The 1992 accord limited state subsidies for the development of new aircraft, including indirect subsidies through defense contracts, to 33 percent of the total development cost of an airliner (applicable to EU support for Airbus) or alternatively three percent of the turnover of the civilian aircraft industry of a party or four percent of the value of a company's civilian sales. These clauses were meant to limit cross-subsidies from U.S. defense contracts. Subsidies had to be repaid with market-level interest rates within 17 years.[239] The aircraft issue resurfaced in the final stages of the Uruguay round negotiations. As the Agreement on Subsidies and Countervailing Measures (SCM) took shape in which would curtail subsidies even more than the 1992 accord, the EU tried to gain an exemption for he civilian aircraft industry. The U.S. refused, however, and the issue was left unresolved. Attempts to bring the 1979 GATT Agreement on Trade in Aircraft in line with new WTO regulations also failed.

This left the question of the legality of aircraft subsidies in a gray zone. The U.S. repeatedly suggested that any Airbus subsidy would have to be in accordance both with the bilateral LCA agreement and the SCM agreement but it stopped short from testing its case by filing a formal complaint at the WTO. The EU, meanwhile, argued that indirect support by U.S. government agencies to Boeing's civilian aircraft division, mostly the Pentagon and the National Aeronautics and Space Administration (NASA) exceeded the three percent limit set by the 1992 agreement. For example, the defense department financed the development of new lightweight materials for use both in military and civilian aircraft, the EU charged. The U.S. argued that because these materials were not yet used in commercial jets, the research funding does not violate the agreement. Washington also rebuffed all attempts to renegotiate the terms of the 1992 agreement to clarify such subsidies.[240] The continued standoff kept the status quo in place.

At three different instances during the Clinton presidency, however, conflicts related to the aircraft industry flared up. This was EU opposition to the merger of Boeing and McDonnell-Douglas in 1997, U.S. anger over EU aircraft

---

[239] McGuire 1997, p. 155.

[240] "U.S. Gets Tough To Ensure Boeing, McDonnell Merger," Washington Post, July 17, 1997.

noise regulations, and U.S. criticism against the launch of the Airbus A380 super-jumbo. The first two issues transcended the area of trade policy and involved also the authorities in charge of competition and transport policy on both sides of the Atlantic. While they were resolved just in time to avoid serious damage to the transatlantic relationship, the fight over the A-380 continued well beyond the Clinton administration. Fortunately, the instruments for damage control are in place and are likely to contain the fallout.

4.2.1. The Boeing-McDonnell Merger

By the mid-1990s, the rise of Airbus Industrie had seriously dented the dominance of the U.S. in the aircraft industry. While Boeing continued to hold on to roughly two thirds of the global market for large civilian aircraft, the second aircraft maker McDonnell Douglas (MDD) was in trouble. Due primarily to the problems of its DC-10 wide-body airplane, MDD was down to single-digit market shares in new orders and even loyal customers hesitated to place orders necessary for the launch of the MD-95 airliner, designed to revive MDD's commercial aircraft division. In 1992, a plan to link up with Taiwan Aerospace was blocked by political concern but MDD continued to look for a partner. Meanwhile, the drastic cuts in defense spending following the end of the Cold War forced defense contractors to cut back and to merge – a process that was strongly encouraged by the Clinton administration. In December 1996, Boeing and MDD, both major defense contractors, proposed a merger in which Boeing would acquire its smaller rival in a deal worth about $15.5 billion.

The announcement raised concerns in the Federal Trade Commission (FTC), one of two U.S. anti-trust authorities, because of the large market share of the combined group both in the defense and civilian sectors could result in a loss of competition. Yet, most observers expected the deal to go through. The administration wanted a further consolidation of the defense industry and in the civilian aircraft sector MDD had become a "non-factor."[241] In 1996, it had gained only three percent of new aircraft orders in the world.

Boeing and MDD also had to keep the EU in mind. Under the 1989 Merger Regulation, the EU Commission gained the right to investigate any big merger, even if none of the companies were based in Europe, as long as the combined group had global sales of more than Ecu5 billion and each company had at least Ecu250 million turn-over in the EU. In 1991, the U.S. and the EU signed a cooperation agreement to exchange information and coordinate timetables in merger cases.

In the past, the Commission had interfered in the merger of two U.S. companies. It required the North American groups Kimberly-Clark and Scott

[241] "Too big to fly?" Washington Post, May 4, 1997.

Paper to sell operations in Britain, just as the U.S. authorities imposed tough conditions on the merger of Ciba-Geigy and Sandoz, that later became Novartis. It was understood that either side would allow the "home regulator" to reach a verdict first and in most cases, follow their lead. Usually, the Commission settled the issues through negotiations. Until 1997, only seven out of 500 mergers were blocked in Brussels. As Boeing and McDonnell had no manufacturing facilities in Europe (only sales and support offices), the two companies assumed that the Commission would wait for the FTC ruling, request perhaps some modifications, and then approve the merger.

Before the FTC came to a decision, the EU commissioner for competition, Karel van Miert, publicly declared in May 1997 that the takeover was "clearly unacceptable as it now stands" and threatened to block it without major modifications.[242] He did so even before his own advisers were certain that the deal came under EU merger regulations.[243] Van Miert expressed several concerns: with a market share of well over 60 percent, any strengthening of Boeing's position posed a threat to Airbus and carried the danger that only one aircraft maker would remain in the world. Taking existing airplanes into account, Boeing and MDD actually had a market share of 84 percent. Van Miert feared that Boeing could use the necessary sale of services and spare parts to existing MDD customers to sell its own airplanes. He also worried that the acquisition of McDonnell's defense business would give Boeing even more access to Pentagon funds that could cross-subsidize its civilian aircraft business. His strongest objection was directed against the exclusive sales contracts that Boeing had signed with AMR Corporation's American Airlines and Delta and was about to conclude with Continental. In return for guaranteed price discounts and favorable terms of delivery, the airlines agreed not even to consider rival bids from Airbus for 20 years.

The last objection left U.S. anti-trust experts flabbergasted. It affected voluntary contracts between consenting adults that were illegal under EU law, but perfectly acceptable in the U.S. (although some U.S. anti-trust experts regarded them as anti-competitive).[244] The exclusive sales contracts had been initiated not by Boeing, but by the airlines that were in any case unlikely to consider ever even purchasing an Airbus plane. Most airlines were moving toward a single-supplier aircraft fleet to save on maintenance and training costs. Moreover, the U.S. side argued that the contracts were unrelated to the merger and should therefore not be part of the EU investigation. Finally, none of the world's major airlines that would have been affected by a loss of competition

[242] "EU Antitrust Chief Demands Changes in Boeing Takeover of McDonnell," International Herald Tribune, May 13, 1997.
[243] "Storm over the Atlantic," Financial Times, May 21, 1997.
[244] "Too big to fly?" Washington Post, May 4, 1997.

expressed concern about the merger. Former customers of MDD actually welcomed it because the takeover would assure continued service and spare-parts production.[245] Even though the FTC shared some of van Miert's concerns and called the exclusive deals "potentially troubling,"[246] the U.S. government took the position that the EU had no right to meddle in major American business decisions. "At least from the U.S. side, this looks like an extraterritorial attempt to impose European law," said Ray Waldman, Boeing's vice president for international business.[247] Ironically, this was the same charge that Europeans had levied against the U.S. in the case of its Cuba and Iran-Libya sanctions laws.

The U.S. side also accused van Miert of using anti-trust law to lend additional support to Airbus Industrie. This suspicion became even stronger when trade commissioner Brittan made another effort in May to reopen the 1992 LCA agreement, charging violations through excessive U.S. defense subsidies. Van Miert emphasized that he was fighting primarily for the interests of the airline industry and consumers, though he also argued that their long-term well being depended also on the survival and health of AI.

Industry observers pointed out that the exclusive sales contracts constituted a major hurdle for Airbus's plans to launch its super jumbo, called A-3XX at the time, to challenge Boeing's 747 monopoly. The contracts would have closed off more than ten percent of the global airline market as potential customers, raising the risk of the billion-dollar project. Airbus could not match the monopolization of the crucial U.S. market by Boeing in Europe. EU competition law did not permit these practices, and moreover, Airbus did not yet have a complete "family" of aircraft like Boeing: it still missed a jumbo with 400-plus seats. European aviation executives feared that if Boeing succeeded, Airbus would never manage to fill this gap and might eventually go out of business.[248] Van Miert was keenly aware of these dangers. "Van Miert is convinced this deal is anti-competitive and if it goes through, there will only be one airplane maker in the world," said one expert on U.S.-European relations, "I think he really wants to be known as the commissioner who would not let Boeing destroy Airbus."[249]

Van Miert first demanded that Boeing sell MDD's civilian aircraft division completely. Boeing argued that such a spin-off would unsettle existing McDonnell customers and raise the cost of spare parts by up to 25 per cent. Moreover, there was no serious buyer in sight. Van Miert later accepted a compromise under which Boeing would keep MDD's civilian aircraft business, including the service and spare parts arm, as a legally separate entity and refrain

[245] "Storm over the Atlantic," Financial Times, May 21, 1997.
[246] "Brussels Vs. Boeing," *Economist,* July 17, 1997.
[247] "Boeing, Threatened, Sees Trade War," New York Times, May 21, 1997.
[248] "Airbus und Boeing drohen sich gegenseitig mit Sanktionen," Handelsblatt, June 17, 1997.
[249] U.S. Gets Tough To Ensure Boeing, McDonnell Merger," Washington Post, July 17, 1997.

from any joint marketing efforts. Boeing also satisfied the Commission on cross-subsidies by promising more transparency. Finally, Boeing also offered to reduce the length of the exclusive sales contracts from 20 to 15 years, and to limit future exclusive contracts to ten years. None of that was acceptable to van Miert as it still would have stifled the A3XX launch. He set a deadline until July 23, 1997, when the EU Commission would rule on the merger. Boeing was pressing the FTC to announce its verdict before that date. It did so on July 2nd, without setting any conditions.

By that time, the merger had become the dominant issue in transatlantic relations. If the EU Commission were to declare the deal illegal, Boeing's European business would have been severely affected. According to EU rules, the Commission could have levied a fine of up to 10 per cent of total group turnover on the new Boeing, amounting to well about $4.8 billion. It could have given order to impound any new Boeing aircraft arriving in Europe, effectively shutting Boeing out of a market that represented one third of global aircraft sales.

As the deadline approached, both sides stepped up their rhetoric. In Europe, Van Miert first rallied the whole 20-member Commission behind him, and then gained the support of the anti-trust authorities from all 15-member countries. Both French President Jacques Chirac and German Economics Minister Günter Rexrodt publicly endorsed his defiant stance. Chirac was particularly forceful, calling the merger "an attack" on Europe's commercial interests and appealing to other EU countries to remain firm.[250]

In the U.S., the issue also became increasingly political. In May, seven prominent senators wrote to president Clinton complaining about the EU investigation as a biased attempt to help Airbus and Vice President Al Gore promised went to Seattle to fire a warning shot against Brussels. "We haven't been bashful about our advocacy of the rights of American businesses overseas," Mr. Gore said, "We will be watching the outcome of their deliberations extremely carefully, and we will take whatever action is appropriate to assure justice and fairness."[251]

At a meeting in the White House on July 15th, Clinton's top economic and trade officials discussed possible actions against the EU. This included the imposition of steep countervailing tariffs on Airbus aircraft based on anti-dumping charges, limits on flights between the U.S. and France, and a formal complaint at the WTO.[252] The next day, Clinton himself warned the EU Commission of blocking the deal. "We have a system for managing this through

---

250 "Clinton steps into Boeing deal row," Financial Times, July 17, 1997.
251 "Boeing, Threatened, Sees Trade War," New York Times, May 21, 1997.
252 "U.S. Gets Tough to Ensure Boeing, McDonnell Merger," Washington Post, July 17, 1997.

the World Trade Organization, and we have some options ourselves when actions are taken by Europe in this regard."[253]

The U.S. stepped up the pressure on van Miert. Joe Klein, the main anti-trust official in the justice department reminded him that vital U.S. interests were at stake in the merger.[254] Eizenstat phoned van Miert and proposed a joint U.S.-EU monitoring of Boeing to prevent it from using the exclusive contracts from locking up the American markets.[255] The final meeting took place on Friday, July 18, 1997, between Boeing executive vice president Richard Albrecht and van Miert. The U.S., company was still searching for a compromise and offered to cut the length of the contracts to 13 years and to forgo any further exclusive deals. But van Miert remained firm: only scrapping the contracts would stop the Commission from banning the merger.[256] Meanwhile, Clinton spoke with several European leaders asking for help to stop a trade war, while commerce department officials prepared an anti-dumping suit against Airbus.[257] More importantly, senior U.S. officials pressed Boeing to go the extra mile toward an agreement. On Tuesday morning, just hours before the deadline, a fax arrived from Seattle in which Boeing offered to abandon the exclusive sales contracts. The next day, the Commission gave green light to the merger.

The outcome was hailed as a victory for the EU Commission, but analysts pointed out that while Boeing may have been humiliated, it did not really give up anything of value. Even without the contracts, the three U.S. airlines were still committed buying hundreds of Boeing aircraft in the following years. Europeans continued to fear that the merger would make Boeing strong enough to crush Airbus. "The point is that the Americans are leaving us behind in the aerospace industry and aerospace technology as a result of that merger," Germany's foreign minister Klaus Kinkel said on German radio, "We must make a decision regarding European industrial policy, and that can only mean that we strengthen Airbus."[258]

The subsequent development proved Kinkel's worries futile. At the height of the boom in the aircraft market in the late 1990s, Boeing committed major management mistakes, suffered production difficulties and was unable to fill

---

[253] "Clinton Warns EU of Trade Conflict Over Boeing Deal," International Herald Tribune, July 18, 1997.
[254] "U.S. Gets Tough To Ensure Boeing, McDonnell Merger," Washington Post, July 17, 1997.
[255] "Clinton Warns EU of Trade Conflict Over Boeing Deal," International Herald Tribune, July 18, 1997.
[256] "Boeing Hides its Hand as an EU deadline Nears," International Herald Tribune, July 21, 1997.
[257] "Boeing Yields to Key EU Demand To Win Approval of McDonnell Deal," Washington Post, July 23, 1997.
[258] "Europeans Agree To Boeing Merger," International Herald Tribune, July 24, 1997.

large orders. Helped by higher productivity and better technology, Airbus scored one sales success after another. By 1999, it for the first time surpassed Boeing in the number of new aircraft orders, even though the pecking order was reversed again in 2000. The major EU countries finally succeeded in overcoming their internal rivalries and reorganized Airbus into a normal commercial company. The merger of three parent companies into the European Aeronautics Defense and Space Company (EADS) and its subsequent stock market flotation completed that process.

None of the setbacks for Boeing were related to the concessions made in 1997, and neither did they dramatically help Airbus in its subsequent endeavors. Even with the exclusive contracts out of the way, the commercial viability of the A3XX remained cloudy. In hindsight, the economic stakes look far smaller than at the time but even then, the disputed points were not generally seen as a life-or-death issue for either Boeing or Airbus. It would have possible to negotiate quietly a compromise. However, given the high profile of the aircraft industry, it was not surprising that the dispute turned into a political battle of wills. As the Economist wrote, "The lethal cocktail of politics, national champions and defense interests ensured it turned into a blurred, politicized mess."[259]

Boeing was hoping until the 11th hour that the Commission would blink first, but van Miert proved to have better nerves. Faced with his brinkmanship, a political damage-control mechanism went into action. While French President Chirac continued to advocate a tough line, Germany's foreign minister Kinkel warned, "We cannot let a trade war happen just because the concerned parties have little notion of reality."[260] Ultimately, it may have been the Clinton administration that gave Boeing the final push to retreat. The objectives of consolidating the defense industry and averting a trade war were more important than denying the Europeans a psychological victory. Just like in the case of the political sanctions, the mechanism of damage control wobbled but did not break down.

4.2.2. Aircraft Noise

In 1998, a new aircraft dispute emerged from an unexpected corner: EU legislation that would ban certain types of noisy aircraft from European airports, seen in the U.S. as an unfair discrimination of U.S. airlines and engine makers. The fight over "hush kits" pitted European concern for consumer protection against U.S. economic interests, though hovering in the background was the

---

[259] "Distrustful," *Economist*, July 24, 1997.
[260] "Peace in our Time," *Economist*, July 24, 1997.

charge that the controversial EU rules were just another way to help Airbus Industrie against Boeing.

Airport noise has long been a strong concern in densely populated Europe where airports are sometimes closer to metropolitan areas than in the U.S. A global industry like aviation requires international standards and the International Civil Aviation Organization (ICAO), a United Nations agency, sets them. In 1977, the ICAO established new, stricter "Chapter 3" standards for aircraft noise, and in 1990, the ICAO members agreed to make these standards obligatory world-wide by 2002. This would have meant the phasing out of older and louder "Chapter Two" aircraft such as Boeing 707, the DC-9 and some older versions of Boeing 737. In contrast, all Airbus aircraft met the stricter Chapter 3 standards because they were younger. U.S. engine manufacturers developed a technology that allowed older aircraft to meet the new noise standards and thus stay in use beyond 2002: engine mufflers called "hush-kits". U.S. authorities moved the introduction of the new noise standards forward to 2000, which triggered a rush by airlines to outfit their older planes with hush-kits before that date. The main beneficiary was United Technologies' Pratt & Whitney unit.

European authorities did not like this trend. They would have preferred if airlines replaced their older fleet with safer, less polluting and more fuel-efficient new aircraft. Consumer groups complained that hush-kitted airplanes might meet the formal noise requirements, but had a more whining noise that appeared louder for the people living under their flight paths. European airlines, enjoying years regulated higher ticket prices, had generally more modern fleets than the U.S. and did not need hush-kits. While few of the hush-kitted American jets were flying to Europe, authorities feared that these planes would be later sold to airlines in other countries that would then land and take off on European airports.

Faced with growing pressures from local residents and environmental groups, separate EU members and even individual airport authorities began in the mid-1990s to draft their own noise standards, some of them banning hush kits. The European Commission feared a fragmentation that could hamper the functioning of the single market and decided to write an Airport Noise Directive to stop the proliferation of "re-certificated civil supersonic jet airplanes" in the whole EU.[261] It received broad support from all 15 EU governments and public opinion. In December 1998, a divided Commission voted to halt the registration of hush-kitted aircraft in the EU as of April 1, 1999.[262] More importantly, it decreed that as of that date, any hush-kitted aircraft from third countries that

[261] Common Position (EC) No. 66, 1998, Official Journal of the European Communities, December 23, 1998.

[262] Joncquières 2001.

was not operating in the EU would be banned from flying to Europe as of April 2002.

The proposed regulation caused uproar in the U.S. As few airlines would buy jets that could not land in Europe, the rules would lower the resale value of existing aircraft in the secondary market. Moreover, hush-kit makers would lose a lucrative market because airlines would be forced to replace their aging fleet with newer aircraft. The U.S. government estimated the economic loss for its industry first at over $1 billion, later at more than $2 billion: $1.6 billion for lost sales of hush-kits and engines, and $500 million for lower resale value of existing planes.[263]

By forcing U.S. airlines to replace their aging aircraft with new jets, the U.S. officials declared the directive a boon for Airbus, who at that time had already half the world market share. The Clinton administration shared some of the European concerns over aircraft noise, but the solution chosen by Brussels was "too cute a play," said David Aaron, U.S. undersecretary of commerce for international trade.[264] The technical standard used by the EU, the bypass ratio that measures airflow through the engine, has "no correlation" with sound levels, he added.[265] On principle, Washington objected to EU regulation that would discriminate against one specific technology that happened to be American. "Rather than focusing on performance levels the Europeans are mandating a specific design solution, which constitutes a clear, anti-competitive act," warned the U.S. trade expert Clyde Prestowitz[266].

Still, widespread public concern about aircraft noise in Europe and strong pressure from the European Parliament that was deeply involved with the issue left the Commission with little room for maneuver. On February 10, 1999, the European Parliament approved the new rules. EU transportation commissioner Neil Kinnock suggested that the hush-kit ban was needed to forestall even tougher restrictions in Europe: "Local authorities and national governments are already introducing noise stipulations which risk fragmenting the market. It is better to have EU regulation that would ensure there was transparency."[267]

But at that point, the U.S. Congress also became involved and threatened retaliation. The Senate and the House of Representatives introduced legislation that would ban the Concorde supersonic jet from U.S. airports. For three decades, British Airways and Air France had operated the loud supersonic jets under a waiver of noise regulations. Worried about another trade war, the U.S.

---

[263] "U.S. Asking U.N. to Settle Aircraft Noise Dispute with Europe," New York Times, January 19, 2000.

[264] Interview with David Aaron, U.S. deputy secretary of commerce for international trade from 1997 to 2001, on April 10, 2002 in Washington, D.C.

[265] "Kinnock defies US over Curbs on Noisy Aircraft," Financial Times, February 11, 1999.

[266] "Flying the face of the market," Financial Times, May 12, 2000.

[267] "Kinnock defies US over Curbs on Noisy Aircraft," Financial Times, February 11, 1999.

government appealed to the EU to delay any further action to give negotiations a chance.[268] On March 29, 1999, just two days before the deadline, the EU transport minister postponed the legislation for a month but stated that the regulation would go into effect on April 29. The U.S. complained that this did not leave enough time to even start bilateral talks. In return, Kinnock said that the ban could subsequently be amended if the two sides reached an agreement before April 2002.[269]

The EU action did not satisfy Congressional leaders. Senator John McCain, the chairman of the U.S. Senate Commerce, Science and Transportation Committee, wrote a letter to Kinnock threatening not only a ban on Concorde flight but general restrictions on European airlines as well. He pointed out that a complaint by Northwestern Airlines, who had a large number of hush-kitted jets, was based on a law that authorizes the government to "deny, amend, modify, suspend, revoke or transfer" a foreign airline's permit to fly to the United States. As the new trade dispute coincided with other transatlantic spats on data privacy and the EU ban on American beef imports, McCain and others warned of a larger trade war.[270]

Faced with these threats, the EU took a slightly more conciliatory position. On April 29, 1999, the transport ministers approved the new regulation while delaying the implementation of the hush-kit ban for third countries for a year, May 4, 2000. U.S. officials call the move "a very constructive step" and offered to work with the EU on a new set of global noise regulations to be finished within the ICAO by September 2001.[271] This left both sides a year to settle the dispute. As negotiations on new aircraft noise standards continued, the EU transport minister signaled in October 1999 to further delay the implementation of the hush-kit ban.[272] By the end of the year, the talks got bogged down in technical and procedural details.

As the May 4 deadline approached, the Clinton administration decided to increase the pressure on the EU. On January 19, 2000, it announced that it would file a complaint with the ICAO under Article 84 of the Convention on International Civil Aviation against the EU rules. "We have to defend our interests now," said Commerce Secretary William Daley, "We all want more quiet aircraft, but we are not going to let Europe set the standards unilaterally." What looked like a formal initiative was actually a potent weapon. Since the

---

268 "US congressmen urge ban on Concorde flights," Financial Times, February 25, 1999.

269 "EU offers olive branch on aircraft noise," Financial Times, March 30, 1999.

270 "Senator Warns EU On Banning Aircraft," International Herald Tribune, April 19, 1999.

271 "EU Relents in Aircraft Noise Dispute with US," Financial Times, April 29, 1999.

272 "Retreat by EU in hush-kits dispute," Financial Times, October 7, 1999.

ICAO insisted on global standards, the EU was bound to be overruled and could be punished by losing its voting rights in the U.N. body.[273]

The U.S. move raised the temperature on both sides of the Atlantic. EU officials tried desperately to stop the complaint procedure at the ICAO, but were unwilling to abandon the hush-kit ban for good before agreement on new international standard was reached. The U.S., however, would not withdraw its ICAO complaint as long as the threat of the hush-kit ban remained. The EU offered a three-pronged solution: the U.S. should suspend its complaint, the EU would suspend the ban, and the two sides would work toward a joint declaration of cooperation on aircraft noise standards.

When Washington was slow to react to a new EU offer, the new EU transportation commissioner Loyola de Palacio set a one-day ultimatum on March 12, 2000: if the U.S. did not send "a clear signal" the next day that the offer was acceptable, it would be too late for a deal to gain approval from EU governments and the European Parliament by May 4th, permitting the hush-kit ban to go into effect. Angry over U.S. sanctions over bananas and beef, Europeans were not in a mood to compromise. "You should not underestimate the parliament's opposition to US bullying," remarked David Bowe, a British Member of the European Parliament and spokesman on aircraft noise in the Socialist group.[274]

Behind the scenes, Aaron and Palacio had effectively reached agreement along the lines of the EU offer. The affected U.S. airlines, however, did not want to go along. Federal Express was so angered by the European tactics that it demanded from the Clinton administration to go ahead with the ICAO complaint to "teach the Europeans a lesson."[275] When Aaron sought political cover for a deal in the White House, he could not get the president's attention. The assistant familiar with the issue had just left and in the post-impeachment atmosphere the issue was too small to be taken up by anyone else. The deal broke down, and on March 14, 2000, the U.S. government filed the complaint at the ICAO. Outside observers were puzzled about the escalation of the conflict that seemed more about pride than principle.[276]

The two sides continued to run in circles. On March 28, 2000, the EU transport minister effectively repeated their earlier offer, signaling that there was still time enough before May 4 to reach an agreement.[277] However, there

---

273 "U.S. Asking U.N. to Settle Aircraft Noise Dispute with Europe," New York Times, January19, 2000.

274 "US faces EU deadline on use of jet hush-kits," Financial Times, March 13, 2000.

275 Interview with David Aaron, U.S. deputy secretary of commerce for international trade from 1997 to 2001, on April 10, 2002 in Washington, D.C.

276 "EU-US aircraft noise dispute spinning rapidly out of control," Financial Times, March 22, 2000.

277 "EU proffers new solution to dispute on hushkits," Financial Times, March 29, 2000.

was still no agreement on the exact nature of the EU suspension. As industry leaders reported that the threatened ban already affected the resale value of older aircraft, Washington wanted to see the ban go for good. On May 4th, the clock started ticking: any hush-kitted aircraft not registered that day would be banned in 2002.[278]

The dispute now turned to the ICAO, where the EU challenged the legality of the U.S. complaint. In mid-November 2000, as the outcome of the U.S. presidential elections were in doubt, the ICAO dispute panel, chaired by ICAO Council President Assad Kotaite, ruled that it had jurisdiction to hear the U.S. complaint. EU lawyers began preparing their briefs to defend their action, while Kotaite began an unsuccessful mission of shuttle diplomacy between Brussels and Washington.[279] EU officials apparently decided to delay a settlement until a new administration was in, ensuring that it would also be committed to the deal.[280]

The conflict was finally resolved in October 2001, when the U.S. and the EU managed to reach agreement on new standards for aircraft noise at an ICAO conference in Montreal. The accord did not permit a blanket EU ban, but created a mechanism under which individual states could introduce specific restrictions on some Chapter 3 airplanes at "airports with severe noise problems."[281] On October 29, 2001, five months before the ban on hush-kitted jets would have gone into effect, the EU scrapped the controversial regulation. "This is a victory for Europe because the US will withdraw their complaint and the threat of economic sanctions," explained a spokeswoman of Belgium EU presidency. The view from Washington was quite different. "They were looking for some sort of cover," said one U.S. official, "They didn't want to say that they lost and we won."[282]

EU experts still insisted that without their hardball tactics, the U.S. would have never gone as far as it did to fight aircraft noise. Even so, the fruits of the acrimonious dispute were quite modest. Even when the outline of a compromise was clear to everyone, the two sides continued to escalate the conflict. The conflict was only contained because the built-in time delays – the grace period for hush-kitted airplanes in the EU, and the lengthy procedure at the ICAO – gave both sides enough time to work out a face-saving compromise. Still, the

---

278 "Brussels defends hush-kit ban against US complaint," Financial Times, November 21, 2000.

279 "Brussels defends hush-kit ban against US complaint," Financial Times, November 21, 2000.

280 Interview with David Aaron, U.S. deputy secretary of commerce for international trade from 1997 to 2001, on April 10, 2002 in Washington, D.C.

281 ICAO news release, October 5, 2001.

282 "EU to withdraw ban plan on noisy aircraft," Financial Times, October 30, 2001.

course of the dispute showed that by the end of the Clinton administration, the ability on both sides to solve bilateral problems was fading fast.

4.2.3. The Launch of the Airbus A380

In the mid-1990s Airbus was able to challenge Boeing in all segments of large civilian aircraft, with the crucial exception of the jumbo jet. The Boeing 747, first developed in the 1960s, was "a license to print money": the company made $45 million on every $150 million aircraft that it sold.[283] The 747-400 was the only plane that could carry more than 400 passengers. While Airbus was working on a stretched version of its A340 model that could carry 380 passengers, Airbus executives had plans for a completely new aircraft that would take the company into the 500-plus segments.[284] Boeing also had plans for a super-jumbo. In 1992, it approached the parent companies of Airbus - France's Aerospatiale, Germany's Daimler-Benz, British Aerospace and Spain's CASA – with plans to build an aircraft that could carry 800 people but no agreement was reached. In the following years, Boeing went back and forth on the question of super-jumbos. When travel in Asia, where the demand for jumbos is greatest, grew briskly, it developed plans to build an extended version of its 747-400 that could carry up to 500 passengers. In the wake of the Asian crisis, Boeing argued that the growth market lay actually in aircraft slightly smaller than the 747-400, such as Boeing's new 777 model.

Despite this, Airbus, buoyed by the constant growth of its market share, pushed ahead with its plans to develop a super-jumbo dubbed the A3XX that would be able to carry between 550 and 600 passengers. For a slightly higher price tag, it promised the airlines significantly lower operating costs, making the aircraft superior to the aging 747. By breaking Boeing's monopoly in this segment, Airbus hoped to achieve similar profitability and to give airlines the option to use exclusively Airbus jets.

But the A3XX also gave the U.S. another chance to challenge the EU subsidy policy. It was the first new Airbus development since the 1992 LCA agreement; the extension of the A340 into the A340-500/600 did not generate major development costs. For the A3XX, European governments were expected to foot $4 billion of the $12 billion development bills through state-guaranteed loans. Airbus claimed that this launch aid was in line with the 1992 accord that limited development subsidies to one third. The U.S., however, raised two objections. First, it argued that the 1992 agreement had been superseded by the stricter terms of the SCM agreement in the WTO. Second, the U.S. challenged the commercial assumptions of the A3XX project. Launch aid is paid back to

[283] "Peace in our Times," *Economist*, July 24, 1997.
[284] "World Skies are Dominated by US," Financial Times, September 22, 1997.

the governments as a royalty of sales, so the repayment depends on the commercial success of the model. In the case of the highly successful A320, the governments made a profit of roughly 100 per cent on their original investment.[285] The 1992 agreement stated that launch aid was only permissible if "there is a reasonable expectation of recoupment within 17 years." Boeing claimed that the market for the A380 was far too small for the government loans ever to be repaid. Rather than the 1500 orders over a ten-year period predicted by Airbus, Boeing saw the market for such large planes only at 300 to 400. The main growth would come in smaller jets serving more comfortable point-to-point routes, the company argued.[286]

Whether or not the A3XX would ever become commercially viable also depended on the actions taken by Boeing. Even before Airbus launched the super-jumbo, the U.S. aircraft maker offered a stretch version of its 747-400 that would make room for more than 500 passengers. Yet, Boeing did not receive a single order for this derivative of a 30-year-old technology. So after Airbus finalized the launch of its super-jumbo, now called the A380, in December 2000, Boeing dropped plans for the A747X and conceded the market for the largest airplanes to Airbus. Instead, the U.S. aircraft maker started to work on a smaller jet that would fly just under the speed of sound, fifteen to twenty percent faster than conventional planes. Moreover, Boeing offered a quieter, longer-range version of its 747-400 to meet stricter noise standards. This move gave a new facet to the Boeing-Airbus rivalry. Was the Airbus super-jumbo or the Boeing sonic cruiser the plane of the future, or was there a market for both? The prospect for both projects, particularly the A380, were dented by the sharp downturn in global air traffic after the terrorist attacks on the New York World Trade Center and the Pentagon in Washington in September 2001. Airbus, deeply committed to the success of its super-jumbo, remained confident that it would make a profit from the huge plane.

Washington was not willing to wait to see whether Airbus' market forecasts proved true. It strongly objected to the plans of the German, French, British and Spanish governments to grant Airbus around $2.5 billion in launch aid for the A380 that constituted about a quarter of the total development costs of $10.7 billion. When the British government moved in March 2000 to commit 530 million Pound to the Bae Systems, one of the major shareholders in Airbus Industrie, the U.S. demanded details on the aid package.[287] In May 2000, USTR Charlene Barshefsky threatened to take the case to the WTO.[288] Recent WTO rulings that had found Canada in violation of the SCM agreement by giving too

---

[285] "Super-jumbo trade war ahead," *Economist*, May 4, 2000.
[286] Ibid.
[287] "Airbus Project Package Attacked by US," Financial Times, March 14, 2000.
[288] "Super-jumbo trade war ahead," *Economist*, May 4, 2000.

much aid to regional jet maker Bombadier made U.S. experts confident that they could gain a similar verdict against Airbus.[289]

President Clinton repeated the warnings after the official launch of the A380 in December 2000 and the dispute over aircraft subsidies, coming on top of the banana and beef sanctions, added to the feeling of gloom at the last US-EU summit of the Clinton era in Washington.[290] At a meeting of technical experts from the U.S. and the EU on January 12, 2001 in Washington, the two sides remained far apart. EU officials made it clear that they would counter a U.S. complaint at the WTO with their own complaint against cross-subsidies from the military and NASA for Boeing that they claimed exceeded the three per cent limit of the 1992 agreement. "If the US were to choose the path of launching legal action under the WTO, the Commission would not hesitate to propose that the EU mirrors that action," said Gunnar Wieland, the EU's spokesman for external relations.[291] According to EU figures, Boeing received $2.3 billion annually or 7.5 per cent of its annual turnover. The U.S. disputed the claim, putting the figure at less than one percent of turnover.[292]

The U.S. continued to criticize the Airbus aid and raised the issue at every bilateral trade meeting while holding off from any action at the WTO. Even Boeing was divided on whether it should push the government into a process that could result in a major trade war. The reasons were the same as in 1992 when Boeing lobbied for a compromise agreement: with European airlines making up about a third of the global aviation market, Boeing was afraid of being locked out. Moreover, the U.S. and European aircraft industries were becoming highly integrated, with Boeing and Airbus spending about $5 billion a year buying parts and services and supporting around 100,000 jobs on each other's soil.[293] While strong words continue to fly over the Atlantic, the aircraft dispute appears to remain a tightly controlled conflict for the foreseeable future.

4.3. Personal data protection and the Internet

The U.S.-EU dispute over personal data protection regulation had all the features of a modern trade conflict. A new technology posed new social and legal challenges to which the EU reacts with far-reaching regulation with an extraterritorial reach. The U.S. opts for self-regulation, and while the outline of a compromise is quickly reached, the conflict lingers on for several years.

---

289 Interview with an anonymous aerospace expert from the International Trade Administration in Washington, March 2002.
290 "US and EU still split on beef and bananas," Financial Times, December 19, 2000.
291 "Storm clouds greet newest Airbus," Financial Times, December 20, 2000.
292 "Brussels defends grants to Airbus," Financial Times, January 13, 2001.
293 "Super-jumbo Trade War ahead," *Economist*, May 4, 2000.

Anticipating the growth of the information technology, the European Commission began in 1990 to work on a directive that would harmonize European rules for the protection of personal electronic data. At that time, data transfer was limited to large mainframe computers by major companies, so the directive was not much concerned about the possible exchange of million of personal data among decentralized personal computers through the internet. Even when EU communications minister approved the directive in 1995,[294] it was heralded as a trade-liberalizing move. It would strengthen the single market by reducing discrepancies between national privacy rules that were far stricter in the northern EU countries than in the southern ones.[295] The law put strict limits on the use and transfer of personal data collected by public institutions and companies and gave individual citizens the right to find out what kind of information is collected about them. Data registrars in each EU country would be set up to enforce the rules.

To close a major loophole in the protection of privacy, the directive authorized the severance of information flows to non-EU countries that did not have "adequate" data protection arrangements. While the meaning of "adequate" was never clearly defined, the EU Commission said in 1998 that it had only identified about ten countries that would meet the criteria. The U.S., with a patchwork of loose forms of self-regulation, was not among them.

The directive therefore raised the prospect of a cutoff of transatlantic data flows, disrupting electronic commerce and transatlantic trade. Most strongly affected would have been airlines, tour operators and other providers of consumer services that heavily depended on the international transfer of customer data, and U.S. multinational companies collecting personnel data from European subsidiaries. The directive was set to go into effect on October 25, 1998, and then it still had to be implemented in 15 different national laws. By mid-1997, with the Internet boom in full swing, U.S companies and officials were already extremely worried.

The Clinton administration recognized that there may be a problem with data privacy in the U.S. and just like its EU counterpart, it was under pressure from consumer groups to tighten the rules against the misuse of personal information. However, it rejected both Brussels's heavy-handed regulatory approach and the EU attempt to force its laws onto the U.S. Washington considered an appeal to the WTO, and some members of Congress suggested a "blocking statute" that would prohibit U.S. companies from complying with the EU rules.[296] Clinton's Internet advisor Ira Magaziner, who started the talks with the EU Commission

---

[294] See *www.privacy.org/pi/intl_orgs/ec/eudp.html*

[295] "The Changing of the Guards," Financial Times, July 9, 1998.

[296] "Data Protection Dispute Exposes Core Differences," Financial Times, June 9, 1999.

in 1997, set out to devise a system of self-regulation that would be acceptable to the Europeans.

A year later, an agreement was still not in sight. Some Europeans were critical of the impending EU system, claiming hazy legal rules, high expenses and a regulatory overkill. The situation in the U.S. was worse. There were 90 different data privacy bills pending in Congress, mainly intended to protect children and medical records. Private pressure groups criticized existing data protection rules as totally inadequate. For example, a report charged a leading pharmacy retailer with selling names, addresses and purchasing details of its customers to a marketing company.[297] Yet few in the U.S. were willing to go as far as the Europeans to prevent the wide-spread use of personal data, a multi-billion-dollar business in the U.S. "What is boils down to is that Americans don't mind junk mail, and we do," summarized a Commission official of the dispute.[298]

The Clinton administration was on one side pressuring the private sector to come up with better safeguards and on the other side, asking the EU to accept current regulations as adequate. A breakthrough seemed at hand in September 1998, when the government endorsed a proposal by a private alliance to set up a system of "safe harbors" for the protection of personal data.[299] U.S. companies were also working on a "seal of approval" for web sites that promised to adhere to private rules. While the EU accepted these systems of voluntary codes and self-regulation in principle as "a reasonable approach," it remained skeptical on its implementation and demanded more information.

In early October, Commerce Secretary Wiliam Daley said he was "confident and optimistic" that an agreement could be reached before the EU directive would take effect but by October 25, 1998 there was still no agreement. The two sides haggled specifically over two issues: the EU insisted on citizens' right to find out about personal information in a database and, if necessary, to correct it. U.S. companies said that would be far too expensive. The U.S. offered only "limited access" for such requests, "based on their importance to the individual, the ease of retrieval and the cost to the company."[300] U.S. companies were concerned that rivals or pressure groups could disrupt its operations through a flood of requests.

The directive also required each outside country to have an independent arbitrator to decide in a dispute between an individual and a company. The U.S. had no intention to set up such an institution.[301] Negotiations between the U.S. and the EU continued after October 25th, with the threat that some countries

---

[297] Ibid.
[298] Ibid.
[299] "Bid to avert threat of 'cyber trade war," Financial Times, September 9, 1998.
[300] "Little progress in talks on data protection," Financial Times, January 28, 1999.
[301] "Privacy Rules Send U.S. Firms Scrambling," Washington Post, October 20, 1998.

would cut off data transfer to the U.S. now suddenly real. Observers feared that consumer-protection groups in some countries would pressure its government to set an early example to prevent the law from being ignored. Meanwhile, negotiations between the Clinton administration and the private sector got stuck. The first government draft for a set of self-regulatory principles was rejected by some companies and lawyers as being too vague. When the commerce department tried to clarify the rules, several large companies, including America Online and Walt Disney, complained that the ideas were too specific and potentially too costly.[302] By the time of the WTO summit in Seattle in December 1999, the U.S. and the EU had already missed several deadlines and were still far apart on the issues.

Meanwhile, other internet-related disagreements began to surface. The EU had long criticized the U.S. ban on some encryption technology on national security grounds, arguing that better encryption technology would increase consumer confidence in e-commerce.[303] And while EU officials had at first endorsed the U.S. idea of a tax-free world wide web, the explosive growth of e-commerce made EU governments and the Commission worried about losing too much government revenue and therefore reconsider its position on an internet tax.[304]

In early 2000, an agreement finally took shape. In mid-January, U.S. officials invited representatives of EU member countries to Washington for a demonstration of the proposed system of self-regulation.[305] The two sides missed again a March 31 deadline, but by early summer the differences had been bridged. On May 31, 2000, a committee of EU data protection experts voted to accept the U.S. "safe harbor" model;[306] a month later, the European Commission approved the deal.[307] The safe harbor scheme did not work as well as its designers hoped. By the time a EU moratorium on taking action under the data protection directive ran out on July 1, 2001, only 78 U.S. organizations and companies had signed up. Even though this included many of the largest U.S. corporations, thousands of American companies in Europe were theoretically threatened by a data cutoff. Financial service providers were not included in the safe-harbor agreement because U.S. and EU regulators still wanted to negotiate separate regulations for this sector. Other companies feared litigation in U.S. courts by consumer groups if they were found not adhering to any safe harbor principle.[308] Moreover, the European Parliament objected to a lack of

---

302 "Companies Resist U.S. Proposals On Privacy," Washington Post, March 16, 1999.

303 "Europeans clash with US on Security for Internet," Financial Times, July 8, 1997.

304 "US and EU at Odds on Taxing E-Trade," Financial Times, December 17, 1999.

305 "US attempts to break deadlock on data privacy," Financial Times, January12, 2000.

306 *www.export.gov/safeharbor*

307 "Brussels Ends Data Protection Dispute with US," Financial Times, July 28, 2000.

308 "Legal Threat to Information Sharing," Financial Times, July 30, 2001.

safeguards against "spam," i.e. unsolicited e-mails, and voted against a follow-up directive in September 2001. Still, on the level of official US-EU relations, the issue was settled.

The dispute over data protection had some similarities with the fight over hush kits – a EU consumer protection directive ran foul against U.S. commercial interest - but it was solved in a much calmer and constructive atmosphere, without any threats and counter-threats. The two cases therefore offer an instructive comparison of the different dynamics within trade disputes. Unlike aircraft noise, individual EU members had no specific interests on data privacy, giving the Commission more room to bargain. On the U.S. side, a large number of major corporations had a general concern about the potential cutoff of data flows, though they did not see the issue yet affecting their bottom lines. Those that were active in Europe had also learned to live with stricter privacy rules. They gave the Clinton administration a much freer hand in its dealings wit the European Commission.[309] Congress also failed to develop an interest in that complex issue. Largely isolated from domestic politics and corporate lobbying, negotiators faced no real deadlines and had plenty of time to work on the technical issues.

4.4. Macroeconomic coordination, exchange rates and financial crises

Macroeconomic coordination and exchange rate policy has long been an area of cooperation and conflict between the U.S. and the main European governments. Starting the in the late 1970s, U.S. leaders demanded at various times that European governments boost economic growth by cutting interest rates and undertake structural reforms. The main target of U.S. criticism was the Deutsche Bundesbank, the German central bank, and its nearly exclusive focus on keeping inflation down. Starting in the mid-1980s, most West European countries adopted the same anti-inflation policies and had their central banks shadow the interest-rate policies of the Bundesbank. The increasing European coordination was formalized in the Treaty on the European Union signed in Maastricht in 1991 that called for the establishment of a full-fledged monetary union by 1999.

The policies of economic convergence required under the Maastricht Treaty brought the main EU countries even closer together and forced them into a strict fiscal austerity policy as of the mid-1990s. While budget deficits and inflation rates declined all over Europe, economic growth fell short of its potential, while economic growth rates accelerated in the U.S. starting in 1996. However, the

309 Interview with David Aaron, U.S. deputy secretary of commerce for international trade from 1997 to 2001, on April 10, 2002 in Washington, D.C.

positive economic outlook for the U.S. gave the Clinton administration little reason for concern over the sluggish performance of the EU and Japan.

On the question of exchange rates, the ups and downs of the dollar compared to the main European currencies since the early 1970s have at various times caused tensions between the trading partners. In the late 1970s, the Europeans resented the decline of the dollar as harmful to their export industry, while the even sharper rise of the dollar rate in the first half of the 1980s raised concerns in the U.S. about declining productivity and an exploding trade deficit. Two agreements on exchange-rate coordination within the Group of Seven – the Plaza accord of 1995 and the Louvre agreement of 1997 – took the bite out of exchange rate policy. It was not until 1995, when European leaders, and particularly the French, began fretting about the Clinton administration's "benign neglect" for the steady decline in the dollar rate that they said gave the U.S. an unfair trade advantage.[310] The dollar recovered in 1996 and 1997, particularly against the Japanese yen, but it declined again significantly in the wake of the 1998 financial crisis. In 1999, however, the trend was reversed as the newly established Euro set out to lose almost thirty percent of its value against the dollar. The Clinton administration saw the strong dollar as an expression of U.S. economic superiority and the consequence of massive capital inflows into the country. Despite the persistent trade deficit, the government did not interfere in the currency markets and left exchange rate coordination off the international agenda.

The coming of the Euro was greeted with mixed feelings across the Atlantic. While the U.S. government continued to support the move toward closer European integration, most policy-makers shared the skepticism expressed in academic journals about the feasibility and the sustainability of a monetary union among countries that did not form an "optimal currency area."[311] Others worried about growing economic assertiveness of the European countries[312] or a shift of foreign-exchange reserves from dollar to euro. The most alarmist reaction came from the Harvard economist Martin Feldstein, chairman of the Council of Economic Advisors under President Ronald Reagan, who in a widely noted *Foreign Affairs* article predicted war in Europe as a consequence of monetary union.[313] Still, the arrival of the Euro was given surprisingly little attention in the U.S.[314]

---

310 "Europeans Say Weak Dollar Gives U.S. Unfair Trade Advantage," Washington Post April 7, 1995.
311 Henning/Padoan 2000.
312 Bergsten 1999.
313 Feldstein 1997.
314 "Will Dollar be Dethroned?" Euro may Herald End of an Era," International Herald Tribune, December 10, 1998.

Macroeconomic policies became a point of transatlantic dispute only in August 1998, when the Russian crisis led the world to the brink of financial meltdown. The first financial crisis, the breakdown of the Exchange Rate Mechanism of the European Monetary System (EMS) in 1992 and 1993, was a purely European affair. In the Mexican crisis of 1994 and 1995, the U.S. government was on its own when it arranged a huge loan package to prevent Mexico from defaulting. Given the proximity of the two countries and the close trade relations, the Clinton administration did not ask for support from other G-7 countries.

The Asian crisis, however, was global in scope. Beginning in July 1997 in Thailand, it had spread by 1998 not only to most of East Asia but also to other emerging markets like Russia and Brazil. In September 1998, the rising spreads on emerging market debt brought the huge hedge fund Long-Term Capital Management (LTCM) to the verge of collapse. With $200 billion exposure, the crisis at LTCM threatened the global banking system. In a dramatic late-night session, U.S. Federal Reserve Chairman Alan Greenspan cajoled the leading U.S. banks into a rescue operation for LTCM.[315] Again, the U.S. did not ask for any help from Europe, nor did it receive any, even though some of the banks most strongly exposed to LTCM were European, such as Switzerland's UBS.

Yet there were other reasons for growing U.S. frustration about its European partners. As the Russian ruble collapsed and Russia defaulted on part of its debt in August 1998, there were growing calls for Europeans, and particularly Germany, to step in and held the ailing power at its doorstep. Stanley Fischer, the influential vice president of the IMF, charged the German government for blocking a bailout package for Russia.[316] The view form Washington was that Europe was preoccupied with the launch of the Euro and did not shoulder the international responsibility that goes with being a world economic power. U.S. officials also did not like the ideas on the international economy that came from Europe. They regarded proposals by the leftist German finance minister Oskar Lafontaine for a new international financial order as counterproductive and even dangerous. Furthermore, the sustained opposition in the Republican-dominated Congress against the $18 billion increases in U.S. contributions to the IMF requested by the White House cast a shadow on Washington's willingness to do its part.

The Asian crisis caused a collapse in demand for industrial goods in East Asia, one of the main markets for U.S. exports in previous years. With a shrinking domestic market, East Asian manufacturers of machinery and steel were looking for foreign buyers and, helped by the devaluation of their currencies, stepped up their exports to the U.S. The consequence was a flood of

---

[315] "Long-term sickness?" *Economist*, October 3, 1998.

[316] "View from Fortress Europe," Financial Times, August 26, 1998

imports and a widening of the U.S. trade deficit in 1998. This gave rise to the charge that Europeans were keeping both their domestic demand down and their markets closed through a complex web of anti-dumping rules and non-tariff barriers.

"There is a view in the U.S. that Europe is not doing its part with respect to absorbing imports, particularly from Asia," said the USTR Charlene Barshefsky in October 1998. "Slowly, we are seeing the U.S. not only as the market of last resort, but the market of first resort. Politically, in the longer run, this will not be sustainable."[317] Specifically, Barshefsky asked the EU to lift its curbs on Japanese auto sales that kept the market share of Japanese models to 11 percent before its expiration date of the end of 1999. The demand to open up the European market for Japanese cars was ironic, given that three years earlier the EU had strongly objected to U.S. sanctions against Japanese luxury car imports.[318]

The acrimony reached its peak at the meeting of the Transatlantic Business Dialogue (TABD) in Charlotte, North Carolina, on Nov. 5-7, 1998, where Vice President Al Gore, Deputy Treasury Secretary Lawrence Summers and Commerce Secretary William Daley told the EU it had to boost growth and open markets.[319] Gore said "the United States cannot carry the burden alone…It is vital that Europe look outward as well as inward. It must look for ways to restore healthy trading programs."[320] Failing that, the U.S. would revert to protectionism, warned Daley. EU leaders were familiar with these complaints and warnings. The anti-European rhetoric did not signal any imminent actions.[321] The prospect that worried Europeans most was the possible imposition of steel import tariffs.

4.5. Steel

The U.S. steel industry has fought for and received protection from imports since the late 1960s, when European and Japanese imports for the first time threatened the health of the major integrated still mills such as U.S. Steel, LTV and Bethlehem Steel. From 1974 to 1992, employment in the steel industry dropped from 512,000 to 140,000, as many of the companies permanently closed mills or filed for bankruptcy.[322] U.S. steel executive and union leaders

---

[317] "US urges EU to help boost global growth," Financial Times, October 19, 1998.

[318] "U.S. Fails to Win EU Support for Anti-Japan Trade Sanctions," Washington Post, May 25, 1995.

[319] "Nerves are taut as leaders hint at an EU-US trade war," Financial Times, November 9, 1998.

[320] "Gore Asks Europeans To Help Stem Turmoil," Washington Post, November 6, 1998.

[321] William/Zielonka 1998.

[322] Krueger 1996, p. 73-75.

usually blamed unfair trade practices in other countries for their ills, pointing to pervasive subsidies for steel producers that resulted in a global overcapacity and the "dumping" of steel in the U.S. market. Over the years, steel companies lobbied for all forms of protection, from anti-dumping and countervailing duties over voluntary export restraints (VER) to various forms of subsidies. Even though Congress did not meet all of the industry's demand, legislators were usually quite open to their arguments and lobbying power and created a whole web of import barriers for foreign steel.

In Europe, a number of state-owned steel companies were privatized in the 1980s and 1990s and underwent a wrenching process of consolidation and downsizing. As part of the privatization process, national governments often assumed the heavy debt loads of these companies to make the fit for public flotation. The combination of debt forgiveness and radical restructuring left European steel producers overall more competitive than their U.S. counterparts.

Rising domestic demand for steel, a rise in steel prices and the continued protection from import barriers in the 1990s allowed most U.S. steel companies to delay layoffs, plant closures and mergers. Steel wages actually rose faster than other blue-collar compensation, as managers tried to keep the powerful unions content.[323] Steel plants that were shut down by the big firms were resurrected as independent steel producers and agricultural-dependent states looked to steel as a venue for high-paying industrial jobs. Meanwhile, new technology allowed American "mini-mills" such as Nucor to convert scrap metal into steel of acceptable quality at much lower costs.[324] This structure left the major steel mills highly vulnerable to the onslaught of steel imports in the wake of the Asian crisis. Steel imports rose 6.8 percent to a record of 31.2 million tons in 1997 and jumped then another 33.3 percent to 41.5 million tons in 1998 (American Iron and Steel Institute). Sharply lower currencies allowed Japan, South Korea, Russia and Brazil to sell steel at far lower prices than those charged by U.S. steel mills. As the mid-term Congressional elections approached, the Clinton administration came under increasing pressure to stop the flood. On September 10, 1998, the major U.S. steel producers filed a demand for anti-dumping measures against Brazil, Russia and Japan and started an advertising campaign to press the White House into further action.

Although European steel producers were not specifically targeted, the issue spilled over into the already tense transatlantic trade relationship. The EU was itself hit by a sharp increase in steel imports and for the first time in history became a net importer of steel. But it had agreed to import restraints with Russia and the Ukraine who desperately needed to earn foreign exchange. This diverted Russian exports to the more open U.S. market. In October 1998,

---

[323] Hufbauer/Goodrich 2002.

[324] "In America's fiery Furnace," *Economist*, September 17, 1998.

Barshefsky appealed to the EU to lift its import quotas with Russia in order to take pressure off the U.S. markets.[325] Trade commissioner Brittan did not concur and to the disappointment of EU steel makers; he called on Europe to resist any further protectionism.

The anti-dumping cases moved forward with surprising speed. In early 1999, following a recommendation of the International Trade Commission (ITC), an independent federal agency, and the administration imposed prohibitive duties on Japanese and Brazilian steel, while Russia agreed to voluntary export quotas. Clinton offered the steel industry $300 million in tax breaks and promised in his state-of-the-union address to retaliate "when imports unlawfully flood our nation." The steel lobby was far from satisfied. On March 17, 1999, the House of Representatives voted to impose quotas on all foreign steel producers. By that time, imports from Japan and Russia had all but ceased, Canadian and Mexican steel makers were protected through NAFTA: the quota would have hit EU steel producers particularly hard.[326]

The White House signaled its opposition to the bill because it violated WTO rules and threatened to trigger retaliation. Vice President Gore needed the support of steel-producing states as well as House minority leader Richard Gephardt, a champion of the steel industry, for his presidential bid, so the White House kept a low profile. In the end, Clinton did not have to veto the bill, as it was killed by a Senate vote on June 22, 1999. Still, the Senate approved the Emergency Steel Loan Guarantee Act that promised another $1 billion in loan guarantees to the steel industry.[327] The steel industry launched another 20 anti-dumping suits against 18 different countries. In a key question of whether to restrict the import of steel wire rod, one of the major categories of steel, the ITC split its vote, leaving it up to the White House to decide.

On August 5, 1999, the government announced a "steel action plan" to bolster the embattled industry. Commerce Secretary William Daley said the U.S. would raise steel issues in global trade forums and launch a comprehensive review of government subsidies of foreign industries and other "market destroying trade barriers." Moreover, the U.S. Foreign Service and Commerce Department would "aggressively" promote U.S. steel and steel products.[328]

Washington also targeted products made by former European state-owned steel companies, imposed a number of countervailing duties on steel products produced by formerly state-owned steel companies, alleging that they received a continued benefit from earlier government subsidies. As early as 1993, the U.S. imposed such duties on British Steel because of subsidies it had received before

---

[325] "Close to the melting point," Financial Times, October 23, 1998.
[326] "Steel Scrap," *Economist*, March 18, 1999.
[327] "Standing up to Steel," Economist, June 24, 1999.
[328] "US Plans to Bolster Local Steel Industry," Financial Times, August 6, 1999.

its privatization in 1988. The EU challenged these measures in 1998, and a WTO panel ruled in December 1999 that the countervailing duties violated the SCM Agreement.[329] The U.S. withdrew the duties against British Steel, now part of the Anglo-Dutch group Corus, but left other countervailing duties against EU steel markers in place.[330] The EU subsequently challenged them as well.[331]

The sum of measures caused major concern in Brussels. In a letter to Barshefsky, Brittan warned on August 12, 1999 of a "damaging protectionist spiral" and signaled an appeal to the WTO over various U.S. anti-dumping measures. Brittan was particularly concerned about the prospect of a quota for steel wire rod that would then be diverted to Europe, and the loan guarantee that constituted an illegal subsidy under WTO rules.[332] Steel imports into the U.S. declined by 14 percent in 1999 to 35.7 million tons, relieving some of the pressure on the industry and the political leadership. Still, imports started to surge again in mid-2000 after a relatively weak first half.

As the presidential elections 2000 approached, the steel industry began again to flex its muscle with a major advertising campaign. Claiming "serious injury" through imports, it demanded from the White House to initiate trade action under the Section 201 of the 1973 Trade Act that could allow general quotas on imports from all trading partners, including the EU. "We need the Administration immediately to take broad and comprehensive action against the flood of imported steel," the chief executives of about 100 U.S. steel companies told Clinton in a letter. In a decision that may have cost the Democrats the presidency, Clinton declined to go ahead with a 201 investigation. He knew that the imposition of such tariffs would trigger a WTO complaint or retaliatory steps by the EU. Instead, he warned several countries outside the WTO, including Ukraine, Taiwan and China, to restrain steel imports to the U.S.

Clinton's decision to forego action on Section 201 should have calmed the transatlantic steel waters but an unexpected legislative move in Congress caused a new dispute. Robert Byrd, the senior Democratic senator from West Virginia, tacked an amendment to an agricultural appropriations bill that would hand the proceeds of countervailing and anti-dumping duties to the affected companies. The amendment was introduced in the House-Senate committee that settled the differences between two bill versions. It passed without anyone really aware of its international implications. Because anti-dumping and countervailing duties are set at a level to offset unfair pricing by foreign exporters, handing them over

---

329 EU Press Release IP/00/6, January 7, 2000. *http://europa.eu.int/comm /external_relations/ news/01_00/ip_00_6.htm*

330 "US Acts to Curb Steel Imports," Financial Times, October 27, 2000.

331 "WTO Sets Up Panel on Steel Disputes," Financial Times, September 11, 2001.

332 "EU urges US to Refrain from Steel Industry Measures," Financial Times, August 13, 1999.

as subsidies would add another layer of protection to the affected companies. As this clearly violated WTO rules, the White House had previously fought similar measures by Byrd.[333] With the Byrd Amendment passed as part of a bill that was essential for farming states, Clinton had no choice but to sign the Continued Dumping and Subsidy Offset Act into law on October 31, 2000. Barshefsky called it a "bad idea," but said it would be enforced until the Congress came around to repeal it.[334]

Still, for the EU, this was the straw that broke the camel's back. The Byrd amendment, it feared, would give companies an incentive to initiate dumping claims and lead to a proliferation of anti-dumping measures. On December 21, 2000, eight more countries joined the EU in a WTO challenge to the Byrd amendment.[335] In June 2001, the complainants requested a panel that was established on August 23, 2001. Meanwhile, the prospects for a repeal of the law in Congress faded, and the Bush administration decided against picking a domestic fight over the issue. The USTR announced that, "the Byrd amendment is fully consistent with our international obligations under the WTO" and would be vigorously defended.[336] In October 2001, the U.S. treasury began disbursing $200 million in tariff receipts to various U.S. companies. The largest beneficiary was ball bearing maker Torrington who received more than $60 million, while steel producers received $31 million.[337]

The case against the Byrd amendment was just one element of a deliberate EU strategy to challenge the whole range of U.S. anti-dumping legislation at the WTO. The most clear-cut and therefore most successful complaint was against the anti-dumping law of 1916 that imposed treble damages and criminal penalties against persons found to have imported goods at dumped prices. This clearly violated the spirit and the letter of the WTO rules. The law had been little used for decades, but starting in 1988, several U.S. companies discovered the law as a weapon against foreign competitors, including the Wheeling-Pittsburgh Steel Corporation and an Iowa printing press manufacturer, who successfully sued two German companies. The EU initiated the complaint process in June 1988 and was later joined by Japan. A WTO panel ruled against the law on February 15, 2000. The U.S. appealed on grounds that it was an anti-trust statute and should not be assessed under WTO anti-dumping rules. The WTO appellate body confirmed the panel ruling on August 28, 2000, and an arbitrator later ruled that the U.S. had to remove the provision by July 26, 2001.[338] Even though the Bush administration asked Congress to nullify the

---

333 "For the Byrds," *Economist*, October 19, 2000.
334 EABC Abstracts October 20, 2000. *www.eabc.org/abstracts/abstract/1020.htm*
335 "US Law Faces WTO Challenge," Financial Times December 19, 2000
336 EABC Abstracts July 13, 2001. *www.eabc.org/abstracts/abstracts0713.htm*
337 EABC Abstracts February1/02. *www.eabc.org/abstracts/abstracts020102.htm*
338 "WTO Rules on Repeal Deadline," Financial Times, January 28, 2002.

law, arguing that it was "unnecessary given other available trade remedy laws," Congress did not take up the issue by the summer.[339] The EU agreed to an extension of the deadline until the end of 2001.

As Clinton prepared his departure from the presidency, steel was one more of the many trade disputes, which he left to his successor. In hindsight, it became clear to what extent Clinton had maneuvered adroitly between the opposing forces of Congress and the trading partners to keep the lid on the explosive steel issue. The flurry of protective measures irritated the trading partners and triggered an avalanche of WTO complaints, but none of them was big enough to lead to a major fight. From an international trade perspective, Clinton's steel policy was successful damage control. In terms of domestic electoral politics, it was an utter failure. When Republican candidate George W. Bush went to West Virginia and promised to stand up for America's steel interests, he snatched that traditionally Democratic state away from Gore. The five electoral votes from West Virginia were enough to hand Bush the presidency.

In spite of his overall commitment to free trade, Bush went on to make good on his campaign promises: on June 22, 2001, his administration invoked Section 201 of the 1974 trade act and asked the ITC to investigate. The ITC recommended duties of up to 20 percent for most steel products and in March 2002, he went beyond that proposal and decreed tariffs of 30 percent, directed mostly against steel imports from the EU and South Korea. Canada and Mexico were exempted because of NAFTA, while other developing countries received special waivers.[340] By fulfilling his promise to the steel workers of West Virginia and Ohio, Bush created a trade row with Europe that immediately surpassed any of the spats of the Clinton years. In the spring of 2002, the EU filed a complaint at the WTO, imposed its own safeguard measures to protect against an the diversion of steel imports from the U.S. to the European markets, and threatened to impose retaliatory sanctions *before* the conclusion of the WTO dispute-settlement procedure, just as the U.S. had done in the banana case. With one stroke, steel had become the nastiest of all transatlantic trade disputes. In November 2003, the WTO ruled, in effect, that the Bush administration had stretched and abused the WTO rules. Eight nations, led by the EU, stood ready to apply billions of dollars' worth of sanctions against US exports if the US did not back down by the December 15th deadline. Under great international pressure, President George Bush rescinded tariffs on imported steel goods, much to the howl of steel executives and steel union leaders, as

[339] European-American Business Council Abstracts, August 3, 2001. *www.eabc.org/abstracts /abstracts0803.htm*

[340] "Bush Puts Tariffs of as Much as 30 % on Steel Imports" and "Angry Europeans to Challenge U.S. Steel Tariffs at WTO," both New York Times, March 6, 2002.

well as from the many Democratic presidential aspirants.[341] Nonetheless, a nasty transatlantic trade dispute was prevented from turning into a full-scale trade war.

4.6. Music Copyright

A small and little noticed case presented a good example of how WTO arbitration could conceivably defuse transatlantic trade disputes. The 1998 U.S. Copyright Act in Section 110(5) exempted restaurants and bars and shops from royalty payments for playing recorded music on radio or television. In early 1999, the European Commission challenged the compatibility of that law with the TRIPS Agreement on behalf of the Irish Music Rights Organization (IMRO), whose members were particularly hard hit by the loss of royalties. A WTO panel was established in May 1999 and a year later ruled in favor of the complainant. The Dispute Settlement Body officially adopted the report on July 27, 2000 and on January 15, 2001; an arbitrator gave the U.S. until July 27, 2001 to bring its law in line with its WTO obligations, requiring Congress to act.

Just before the deadline expired, the U.S. requested and received an extension until December 20, 2001. At that time, the EU and the U.S. also agreed on a procedure under which the U.S. would set up a fund to compensate European artists for lost royalties until the U.S. law is amended and ask an arbitration panel "under Article 25 of the DSU to determine the level of nullification or impairment of benefits caused by Section 110(5)(B) of the US Copyright Act." European music groups estimated the appropriate compensation at $27 million a year, but in November, the panel set the amount at only $1.1 million per year for a three-year period, giving the U.S. sufficient time to change its laws. On December 18, 2001, the U.S. and the EU agreed on this level of compensation. Lamy called the accord "a good example of how we can manage our problems in a cooperative manner, while keeping in mind our international obligations and commitments."[342] Yet, even this agreement required Congressional approval. The EU requested authorization to impose sanctions, to which the U.S. formally objected, though both sides agreed to suspend any action until March 1, 2002 to give Congress time to act. By April, the matter was still stuck in Congress, while the parties remain engaged in productive discussions with a view to resolving the dispute.[343]

---

[341] "US Steel Tariffs Gave Safeguards a Bad Name," Financial Times, December 7, 2003.
[342] "U.S. Fund to Repay Royalties to EU Musicians," Financial Times, December 19, 2001; and EABC Abstracts, December 21, 2001. *www.eabc.org/abstracts/abstracts1221.htm*
[343] Status Report by the United States by the United States to the WTO DSB on April 4, 2002.

Unlike other issues, this case was easy to settle: it was all about money, and the sums involved were so small that the U.S, government could settle it through financial compensation. Even so, the case dragged on for more than three years and depended and required legislative action. With Congress not interested in the issue and therefore ignoring several deadlines, the domestic policy process came close to endangering even such a minor and simple international agreement. The EU continued to show plenty of patience, but it easy to imagine that under a different international climate and with a more complex case involved, cooperation could have broken down. The structural hurdles to settle narrow trade disputes remain true even here.

CHAPTER 5: TRADE WARS

Whereas the U.S. and the EU were able to resolve or at least contain their most heated trade disputes until mid-1998, this was no longer the case in the following months. A series of conflicts resulted in moves that were perceived as openly hostile by the other side and triggered some counter-action. As the U.S. imposed sanctions on EU products over rows in gluten, bananas, beef, the EU launched the biggest challenge ever of U.S. tax laws at the WTO, talk increased of a trade war. While both sides stayed within the rules of the WTO and also resorted to diplomacy to control the escalation, I argue that the maneuvers taken in course of these conflicts do meet the definition of a limited trade war – the imposition of trade restrictions that are motivated not by economic interests, but by the aim to hurt the other side and force a change of its behavior. The failure to resolve these disputes caused a further deterioration of the transatlantic trade relationship and became a factor for the failure of larger trade negotiations.

5.1. Gluten: The classic trade war

The first trade dispute during the Clinton presidency to escalate into a trade war came in a small and rather obscure area of cereal production – wheat and corn gluten. Wheat gluten is the concentrated form of the protein contained in wheat flour and is an essential ingredient in multi-bread and high-fiber breads as well as pet food. In modified form, it can be used as a meat extender, egg substitute, or as an ingredient in the production of biodegradable plastics. The other major by-product of wheat is starch.

In the mid-1990s, the U.S. Wheat Gluten Industry Council (WGIC) charged that certain measures under the EU Common Agricultural Policy led to a drop in U.S. wheat exports to the EU and a surge of EU gluten exports to the U.S. Specifically, the EU levied an export tax on wheat that increased the domestic wheat supply and lowered prices. This policy shut out U.S. exports from the market. A resulting drop in production was prevented by a refund for gluten and starch production and by an export subsidy on starch that also provided incentives to overproduce.[344] WGIC claimed that with the help of these measures EU producers had doubled their share of the U.S. gluten market to nearly 28 percent by 1996 to 36 million tons. This rose to 41 million tons in 1997. Meanwhile, gluten prices dropped dramatically and even occasionally falling below production costs, causing financial losses in the U.S. industry.

Faced with growing opposition in Congress to free trade and an extension of fast-track authority, the Clinton administration decided to use this issue to demonstrate that it was willing to stand up for U.S. commercial interests. On

[344] "US launches EU wheat gluten probe," Financial Times, January 23, 1997.

March 8, 1997, the USTR launched an investigation on the barriers to U.S. wheat and starch exports under Section 301 of the trade law that permits trade restraints to offset unfair trading practices abroad.[345] Subsequently, the International Trade Commission was asked to study the injury caused by EU gluten exports to the U.S. wheat gluten industry under the Section 201. After the ITC established that the U.S. industry was seriously injured and should receive "safeguard relief," Clinton imposed a three-year quota on EU gluten exports on June 1, 1998. This quota limited the European share of the U.S. market to 24 million tons, but was designed to increase by six percent in the second and third years.[346] The move came just days after the U.S. government announced export subsidies for barley in retaliation to a shipment of 30,000 tons of heavily subsidized European barley.[347] The European Commission called the quota "discriminatory and unjustified," as Australia's quota was set at the 1997 level and Canada was excluded. It claimed that, "the increase in EU exports over the last year is market-driven and is not the result of support to the EU industry."[348] EU experts claimed that the industry's problems stemmed from the competition of much cheaper corn gluten than from EU producers.

The Commission agreed at the time to examine "all appropriate responses" to the action. On July 28, 1998, the Commission proposed a tariff on U.S. corn gluten feed sold in the EU. The Ecu 5 per ton duty would hit 2.73 million tons and raise Ecu 13.65 million, or 15 million dollars. However, the EU took its time in following up on this proposal and other measures. In March 1999, it finally launched a challenge against the U.S. quota at the WTO, starting with a request for consultations with U.S. officials.

While the dispute so far was low key, it heated up in June 1999 when the U.S. declared it would cut the EU quota by 5.4 million tons because of a similar quota overshoot in the first year. Brussels argued that the overshoot was due to the failure of U.S. customs officials to record imports against the quota and report the remaining quota for the year correctly.[349] The Commission asked the WTO for an immediate investigation of the quotas, but was rebuffed. It repeated the request in late July, forcing the establishment of a dispute panel. As U.S. authorities prepared another cut in the quota in June 2000, the WTO dispute panel sided with the EU in an interim judgment.[350] The U.S. appealed, and in December, the appellate body changed some of the legal reasoning used by the panel report. Nonetheless, it upheld the basic finding that the U.S. quota

---

[345] USTR press release March 10, 1997.

[346] USTR press release, June 1, 1998.

[347] "US three-year quote will hit exports from EU," Financial Times, June 1, 1998.

[348] Press release by the Delegation of the European Commission to the U.S., June 2, 1998.

[349] "EU attacks quota cut on wheat gluten," Financial Times, June 4, 1999

[350] United States – Definitive Safeguard Measures on Imports of Wheat Gluten from the European Communities, DS 166, January 19, 2001. *www.ejil.org/journal/curdevs/sr20.html*

violated WTO rules because it had not demonstrated the causal link between increased imports and serious injury to the domestic industry.[351]

When the WTO Dispute Settlement Body adopted the appellate body report on January 19, 2001, the EU imposed its duties on U.S. corn gluten imports. This hurt U.S. exporters particularly hard because the scare over mad cow disease (BSE) had boosted EU demand for cheap U.S. animal feed. The new Bush administration challenged the duties at the WTO, alleging that the EU had not followed WTO procedures correctly while agreeing with the EU to settle the issue by June 2001when the gluten quota expired. Even though the ITC recommended another two-year extension of the wheat gluten quota,[352] the U.S. government Washington decided to let the quota expire. In its place, it offered a $40 million subsidy over two years to wheat gluten industry, "to complete its transition to competitiveness."[353] In return, the EU ended its duties on corn gluten of which the USTR estimated would have cost the U.S. industry $50 million over the same two-year period. The Bush administration called the decision to "monetize" the value of the quota extension "an innovative approach to help the U.S. wheat gluten industry" without triggering further retaliation.[354] EU leaders were satisfied that the combination of WTO complaint and tough retaliation could move the U.S. government to abandon protectionist measures.

The wheat gluten conflict was triggered by a unilateral U.S. move that was covered by U.S. domestic law, but violated WTO rules. Following the ruling of the WTO dispute panel, the U.S. changed its policy to become in line with its multilateral obligations. Given the resolution of the conflict, trade war seems like an extreme categorization. Yet the EU imposition of corn gluten duties was exactly the type of hostile action that only served the purpose to hurt the trading partner and therefore, would qualify as a shot in a trade war. By driving up the price of animal feed, the EU was actually hurting its own cattle farmers, who were suffering from the BSE scare. Retaliation carried a cost for both sides.

The outcome of the dispute also demonstrated the risk of confrontational tactics in trade policy. If the Clinton administration had decided in 1998 to pay a subsidy to the wheat gluten industry instead of imposing quotas, it could have achieved a similar domestic effect without causing any transatlantic tensions and causing – even just temporary - damage to the U.S. corn gluten industry. The "gluten war" never became a major issue for the transatlantic relationship, but its dynamics foreshadowed some of the bigger fights that were about to come.

---

[351] "WTO Upholds Ruling on Gluten Exports," Financial Times, December 23, 2000.
[352] "ITC finds Wheat Gluten Industry Needs Continued Import Relief," International Trade Reporter No. 18:3, March 29, 2001.
[353] USTR Press Release, June 1, 2001.
[354] Ibid.

5.2. Bananas: Trade War as a Farce

The dispute over the EU banana import regime was the best known but probably least understood transatlantic trade issue in the late 1990s. As neither the U.S. nor the EU grow more than a negligible amount of bananas, it seemed strange that the two sides would pick this issue for a trade war involving several WTO complaints, punitive sanctions and a heated rhetoric that came to affect the strategic relationship. As the conflict escalated, both sides argued that more than bananas were at stake but rather numerous key principles in their trading policy. There are several key questions that can be asked in an analysis of the conflict: Why did the U.S. pick bananas among all the controversial EU trade practices for its first full-fledged WTO challenge? Why did the EU not modify its regime once it became clear that it was not WTO-compatible? Did the political damage-control mechanisms work in this case, did they set in too late, or did they just fail? What was the political and economic damage of the dispute?

The banana dispute can be traced back to the system of colonial trade preferences that the European colonial powers continued after World War II, against the opposition of the U.S. As bananas were a major source of income of several colonies in Africa and the Caribbean, granting preferential access for banana exports was a key element of the French, British and Spanish policy toward former and continued colonies. This preference was particularly important because the major banana plantations were run primarily by U.S. companies in Central and South America who were able to produce the fruit at lower costs and often with higher quality. Until the early 1990s, bananas entered the EU, the world's second largest importer of bananas with more than 3 million tons a year, through a hodgepodge of different import policies. France imported bananas from its Overseas Departments of Guadeloupe and Martinique and from former colonies Cote d'Ivoire and Cameroon. Britain received most of its bananas from the Windward Island in the Eastern Caribbean (Barbados, Dominica, Grenada St. Lucia and St. Vincent), while Spain relied exclusively on its domestic production in the Canary Islands. Other EU countries imposed a 20 percent tariff, while Germany, with the world's highest per capita consumption of bananas, bought most of its bananas tariff-free from the major U.S. distributors, Chiquita Brands International, Dole Foods and Del Monte Produce.[355] The various banana privileges were in line with the system of trade preferences enshrined in the Lome Convention, the trade-and-aid agreement signed by the European Community in 1975 with African, Caribbean and Pacific (ACP) countries.[356]

---

[355] Harahan 1999.
[356] Dinan 1999, p. 505.

The completion of the EC single market in 1992 forced the Europeans to harmonize its banana regime. This became a controversial topic within the Community. While Germany wanted to preserve access to cheap "dollar bananas," Britain and France rejected any change that could have hurt its former colonies. The internal negotiations resulted in an extremely complex compromise that combined tariffs, quotas and a system of import licenses. The 404/93 regime established four categories of suppliers:

1. EU producers covered by internal aspects of the common market (mainly Canary Islands, Martinique and Guadeloupe). For these regions, income support up to 854,000 tons was guaranteed in case prices fall below the costs of production.

2. Traditional ACP countries, i.e., the ACP banana suppliers in the years preceding the single market, received duty-free access up to a maximum amount of 857,700 tons per year.

3. Non-traditional ACP countries (e.g. Dominican Republic) had access to the general quota of 2.2 million tons for duty-free exports.

4. Third countries, the so-called 'Dollar' countries shared the quota of 2.2 million tons with Category 3 countries, but faced a tariff of 75 Ecu a ton.

In addition, the regime also favored the ACP countries in the allocation of import licenses. U.S. companies received only 66.5 percent of the licenses, while 30 percent went to established operators in the EC or in ACP countries. The final 3.5 percent was reserved for newcomers, particularly those espousing "fair trade" policies. "The allocation of Dollar quotas to the ACP companies was designed to cross-subsidize the expensive ACP bananas with some Dollar banana quota rent and thus strengthen the position of the ACP companies in relation to the Dollar companies. At the same time, it led the *Dollar companies to invest in ACP countries* to build rights to future Dollar quota allocation within this category.[357]

The regime was disappointing for the U.S. banana companies who had hoped for the opening of the European banana market. Not only did the trade preferences remain, the system of import licenses was clearly stacked against them. In particularly, Chiquita, with a 26 percent share as the world market leader in bananas, was bound to lose some of its dominance in Germany, the

---

[357] Kasteele 1998, p. 11.

Netherlands, and Denmark as the licensing system favored European importers and even ripening companies who had never been involved in the banana trade.

The first to challenge the system was Germany who appealed to the European Court of Justice to stop its implementation to no avail: the regime was put in place in July 1993. Shortly afterwards, five Latin American bananas growers (Costa Rica, Venezuela, Columbia, Guatemala and Nicaragua), protested against the system in the GATT. A GATT panel first ruled on May 19, 1993 against the existing restrictions of EU member countries on banana imports ("Banana I") and on January 18, 1994, against the new EU-wide regime ("Banana II"). As GATT findings had to be adopted unanimously by all members, the resistance of the EU and the affected Caribbean countries made the ruling unenforceable. Instead, the EU offered to negotiate a 'Framework Agreement' with the complainants that would have eased the impact of the regime. All countries except Guatemala signed the accord. It reduced in-quota tariff for their banana exports from 30 percent to 20 percent and allocated export licenses to the national governments.[358] The U.S. companies saw this arrangement as even more damaging to their interests. In particular Chiquita decided to actively oppose the system and use its influence in Washington to force a change.[359]

When Chiquita spoke up, Washington politicians listened. Carl Lindner, a controversial rightist businessman with strong political clout within both parties, led the Cincinnati-based company concern. At a time when "soft money" donations to the national parties in the U.S. were exploding, Lindner became one of the main contributors to both Democrats and Republicans. In 1993 and 1994, Chiquita and Lindner was the second largest contributor of soft money, giving $525,000 to Democrats and $430,000 to Republicans. Thanks to this largesse, he gained the support of such influential senators like Robert Dole (R-Kansas) and John Glenn (D-Ohio) and the Democratic leader in the House of Representatives, Richard Gephardt (D-Missouri). This made the White House also receptive to Lindner's complaints about EU trade policy.[360]

USTR Mickey Kantor took up the fight against the EU banana regime. On September 2, 1994, Chiquita and the Hawaii Banana Industry Association filed a petition under second 301 of the 1974 Trade Act claiming that the EU policy and the Framework Agreement are "unreasonable and discriminatory" and a "burden and restriction on U.S. commerce." On October 17, Kantor initiated an investigation into the EU practices and called upon the Latin American countries to withdraw from the Framework Agreement. While Venezuela and

[358] Hanrahan 1999.
[359] Kasteele 1998, p. 12.
[360] "The Riled Bunch," Washington Post, October 20, 1995.

Nicaragua abandoned the agreement under U.S. pressure, Columbia and Costa Rica implemented it on January 1, 1995.[361]

The U.S. then proceeded on two fronts. Following the completion of its investigation Kantor announced on September 25, 1995 that the U.S. would use the newly established dispute settlement mechanism (DSM) at the WTO to challenge the EU regime.[362] In Congress, Dole prepared legislation that would punish Columbia and Costa Rica with the elimination of vital U.S. trade concessions if they did not withdraw from the Framework Agreement.

Europeans were baffled by the U.S. decision to pick this narrow issue as its first major case to use the WTO. The EU ambassador to the U.S., Hugo Paemen, phrased it in the following way: "The Latin American banana producers had 85 percent of the European market, and for the remaining 15 percent, the U.S. was ready to go to war".[363] While acknowledging the shortcomings of the EU regime, he and other EU officials noted a "major discrepancy between objective and mean." U.S. trade experts were equally critical. Jeffrey Scott from the Institute for International Economics asked, "With all the problems that Mickey Kantor has, does this deserve his priority attention?"[364] He and others saw the move as proof of the damaging power of special interests and campaign contributions.

Yet U.S. trade officials argued that they had a strong and important case to make. "The real issue was not bananas, but the U.S. rights for distribution under the General Agreement of Trade in Services, the GATS," said Kantor's deputy and successor Charlene Barshefsky, "This was an important case of precedence."[365] The USTR also referred to the 16,000 people employed by Chiquita, Dole and Del Monte in the U.S. of which 7,500 were involved in the banana trade.

It was striking, however, that only Chiquita chose to challenge the EU directly. Dole and Del Monte took advantage of the new rules and actually became some of the main beneficiaries of the import regime.[366] Thus, the U.S. not only battled its European partners in the subsequent trade conflict, but also the Caribbean banana exporters, Costa Rica and Columbia and two of its three major banana companies, all in the interest of the market leader. The conflicting interests between Chiquita and Dole became particularly important in 1999when the U.S. and the EU finally sat down to settle the dispute.

---

[361] USTR Press Release, January 9, 1995.
[362] USTR Press Release, September 25, 1995.
[363] Interview with Hugo Paemen, EU ambassador to the U.S. from 1993 to 1999, on April 10, 2002 in Washington, D.C.
[364] "The Riled Bunch," Washington Post, October 20, 1995.
[365] Interview with Charlene Barshefsky, United States Trade Representative from 1996 to 2001, on March 19, 2002.
[366] Kasteele 1998.

On February 5, 1996, the U.S. along with Ecuador, Guatemala, Honduras and Mexico formally asked for consultations with the EU on the banana issue, a first step in the complaint process. On April 11, it filed a request for establishment of a WTO dispute settlement panel that was later established on May 8. The U.S. argued that the banana regime violated the GATT, the GATS and the Agreement on Import Licensing Procedures. It focused not on the preferential access for the ACP countries, but rather on the accompanying license agreements and the preferential tariffs provided to the Latin American countries through the Framework Agreement.

The EU argued that the waiver extended to the EU's Lome Convention in the Uruguay Round Agreement covered not only trade preferences for the ACP countries, but also the measures necessary to fulfill these obligations. This included the import licenses and the trade preferences for the framework countries.[367]

The WTO panel rendered its verdict in March 1997 and released its finding in a public report on April 30, 1997. As expected, it found that major aspects of the banana regime, particularly the system of allocation import licenses, discriminated against growers and distributors in Honduras, Guatemala, Ecuador, Mexico and the United States. The ruling did not find any fault with the principle of Lome Convention trade preferences. The EU appealed the verdict but an appeal panel on September 9, 1997 effectively reaffirmed the earlier judgment. On January 8, 1998, a WTO arbitrator gave the EU until January 1, 1999 to bring its regime in line with WTO requirements.

The EU Commission set out to modify the banana regime, though it quickly realized that any model had limited maneuver room. Britain and France insisted on maintaining the system of preferences for its former colonies both in production and distribution. A move toward a tariff-only regime, or one in which the quotas were distributed on the basis of the "first- come, first-served" principle, was unacceptable to them. Pressure came also from the Caribbean states that feared any change within the existing regime could wipe out their fragile banana industry. They depended on banana exports for about 60 percent of their exports earnings, but their small hilly farms had far higher production costs than the Latin American plantations. They frantically lobbied both in Washington and Brussels and warned of an economic collapse and a growth of drug production if their banana privileges were curtailed. Germany, who had originally opposed the system, had meanwhile gained a commercial stake in it. Port authorities and trading companies in Hamburg and Antwerp made major

---

[367] Hanrahan 1998.

investment to accommodate the banana trade through the new licensing system and did not want any change.[368]

The Commission proposal presented on January 14, 1998 only made the minimum changes to the regime deemed necessary to make it WTO-compatible. It proposed to increase the import quota from 2.2 million tons by 353,000 tons to 2.5 million tons to reflect the accession of Sweden, Finland and Austria to the EU. It created a further "autonomous" quota of 353,000 tons at a duty of Ecu300 a ton. While the total tariff-free quota for the ACP countries was to stay at 857,700 tons, any further country-specific division would be eliminated. As a concession to the U.S., the EU proposed the elimination cross-subsidies through the granting of 'B' import licenses for dollar bananas to ACP producers. As compensation, these countries would receive Ecu360 million in additional aid.[369]

The U.S. did not like what it saw. The increase in the import quota to 2.5 million tons was no concession, it argued, as it did not exceed what had already agreed ahead of the 1995 EU enlargement. The major problem, however, was the allocation of import licenses. Absent of a first-come, first-served system or an auction, the Commission had to use some historical pattern to distribute the valuable rights of which were around $1 billion. The U.S. wanted a return to the pre-1993 market shares, but the EU proposal used the figures from 1994 and 1995, when the WTO-incompatible regime was already in place, as the basis for the allocation. In this way, "past discrimination would be perpetuated.[370] In the following months, the EU rebuffed the U.S. and the Latin American complainants' attempts to negotiate on the banana regime, a matter Brussels considered internal. On June 26, 1998, the EU Agricultural Council adopted the Commission proposals with only minor changes. While Germany, Belgium, the Netherlands and Denmark pushed for more radical changes to open the banana market and forestall the threat of U.S. retaliation. Eventually, only the Netherlands voted against the proposal. Still, Commission officials expressed confidence that the system would now survive any further WTO challenge.

Washington strongly disagreed with this view. It regarded the reforms as cosmetic changes that did not address the deeper issues that the WTO report raised. Unfortunately, the two sides now entered into a black hole in regard to WTO procedures that address the question of compliance with dispute-settlement rulings. The different legal interpretations about the correct way to test the WTO compatibility of the new EU banana regime triggered one of the

---

368 Interview with Hugo Paemen, EU ambassador to the U.S. from 1993 to 1999, on April 10, 2002 in Washington, D.C.

369 "Brussels Farm Ministers Push on with Search for Banana Imports Deal," Financial Times, June 22, 1998.

370 "A New EC Banana Regime: WTO-Consistent Alternatives," United States Mission to the European Union, November 1998.

harshest transatlantic disputes ever. The EU wanted the complainants to go the regular route for dispute procedures. This meant that the U.S. would have to wait for the new regime to go into effect on January 1, 1999, and then to start the lengthy process of consultations before a new panel could be established. Washington argued that the changes in the banana regime were so minor that no new dispute settlement case had to be started. They argued that the original panel should quickly render a verdict on the WTO-compatibility of the modified banana regime.

When the EU rejected these overtures, the U.S. became convinced that the Europeans were exploiting procedural loopholes in the WTO to delay or even evade compliance with a binding ruling. As U.S. special trade negotiator Peter Sher argued, the EU was "undermining the multilateral process...The fundamental premise of the WTO when it was enacted several years ago was that it would not be like the GATT; that countries could not simply block decisions, could not ignore rulings, that they would have a reasonable time to comply before they would have to pay the price for not complying."[371] From July to November, Brussels rebuffed several attempts by the USTR to reconvene the original panel and charged the U.S. with "legal harassment."[372] At that point in time, the banana dispute was no longer an isolated incidence but part of a seeming increasing pattern of transatlantic conflicts. The list of quarrels seemed to increase day by day: aircraft noise, Airbus subsidies, Internet privacy, steel, wheat gluten, and U.S. export subsidies. Most importantly, following another WTO ruling the EU also found itself on the losing end in the decade-old dispute over import restrictions for U.S. beef. The financial crises and the impending launch of the Euro added another layer of uncertainty and gloom. While neither side tried to create any linkage between the various issues, the width of conflicts made policy-makers on both sides less willing to compromise and work toward solutions.

This was certainly the case in the subsequent pursuit of the banana conflict of which some commentators compared to the "inexorable, blinkered logic of the European great powers mobilizing their forces for World War I."[373] While the EU stalled, the White House told Congressional leaders that the U.S. would announce retaliatory actions against the EU by December 15, 1998 unless the banana regime was "in full compliance with WTO rules." U.S. officials felt they had the right to act even without specific WTO authorization under its own Section 301 legislation that was covered by WTO rules.

---

371 Transcript of Press Conference on November 19, 1998 in Washington. *www.useu.be/archive/scher1119.html*

372 "US and EU Clash at WTO Meeting," Financial Times, September 22, 1998.

373 Reginald Dale, "Trade War's Logic is Vintage 1914," International Herald Tribune, March 9, 1999.

The administration itself was under pressure from Congress where both Chiquita chairman Carl Lindner and farm lobbies were pushing for sanctions legislation against the EU.[374] This came just as the impeachment procedures against Clinton over his affair with White House intern Monica Lewinsky reached its climax. Some European observers hoped that the threats were just a form of posturing ahead of the mid-term elections in early November. Yet, even after Clinton's Democrats did better than expected at the polls, the administration did not relent. The case had taken on a life of its own.

On November 10, 1998, the U.S. published a preliminary list of products that would be slapped with punitive tariffs of 100 per cent, making them prohibitively expensive in the U.S. market. They included cheese, fruit juices, breads, clothing, packing containers, paper and paper products, toiletries, candles, linen, scissors, domestic appliances such as vacuum cleaners and food processors, electrical lighting equipment, photographic equipment, toys, writing implements, champagne and other alcoholic beverages. U.S. trade officials explained that they were targeting "product areas that will focus the attention of EU member states on the importance of reforming the banana regime,"[375] while avoiding actions that could hurt U.S. companies or deprive the country of important inputs. The focus was on British, French and Spanish products, while goods from Germany, Denmark, Sweden and the Netherlands were mostly exempted. EU officials estimated the impact of the proposed sanctions at $1.6 billion, more than the $1 billion the U.S. claimed the EU banana regime had cost its industry. The U.S. declared that the precise list of sanctions would be published on December 15 and that they would go into effect on February 15, 1999.

This move aroused an angry reaction in Brussels, where trade commissioner Brittan charged the U.S. of "playing with fire." From the EU viewpoint, the U.S. course was just another example of unilateral action, similar to the secondary sanctions under the Helms-Burton and D'Amato Acts that had only months before been removed as a threat. Earlier dissent within the ranks of EU member countries had by now disappeared. The so-called 113 Committee of the Council gave full backing to the Commission in its fight against the U.S.[376] "The U.S. does not share our view about the WTO compatibility of the new regime," Brittan said, "It has the right to challenge this if it wishes, but only according to the WTO procedures established to deal with precisely this sort of disagreements." There were not any clear procedures nor was there any

[374] "US May Face Trade War with EU over Beef and Bananas," Financial Times, October 15, 1998.

[375] "Trade War Edges Closer as US Plans Action against EU Exports," Financial Times, November 9, 1998.

[376] "Handelskonflikt mit Washington," Handelsblatt, November 14, 1998.

precedence for such a case in the WTO books.[377] However, WTO experts agreed that the unilateral impositions of sanctions without authorization by the dispute settlement body violated WTO guidelines.[378] Both parties charged the other side of undermining the WTO: The U.S. said Europe refused to comply with a binding panel ruling, the EU said the Americans were taken the law into their own hands.

At a WTO meeting on November 25, 1998, the EU pursued several venues against the U.S. It offered to reopen consultations on the WTO-compatibility of its banana regime if the U.S withdrew its threat of sanctions. A month before such an offer could have broken the jam lock but now the U.S. refused. Adding a stick to its carrot, the EU opened procedures to challenge the U.S. anti-dumping law of 1916 that was applied against steel imports.[379] Japan and nine other WTO members joined that challenge.

As the December 15 deadline approached, the EU repeated its offer to request a WTO panel to test the modified banana regime, but also warned it would immediately challenge the U.S. sanctions at the WTO. As a goodwill gesture ahead of the December 18th summit of U.S. and EU leaders, the U.S. decided to postpone the publication of the sanctions list for a week. Brittan pleaded with Clinton for a further delay to give the WTO panel a chance to give their ruling but the U.S. refused. "This dispute has been going on for six years, and it is time to resolve it," said Stuart Eizenstat, then Undersecretary of State for Economic Affairs, "We have won three panel cases. And there is a question of how long one can be patient before acting."[380] European observers suspected that Clinton also chose a tough line on the banana issue to appease some members of Congress who were inclined to vote for his impeachment.[381]

On December 21, 1998, the USTR published a list of targeted products with a total value of $520 million. It included Louis Vuitton handbags, Cashmere sweaters, the Italian hard cheese pecorino, bath preparations, printed bed sheets, greeting cards, cookies and other consumer products. European wine was taken off the list after U.S. wine producers warned that their efforts to gain access for their own products in Europe could otherwise be derailed.[382] Meanwhile, negotiations under the WTO umbrella got entangled in legal disputes. The EU wanted the DSB to confirm the WTO-compatibility of its banana regime because it had not yet been formally challenged; the U.S. regarded that as just

---

377 "U.S. Threatens to Hit EU with 100% Tariffs," International Herald Tribune, November 11, 1998.

378 Interview with Richard Senti, member of the WTO panel, in Handelsblatt, November 16, 1998.

379 "Verhärtete Fronten im Bananenstreit," Handelsblatt, November 25, 1998.

380 "EU Plea for Delay in Banana Sanctions," Financial Times, December 19, 1998.

381 Pollack/Shaffer 2001, p. 48.

382 "U.S.-Europe Trade War Looms over Bananas," New York Times, December 22, 1998.

another legal maneuver to evade compliance.[383] The EU and its Caribbean allies blocked a planned meeting of the DSB on January 22, 1999 and it was not until January 29th that both sides accepted a compromise proposal worked out by WTO chief Renato Ruggiero. This agreement gave the U.S. the right launch a request for authorization to impose its retaliatory tariffs, while the WTO would not rule on the issue until an arbitrator had decided by March 1st whether or not the amount was appropriate.[384] The arbitrator would be the original panel that had examined the EU's banana regime.[385] Meanwhile, the EU launched procedures to challenge the Section 301 provisions of U.S. trade law on which the U.S. actions were based.

This one-month truce came to a sudden end when the panel told the parties on March 2, 1999 that it needed more time to reach a conclusion, setting a new deadline of April 12th. Clinton had promised Congress, where anger over EU trade policies was mounting, that he would not delay the imposition of sanctions any longer.[386] Another postponement could have triggered the passage of mandatory sanctions against the EU, making a resolution of the conflict even more difficult. The administration therefore took a half step toward imposing these sanctions. On March 3rd, it notified the importers of the targeted goods that they would have to start immediately post bonds for 100 per cent tariffs on all imports. The U.S. would only collect the duties after the WTO arbitrator had reached their verdict.

From Europe, the U.S. had fired the first shot in the trade war. The method, used once before with regard to Japanese cars, was seen as being on the outer limits of legality while effectively killing all U.S. import orders. The trade barriers were in place without WTO authorization.[387] The measure coincided with a move on another trade front, as the House of Representatives passed a resolution to ban Concorde flights if the EU imposed its threatened ban on hush-kitted aircraft.

In response to the sanctions the EU called an emergency meeting of the WTO General Council for March 8, 1999, where it was hoping to build political support for its cause. British Prime Minister Tony Blair, whose country was singled out by many of the tariffs, suggested a shift toward a more conciliatory

---

383 WTO News Release January 12, 1999.

384 United States Mission to the European Union January 29, 1999.

385 WTO News Release January 29, 1999.

386 "Banana decision delay Wrongfoots U.S. sanctions dispute," Financial Times, March 3, 1999.

387 See "US Begins Sanctions as EU Bananas Dispute Deepens," Financial Times, March 4, 1999; "US Trade Fight With Europe Escalates," Washington Post, March 4, 1999; "The Beef over Bananas", *Economist*, March 4, 1999; "Bewildered Europeans Deplore 100 % U.S. Tariffs," New York Times, March 5, 1999, "Im Bananenkonflikt verhängt Washington provisorische Strafzölle auf EU-Produkte," Handelsblatt, March 5, 1999.

position within the EU that agreed to consultations on the banana regime with the U.S. ahead of the April 12 deadline for the WTO report. The U.S. sanctions had hit Clinton's closest ally in Europe where it hurt: Scottish cashmere producers were outraged just before the May 6, 1999 election for a new Scottish parliament.[388] Barshefsky and Brittan also agreed to reopen bilateral talks to settle the dispute outside the WTO.[389] Meanwhile, the U.S. pared the sanctions list to $362 million.

Before the two sides could bridge their difference, the WTO panel announced its findings on April 6, 1999. The arbitrators agreed with the U.S. claims that the modified EU banana regime was discriminatory and harmed the U.S. economy, though it limited the authorized volume of retaliatory sanctions to $191.4 million. To avoid renewed disagreements over what constitutes compliance, the panel made four suggestions for how the EU could change its banana regime to make it WTO-compatible: a tariff-only regime, including duty-free access for ACP bananas covered by a WTO waiver; a tariff-only regime coupled with a quota of ACP bananas; a global quota regime without country allocations, combined with duty-free access for ACP bananas; or a quota regime with country shares negotiated with suppliers.

It was the first time that the WTO or the GATT had formally authorized trade retaliation against a member country under Article 22.6 of the WTO Agreement.[390] However, the EU was also not left empty-handed as the panel reduced the U.S. demand for sanctions by two thirds and reaffirmed the EU's right to give preferences to ACP banana producers in a WTO-compatible form. The EU agreed they would abide by the decision, but would need at least until the end of 1999 to come up with a WTO-compatible alternative. Moreover, it proceeded with its complaints against the unilateral imposition on U.S. trade sanctions on March 3rd, challenged the procedural rules used by the arbitrator, and carried on with the general challenge of the U.S. Section 301 provisions.[391] The two remaining legal disputes ended with a draw. On December 23, 1999, a WTO panel ruled that Section 301 legislation did not violate international trade agreements as long as it was not used to circumvent the WTO.[392]A separate panel concluded on July 17, 2000 however, that the U.S. had acted "prematurely" when it imposed the bond requirement on importers March 3, 1999. Because the duties were never collected, no action by the U.S. was

[388] "Blair Hints at EU Shift on Bananas," International Herald Tribune, March 6, 1999.
[389] "Banana Foes Tiptoe Round Peace Talks," Financial Times, March 11, 1999.
[390] "US Wins Formal Authorization for Sanctions," Financial Times, April 13, 1999 and USTR Press Release 99-38, April 19, 1999.
[391] "EU Needs 8 Months to End Banana Crisis," Financial Times, April 20, 1999.
[392] "US Wins Round in Trade War with Europe," Financial Times, December 23, 1999.

required. The panel, however, rejected the EU's procedural objections and reaffirmed the validity of the U.S. sanctions.[393]

Given the moderate level of punitive tariffs authorized by the WTO, the EU seemed content to live with these trade sanctions, as well as additional sanctions imposed in July 1999 over hormone-treated beef, rather than change the disputed policies. Yet this outcome did not solve the problems for Chiquita. Supported by the cattle farmer and meat exporting industries that had hoped for a lifting of the EU ban on U.S. hormone-treated beef, Lindner lobbied in the Senate for a toughening of sanctions. On September 22, 1999, ten senators, including the Republican majority leader Trent Lott, introduced the Carousel Retaliation Act of 1999 that required the USTR to rotate the retaliation list after 120 days and every 180 days thereafter when a country does not implement a WTO dispute settlement. The bill included a waiver if compliance was imminent or both the USTR and the petitioners agreed that rotation was not necessary.[394]

A constant rotation of sanctions promised additional disruption and loss of market share to European exporters and would have increased the effectiveness of the sanctions. The Clinton administration quietly lobbied against it, fearing an increase in transatlantic tensions. Unfortunately, the law was tacked on a broader bill on trade for African and Caribbean countries that was important to the White House. It was passed on May 3, 2000, and was signed by Clinton on May 18th. The European Commission accused the U.S. of "fanning the flames" and announced an immediate challenge at the WTO against the new legislation.[395]

Many U.S. businesses also claimed that the carousel approach would cause confusion and hardship by continuously raising and lowering tariffs. Reacting to these concerns, Congressman Robert Menendez of New Jersey introduced The Small Business and Trade Protection Act that called for an exemption for small businesses from carousel sanctions. When the USTR invited comments by businesses on the implementation of the bill, hundreds of importers and retailers requests that their line of business should be excluded from the retaliation against the EU.[396]

These requests allowed the administration to delay the implementation of the controversial law beyond the deadlines set by Congress. While the USTR said it planned on publishing a new sanctions list by June 19, 2000, as stipulated by the bill, the day passed by without any action. The USTR claimed that given the many petitions received, it had not completed the list of products. It also missed

---

393 USTR Press Release July 17, 2000.
394 Sek 2001.
395 "US and EU Head for Sanctions Clash," Financial Times, May 8, 2000.
396 Sek 2001.

a self-imposed deadline on July 7th, and continued to dither in the following months. The White House first cited technical problems, though the focus soon shifted to British objections to include $60 million in Scottish cashmere sweater exports on the new sanctions list. British Prime Minister Tony Blair called the plan "unjustifiable" and personally appealed to Clinton to take the cashmere sweaters off the list.[397] Not only was Britain the closest U.S. ally in Europe, but also the main advocate for the lifting of the EU ban on U.S. beef. Meanwhile, intense negotiations on the reform of the banana regime allowed the administration to further postpone the implementation of the carousel sanctions.

By the end of 2000, the U.S. and EU had found common ground on several issues while still falling short of an overall agreement. A proposal endorsed by EU agricultural ministers in December 2000 called for a transition to a tariff-only regime by 2006. Until then, import licenses would be distributed within three different quotas on a first-come, first-served basis.[398] Even though the regime seemed in line with WTO requirements, the U.S. objected because it would have locked in the market shares in which banana importers had gained during the earlier import regimes. This was the worse outcome for Chiquita, whose sales had shrunk drastically during the preceding years. In early 2001, the company decided it would have to file for Chapter 11 bankruptcy protection because of the damage done by EU policies.[399] After nearly a year of negotiations with its creditors, it did so in late November 2001.

Taking on Chiquita's cause, the U.S. wanted import licenses to be distributed according to market shares as they were before the 1993 import regime. According to USTR Barshefsky, the two sides were ready to strike a deal in the final weeks of the Clinton administration, "but Europe decided to hand it over to the new administration as a gift. This was politically right."[400] EU negotiators were also concerned that the Bush administration might try to amend an agreement reached with its predecessor.[401]

The conflict flared up again in the first few months of the Bush administration. The new USTR Robert Zoellick, who had at first taken a conciliatory line on the banana and beef disputes, warned the EU that Washington would start to implement the carousel sanctions if Brussels went ahead with its latest version of the banana regime.[402] Just before the new regime

---

[397] "Blair Plea to US Leader on Cashmere Trade," Financial Times, September 7, 2000.
[398] "EU approves Banana Reforms," Financial Times, December 20, 2000.
[399] "Citing European Banana Quotas, Chiquita Says Bankruptcy Looms," New York Times, January 17, 2001.
[400] Interview with Charlene Barshefsky, United States Trade Representative from 1996 to 2001, on March 19, 2002.
[401] "U.S. and Europeans Agree on Deal to End Banana Trade War," New York Times, April 12, 2001.
[402] "US Ready to Impose Sanctions over EU Bananas," Financial Times, February 23, 2001.

was finalized, he and EU trade commissioner Pascal Lamy finally reached an agreement on the eight-year-old dispute on April 11, 2001. The EU conceded to the U.S. to base the new quotas on the market shares between 1994 and 1996, when Chiquita still had larger sales although 17 percent of the licenses would be left for newcomers to the market or companies that significantly increased their sales since 1996. Moreover, the EU agreed to cut the quota for ACP: bananas by 100.000 tons a year, most of which would be taken up by Latin American producers. In return, the U.S. said it would support a WTO waiver that would permit the EU to maintain preferences for ACP bananas until 2006.[403]

Ironically, this time it was Chiquita's rival Dole that cried foul as it had seen many of its hard won gains in the European banana market of previous years evaporate and would have much preferred the EU first-come, first served model.[404] Ecuador, the co-complainant of the U.S., also disliked the return to historical import patterns, despite the EU's assurance that the country that it would not lose out. Surprisingly, Ireland's Fyffes said it expected to gain from the deal. The new banana regime went into force on July 1, 2001 - the same day, the U.S. banana sanctions were lifted. The sanctions had been in place for just over two years. What drove the banana dispute throughout all these years and why did a marginal trade issue come to dominate transatlantic economic relations? The answer must be sought on four different levels: influence of special corporate interests, the domestic dynamics of transatlantic relations, the workings of the WTO, and the larger international arena.

On the corporate level, studies have shown that the main beneficiaries of the EU banana regime were not the developing countries but rather European marketing companies. The Australian economist and former World Bank expert Brent Borell calculated that the policy imposed a cost of $2 billion a year on European consumers through sharply higher banana prices with only a benefit of $151 million to the ACP countries. Marketing companies swallowed up around $1 billion of the difference and the rest went to the EU in form of tariff revenue or was just lost through inefficiencies. Thus, Borell argued that a tariff of seventeen percent would have created plenty of revenue to compensate the ACP countries for any losses in the banana trade.

403 "US and EU agree on Banana Imports," Financial Times, April 12, 2001.
404 "A Fruity Peace," *Economist*, April 19, 2001.

> "Clearly, the main objective [of the import regime] is not to provide aid to the ACP and EU territorial producers. To have disrupted the market so much and to have imposed such high costs on consumers to have delivered so little makes a mockery of the aid objective," Borell wrote. "It is hard to escape the conclusion that the European Union is pursuing another objective. The most obvious is that it wishes to protect and expand the vested interests of EU based marketing companies. This group is the clear beneficiary of the policy. EU consumers, marketers and Latin American producers are clearly the big losers."[405]

The immediate conclusion is that it was the lobby power of these companies that made the EU adopt such a grossly inefficient system and to maintain it against at such a steep international price. Yet there is little evidence for any major lobbying activity. Fyffes, the largest European banana importer, has no office in Brussels and spends little money on political contributions. Moreover, the system did not produce any windfalls for Fyffes.[406] It was more the ACP countries, and in particular the Caribbean Windward Island, who had exerted heavy pressure on the EU to keep the quota system in place, notwithstanding the small economic benefit they derived.

Evidence of corporate influence was much stronger on the U.S. side. There is little doubt that without Lindner's generous campaign contributions, neither Congress nor the Clinton administration would have exerted so much energy on the banana case, or even chosen it as a cause for an international trade fight. Still, once Chiquita had succeeded to bring the EU regime to the attention of the policy-makers, he did not need to push much further. The EU system was so outrageously distorting and discriminatory that the U.S. had every incentive to carry on what seemed like a clear winner. Even though the banana regime had nothing to do with the controversial EU agricultural policy, Barshefsky noted that there was "an immediate knee-jerk reaction" to the EU's actions because they involved a food product.[407]

The banana fight came to a head at a time when several issues strained transatlantic trade relations. In this climate, the actions of either side, even when they were within the limits of WTO rules, triggered a hostile political reaction. Congress became increasingly frustrated with European intransigence over key trade issues, particularly with EU non-compliance on bananas. The ability of the

---

[405] Borell 1999.

[406] "Trade Feud on Bananas Not as Clear as It Looks," New York Times, February 7, 2001.

[407] Interview with Charlene Barshefsky, United States Trade Representative from 1996 to 2001, on March 19, 2002.

Clinton administration to resist these pressures was constrained by the impeachment process and by worries that Congress might turn against continued participation in the WTO, which came up for renewal in 2000.[408] "We wanted to send a signal to Congress that the dispute-settlement mechanism can pay off," deputy USTR Susan Esserman commented.[409] Pursuing the banana issue was a politically painless way to demonstrate toughness of trade issues.

On the EU side, the banana regime was originally unpopular among several key member states, including Germany. As part of the grand bargaining that was necessary to complete the single market in 1992, the countries with restrictive import regimes carried the day. They cared much more about the interests of their colonial or post-colonial constituencies than the other countries for banana consumers. The system was purposely skewed to benefit domestic distributors but curtailing the profits of the U.S. banana companies, seen by many, as the worst example of the exploitation of poor developing countries by American corporate giants, was also a popular policy. When the U.S. stepped up the pressure on the EU, resisting the "American bully" became even more popular. By early 1999, all governments, the European Parliament and public opinion had closed ranks behind a policy of toughness against the U.S., notwithstanding that it violated those principles of multilateral trade which the EU had embraced and signed. As one EU official pointed out in January of that year, "Any solution to this dispute will be difficult because hard-liners are dug in on both sides of the Atlantic."[410]

Once the battle entered the WTO arena, both sides started to paint the issue as one of preserving the trade organization's credibility. The U.S. was infuriated by what it saw as European dilatory tactics to undermine the WTO dispute-settlement mechanism by taking advantage of delays and loopholes. The EU saw behind the U.S. tactics the familiar unilateralism at work. Both sides claimed to have the interest of the WTO in mind, but both recklessly put the organization at risk.[411] Given the list of trade disputes that were about to be decided by the WTO, both sides had an interest to set the ground rules for coping with WTO findings and to limit the other side's room for maneuver. U.S. trade officials feared that if they would let the EU get away with ignoring a WTO finding on bananas, this would be repeated on beef and other future issues. The EU, meanwhile, wanted to reign in any U.S. tendency to use a WTO finding to bolster its unilateral trade policies. The banana case was an important

408 "Getting out of the Banana Trap," Speech by Willard M. Perry, President of the European-American Business Council, March 19, 1999. *www.eabc.org/jocoped.html*

409 Interview with Susan Esserman, deputy USTR from 1996 to 2001, on April 10, 2002 in Washington, D.C.

410 "Trade goes Bananas," Financial Times, January 26, 1999.

411 "Fruitless but not Harmless," *Economist*, April 8, 1999.

precedence for future trade fights; and by taking it to the furthest extent; the U.S. and the EU at least clarified some major ambiguities in the WTO agreements. The WTO held up surprisingly well under these pressures and may have actually gained in stature and influence from the case.

In hindsight, trade officials admitted that bananas were unsuitable as a first test case for the WTO because of the high political hurdles for the WTO-compatible solution. Esserman noted, "Ideally, we would have started with an issue that would have resulted in compliance." Taking the path of litigation was probably counterproductive. The U.S. may have achieved at least as much and perhaps even more for U.S. banana companies at far lower political costs by engaging in quiet diplomatic negotiations and by using the threat of a WTO complaint only as a bargaining tool.[412] Commentators blamed Barshefsky's experience as a top trade lawyer and the strong presence of lawyers in the USTR, all of which blocked a political approach to solve the issue.[413]

While the banana conflict generated a lot of heated rhetoric, it never quite got out of hand. The punitive tariffs of $191 million imposed by the U.S. were irritating, though without overly damaging to the EU economy. Twice, the U.S. was on the brink of escalating the conflict by tougher and more dangerous measures: the bond requirement on importers in March 1999, and the threat of Carousel sanctions in 1999 and 2000. In the former incident, the Clinton administration overstepped the boundaries of WTO compliance and was later reprimanded for it. However, this lasted only six weeks and caused little economic damage. The Clinton administration regarded the carousel sanctions as a "major headache" created by Congress to disrupt transatlantic relations and never seriously intended to use them. It required plenty of political and legal maneuvering to defuse this bomb.[414]

All these factors kept the banana war from spinning out of control. The EU finally did reform its regime to bring it in line with WTO rules, even though with a three-year delay. The same outcome could have been achieved earlier and with far smaller political costs. Yet given the marginal economic role of banana trade, both sides saw little political risk by staying on a course that they felt was right. On another, broader issue, the political damage-control mechanism might have set in earlier and stopped the escalation in its tracks. On bananas, there was little to lose and too much to gain by continuing efforts to prevail in the fight.

---

412 Interview with Hugo Paemen, EU ambassador to the U.S. from 1993 to 1999, on April 10, 2002 in Washington, D.C.

413 "Objection," *Economist*, January 21, 1999.

414 Interviews with Charlene Barshefsky, United States Trade Representative from 1996 to 2001, on March 19, 2002, and with Susan Esserman, deputy USTR from 1996 to 2001, on April 10, 2002 in Washington, D.C.

5.3. Biotechnology: The future of trade conflicts?

5.3.1. Hormone-treated beef

The transatlantic dispute over the use of growth hormones in cattle goes back more than two decades. In 1980, the Italian government revealed that the hormone diethyl stilboestrol (DES) that was not licensed for use in food products either in Europe or the U.S. had been discovered in baby food and may have caused children to grow breasts and enlarged genitals.[415] This case and other reports of hormone abuse sensitized the European public to the presence of hormones in meat. The EC Council of Ministers banned the use of two DES hormones the next year, though allowed individual state regulations regarding five other hormones to stay in effect until further research was conducted.[416] Consumer groups and the fledgling Green parties in several European countries however, demanded a complete ban of all growth hormones.

When the subsidies under the Common Agricultural Policy (CAP) continued costly-to-store beef surpluses to accumulate during the first half of the 1980s, EC leaders became receptive to any measure that would limit beef imports.[417] Even though a study by European scientists concluded in 1984 that hormones from natural sources did not constitute a health risk if administered in proper dosages, the Council of Ministers passed a directive in 1985 banning all hormones use in slaughter animals within the Community and the import of hormone-treated meat from third countries. This move was targeted at beef imports from the U.S. and Canada, where growth hormones had been used for decades and constituted ninety percent of all feedstock cattle. The U.S. was threatened to lose around $100 million in annual beef exports to Europe, particularly because not a single U.S. beef-processing facility met the stringent EC requirements. The only EC member state openly opposed to the ban was Great Britain.

After a British complaint, the European Court of Justice nullified the directive on procedural grounds but the Council readopted it in March 1988 in its unaltered form, with an effective date of January 1, 1989. As early as 1987, the Reagan Administration had invoked Section 301 of the 1974 Trade Act to investigate the hormone ban as an unfair trading practice. Once the ban was in place, the U.S. imposed punitive tariff on European farm products worth $153.5 million, including tomatoes, citrus fruit, pasta and ham.[418] At a meeting of the GATT General Council in February 1989, the U.S. demanded a panel of

---

[415] Carolyn Rhodes, "The U.S.-EC Beef Hormone Dispute and U.S. Trade Strategy," in Carter 2002, p. 253.
[416] Rountree 1999.
[417] Hanrahan 2000.
[418] Carter 2002, p. 257.

technical experts to investigate the legitimacy of the hormone ban, while the EC wanted a dispute settlement panel to check the legality of the U.S. sanctions. Both parties blocked the other side's request.[419]

Worried that the beef dispute could derail the ongoing Uruguay Round GATT negotiations, the U.S. and the EC created a bilateral task force that on May 3, 1989 announced an interim agreement aimed at facilitating the export of hormone-free beef to the EC. It set up a certification system that would generate a list of U.S. producers of hormone-free beef who would be allowed to export to the EU. United States retaliation on EU products would be reduced according to the amount of beef products shipped to Europe.[420] Although this accord fell far short of U.S. demands, it reopened part of the European market to its beef industry and kept political tensions in check. Most important, the U.S. had its aims set on an agreement within the Uruguay Round that would prevent such forms of "regulatory protectionism" in food trade in the future.[421] The Sanitary and Phytosanitary Agreement (SPS) of December 1993 came close to what the U.S. wanted. It stated that sanitary standards must be based on scientific principles and on international standards when such standards exist. Measures stricter than relevant international standards are allowed to the extent that they are justified on a scientific basis and result from an appropriate evaluation of the risks.[422] This left a loophole, albeit tightly regulated, to nations wanting to set their own higher standards, as the EC did in the beef case. For the ban to continue, the EC had to produce scientific evidence for the harmfulness of growth hormones.

International standards for food safety were to be set by the Codex Alimentarius Commission, a joint body of the Food and Agricultural Organization (FAO) and the World Health Organization (WHO). At their meeting in July 1995 they set standards for residues for the five hormones (oestradiol beta 17, progesterone, testosterone, zeranol and trenbolone) used by U.S. cattle farmers and declared them otherwise safe for human consumption. The Codex rejected European attempts to include "soft" factors like consumer perceptions in their evaluation and insisted on "hard" scientific basis for standards of international trade.[423] An EU conference on the use of hormones in meat production held in late 1995 in Brussels also concluded that "there was no evidence of human health risk arising" from the use of the five hormones but demanded a better global system of surveillance against the illegal use of hormones.[424]

---

[419] Rountree 1999.
[420] Hanrahan 2000.
[421] Sykes 1999.
[422] Rountree 1999.
[423] Rountree 1999.
[424] Hanrahan 2000.

Public opinion in Europe was not ready to accept an end to the ban. Reflecting growing public concerns about modern farming techniques and food safety, the European Parliament in January 1996 passed a unanimous resolution calling for the ban to remain in place. The Commission followed suit with a 14-to-1 vote. Opposition to letting hormone-treated beef into the EU hardened further when British scientists for the first time confirmed a possible link between the "mad cow disease" Bovine Spongiform Encephalopathy (BSE) and a new strain of Creutzfeldt-Jakob Disease (CJD), a debilitating brain disease for humans.[425] The renewed food scare triggered by that news could have also create demand for beef from the U.S., where much more stringent regulations on feeding cattle were in place, and convinced European consumers that growth hormones were much less of a threat than the unsavory feeding methods of an inefficient and poorly supervised European cattle industry. Instead, public opinion turned even stronger against any food technology that was seen as interfering with nature.[426]

With no hope for a negotiated solution, the U.S. took the legal path. In April 1996, the U.S. with Australia, Canada and New Zealand filed a complaint at the WTO against the EU hormone ban – the first case brought under SPS agreement. Not surprisingly, on August 18, 1997, the dispute settlement panel found the EU ban inconsistent with three articles of the SPS agreement. The ban did not rest on scientific "risk assessment," it was not based on international standards and it set up a discrimination or a disguised restriction on international trade.[427] The EU appealed, arguing that "it was entitled to select a risk level of no risk and that, having chosen that level of risk, the precautionary principle entitled [it] to ban the import of hormone-treated beef because there was a perception [among European consumers] that such beef created a health risk."[428]

The Appellate Body confirmed the decision of the panel on January 15, 1998, though left open the option for the EU to conduct its own risk assessment based on scientific evidence. The dispute now turned on the implementation of the ruling. The U.S. demanded that the ban be lifted within ten months. The EU, however, decided it would perform a new scientific assessment that could take as long as four years and would, in the meantime, maintain the ban. An arbitrator gave the EU the usual 15-month period for compliance with dispute settlements. By May 13, 1999, European scientists either had to present a risk assessment or allow the import of hormone-treated beef. The EU put 14 scientists to work and gave no guarantee to meet the deadline.

---

[425] Hanrahan 2000.
[426] Carter 2002, p. 260.
[427] Hanranhan 2000.
[428] Carter 2002, p. 262.

As the deadline approached, the EU signaled in March 1999 that it would not be able to conclude the studies in time and asked for more time. Given the spat over bananas and other trade issues, the transatlantic atmosphere was not conducive to reaching a compromise. Moreover, the EU's negotiating strength was undermined by the resignation of the whole 20-member Commission following a report charging corruption, fraud and nepotism.[429] Brussels rejected an American offer to label U.S. beef for its origin without the labeling it as hormone-treated as inadequate. Similarly, the U.S. refused an increase of the existing import quota for hormone-free beef of which U.S. exporters were not able to fill because of the strict certification requirements. Just as in the banana case, Washington was determined to make take full advantage of its victories in the WTO dispute-settlement system. Scher remarked, "The time has come for Europe to accept its responsibilities and lift this unjustified and unwarranted ban on our exports."[430] On March 22, 1999 the U.S. published a preliminary list of mostly agricultural products from EU countries worth $900 million that could be targeted for retaliatory tariffs if no agreement was reached by May 13.

The tensions increased in late April. Acting as a caretaker, the Commission voted to ban all U.S. beef imports, worth about $20 million a year, as of June 15, because traces of hormones had been found in 12 percent of U.S. deliveries.[431] On May 3, 1999, the Commission announced that its scientific committee had found one of the natural growth hormones used in the U.S., 17beta-oestradiol, must "be considered as a complete carcinogen" that exerted "both tumor-initiating and tumor-promoting effects." The other hormones also posed health risks, according to the interim report of several incomplete studies. Even the scientists themselves recognized that they did not have sufficient data to establish a quantitative risk for any of the hormones.[432] U.S. trade officials were unimpressed by the sweeping but vague conclusions of the EU scientists. They were even more dismayed when consumer affairs commissioner Emma Bonino declared the next day that "there can no longer be any question of lifting the ban" because of the health risks of hormones. Special US trade negotiator Peter Scher accused the Commission of using an incomplete study in a "blatant attempt to politicize" the regulation of food safety.[433] The controversy came against the backdrop of a renewed food scare in Europe caused by reports that Belgian farm animals had been given dioxin-contaminated feed. Just like in the case of BSE, the scandal made consumers wary of any kind of mass-produced

---

[429] "Hoping to Head off a Beef War, Europe to Keep Talking to U.S.," International Herald Tribune, March 24, 1999.
[430] USTR Press Release 99/18, March 5, 1999.
[431] "EU beschließt Importverbort fuer US-Fleisch," Handelsblatt, April 28, 1999.
[432] "Hormone in U.S. Beef Causes Cancer, EU Scientists Conclude," International Herald Tribune, May 4, 1999.
[433] "EU digs in for Beef War with the US," Financial Times, May 5, 1999.

food. The deep-felt opposition to U.S. hormone-treated beef in some European circles was demonstrated as French farmers attacked a McDonald's Restaurant in the summer of 1999 shouting, "Stop McDonald's, Halt Coca-Cola, Down with...hormone-treated beef."[434]

While scientists argued bitterly over the value of the new study and the safety of hormones, the U.S. moved ahead with the process to impose sanctions. On May 14, 1999, it notified the WTO Dispute Settlement Body that it plans to impose punitive tariffs worth $202 million for the U.S. ($51 million for Canada) "in accordance with WTO procedures." Unlike the banana case, the administration was careful to follow these rules to the letter and avoid any unilateral move. The reaction in Brussels was muted, too. Both sides appeared eager to keep the conflict contained and to avoid any inflaming rhetoric. "The EU has responded with resignation rather than indignation...Recent experience has also taught Washington that rushing into combat with all guns blazing would be unlikely to achieve that objective [of lifting the ban] – and prove self-defeating," wrote Guy de Joncquières in the *Financial Times.*[435]

The EU challenged the scale of retaliation and on July 26, 1999, the arbitration panel awarded the U.S. and Canada the right to impose $116.8 million and Can.$11 million, respectively, in punitive tariffs, just over half of the requested amount. The list focused on high-value European food products such as Danish ham, German mustard, Italian prosciutto and French goose liver. These four countries were singled out for being the main fore behind the ban. Scher excluded any products from the United Kingdom "because of its consistent voting record against the EU's import ban."[436]

The EU made a conciliatory gesture toward Washington when it lifted its threat to ban all US beef imports after accepting assurances that the U.S. had improved its controls of hormone residues.[437] Brussels, however, signaled no intention to change its policy. The sanctions were small enough for the EU members "to take the pain rather than risk a political storm by lifting the beef ban."[438] In the following 18 months, EU and U.S. negotiators continued to dance around the same issues in their attempts to resolve the conflict. The sides could not agree on a labeling system that would inform European consumers about possible hormone-treatment without making such branded products undesirable. Fearing that other countries might also ban hormone-treated meat, the U.S. rejected all offers to grant increased access to U.S. producers in other areas in exchange for lifting the ban.

---

434 Carter 2002, p. 260.

435 "Beef will make Bananas Look like Peanuts." Financial Times, May 17, 1999.

436 "Europe Hit by Tariffs In Battle over Beef," Washington Post, July 20, 1999.

437 "European Union postpones ban on all US Beef Imports," Financial Times, June 15, 1999.

438 "Beef will make Bananas Look like Peanuts," Financial Times, May 17, 1999.

Eventually, the U.S. beef industry had come to realize that the Clinton administration would not impose the carousel sanctions that were designed to increase the pain for the EU and that even these measures would not help much to pry open the European market.[439] Thus, the talks focused on ways to improve the system of certification for hormone-free beef and thus increase the market access for U.S. beef producers, who had filled only half of their import quota of 11,500 tons a year. In late 2000, the EU proposed a special quota for U.S. exports for two years that the U.S. rejected as too short to make it worthwhile for producers to invest in hormone-free beef production. Neither the outgoing Clinton administration (who made a last-ditch effort in late 2000) nor the new Bush administration was able to clinch a deal with Brussels.[440]

Meanwhile, European scientists confirmed their earlier finding that the hormone 17 beta-oestradiol was carcinogenic, so the EU Commission voted on May 24, 2000 to ban the hormone permanently, while keeping the prohibitions on the other substances pending "more complete scientific" evidence.[441] The new studies raised hopes in Europe that it could challenge the U.S. retaliation in the WTO without lifting the ban, but worried the U.S. beef industry and made them less receptive for compromise proposals.[442] Well after the U.S. and the EU had settled the banana dispute and other trade conflicts in 2001, the beef standoff continued with no resolution in sight. U.S. trade observers were split on whether that outcome constituted an acceptable compromise – the EU was allowed to pursue its own domestic preferences but was forced to pay a price for it[443] - or whether it was a blow to the credibility of the WTO dispute settlement system. In the absence of carousel rotation, the U.S. sanctions were small enough to keep the conflict contained, but they "also reduced Europe's incentive to deal."[444] Moreover, the measures deprived U.S. importers, distributors, retailers and consumers of desired goods, without offering any U.S. producers relief from unwanted imports.[445] From an economic point of view, it was the least desirable outcome for the U.S, and like in the banana case, the U.S. interest may have been served better outside the WTO venues.[446] In the

[439] "Beef Industry Formula may Solve Dispute wit Europe," Financial Times, October 12, 2000.
[440] "Bid to Solve Dispute on Hormones in Beef," Financial Times, June 11, 2001.
[441] "Brussels Seeks Tougher Bans on Hormone-Treated Beef," Financial Times, May 25, 2000.
[442] Hanrahan 2001.
[443] "Beef will make Bananas Look like Peanuts," Financial Times, May 17, 1999.
[444] Rountree 1999.
[445] Carter 2002, p. 266.
[446] "We should be more careful in deciding which cases to bring to the dispute-settlement process, and to consider more strongly the political milieu of the issues", said Susan Esserman, deputy USTR from 1996 to 2001, in an Interview on April 10, 2002 in Washington, D.C.

case of EU barriers to genetically modified organisms (GMO), the U.S. pursued such alternatives.

Still, the WTO rulings served two larger purposes: it reaffirmed the principle of the SPS Agreement that only scientific evidence can justify import barriers (not consumer preferences) that became critical for the GMO debate. It also underlined the flexibility built into the Dispute Settlement Understanding of the Uruguay Round Agreement that actually allows countries to flout WTO rules for overriding domestic reasons. By setting retaliation always commensurate to the damage, the system is not a mechanism of enforcement but rather one of compensation. Without such a loophole, experts argue, the GATT members would have never agreed to the DSU in 1993. Just as the beef conflict evolved, the U.S. was keenly aware that it might face a similar dilemma soon in the EU complaint against the Foreign Sales Corporations (FSC), who threatened to trigger much larger sanctions. Because trade agreements are incomplete contracts, no one knows in advance what will come into dispute and every country knows that it might one day be on the losing side of a complaint. Thus it is in no country's interest, ex ante, to agree that ex post, either the accuser should be unconstrained in its ability to punish or the accused should be unconstrained in its ability to proceed without punishment.[447] The threat over EU sanctions over FSC made the U.S. government extremely hesitant to step up retaliation by implementing the carousel sanctions.[448]

While the beef hormone dispute can be defined as a trade war, both sides followed rules of engagement that kept actual hostilities to a minimum. In many ways, the style of the conflict was more civilized than even the earlier encounters over Cuba and Iran-Libya. Coming so shortly after the banana dispute, both sides were eager not to repeat the mistakes that had temporarily made that other conflict run out of control. With a U.S. beef industry interested in the European market, and EU policy-makers faced with a highly emotive issue that transcended trade policy, the stakes were high enough to make damage control a high priority, but not high enough to force a solution.

5.3.2. Genetically Modified (GM) Foods

The beef-hormone dispute was widely seen as the prelude to the economically more important and politically even more sensitive conflict over genetically modified organism (GMO). Advances in gene engineering in the 1980s paved the way to technologies to isolate genes from one organism, manipulate them in a laboratory and inject them into another organism. By the early 1990s, biotechnology firms in the U.S. had found ways to change the

---

447 Ethier 2001, p. 4-5.
448 Sek 2001.

characteristics of plants, make them more nutritious, resistant against pests or boosting their yield. Supporters of these technologies consider them to be just an improvement of traditional techniques of seed-selection and crossbreeding.[449]

The Food and Drug Administration (FDA) took this position when it approved the first genetically engineered food in 1992. Because GM foods were not meaningfully different than regular food, the FDA also did not impose any labeling requirements and demanded no testing of new products, just assurances from the producer that they are safe. U.S. farmers rapidly adopted GM crops and by 2000, more than 20 bio-engineered crops were sold commercially and constituted 54% of soybeans production and 25% of corn acreage grown in the United States.[450]

Driven by consumer concerns and pressures from environmental groups, European authorities took a much more cautionary approach to GM products. They focused not only on the safety of individual products, but also on the process by which they are produced. The 1990 EU directive on the release of GMOs into the environment required that the affected member state and various EU authorities must first approve any new crop variety before it can be planted. In 1997, the EU added a labelling requirement for GM seeds; in 2000, the labelling threshold for GM content was set at one percent of the crop.[451] It took massive U.S. pressure and drawn-out negotiations to get U.S.-developed GM crops such as Monsanto's Roundup Ready Soybeans and Novartis' Bt corn approved in the EU. Even so, various member countries, including Austria, Luxembourg and France, refused to go along with the EU approval process and prohibited the important of approved crops on health and environmental grounds. Unwilling to discipline its members on such a sensitive issue, the EU instead stopped approving any new GM products after April 1998, even though its scientific committees declared them to be safe.

The growing barriers to U.S. crops had a massive effect on transatlantic trade. Because the U.S. industry mixed crops from both GM and non-GM sources, a ban on GM products effectively kept American exports out of Europe. U.S. soybean exports to the EU dropped from $2.1 billion in 1996 to $1.1 billion in 2000, contributing to a general decline in agricultural exports to Europe. The EU share of U.S. farm exports declined from 30 percent in 1982 to 15 percent in 2000.[452] The U.S. industry rejected European calls to separate GM crops from ordinary crops as far too expensive and unfeasible.

---

[449] Pollack/Shaffer 2000, p. 47.
[450] Hanrahan 2001.
[451] Pollack/Shaffer 2000, p. 47-48.
[452] Hanrahan 2001.

The massive losses of market share and the prospect of further damage to U.S. interests made the Clinton administration at first take a hard line against the EU. In 1997, agricultural secretary Dan Glickman, himself a strong supporter of GM technology, vowed to lead the fight against Europe. A senior U.S. trade official called the EU restrictions on GM foods "the single greatest trade threat" to U.S. agriculture.[453] Stuart Eizenstat, Under Secretary of State for Economic, Business, and Agricultural Affairs in March 1999 complained that, "Every major, new GMO marketed in by the U.S. becomes the subject of a prolonged and bitter battle to gain entrance to the EU market."[454] In February 1999, negotiations for a Biosafety Protocol to update the 1992 Convention on Biodiversity signed at the Earth Summit in Rio de Janeiro broke down as the U.S. objected to proposals regulating trade in GMOs because "they would have created disguised barriers to trade, would not have protected the environment, and practically speaking would have resulted in a Protocol not capable of being implemented."[455] U.S. trade officials considered challenging the European GM ban as a violation of the SPS Agreement in the WTO.

In the course of 1999, Washington changed course. Media attention given to the U.S.-EU dispute also raised the issue in the U.S., where consumer and environmental groups began to question the safety of GM foods. A May 1999 issue of *Nature* included a report that the GM BT corn variety could kill not only the corn borer, but also the Monarch butterfly larvae. Large U.S. grain traders such as Daniels Midland and A.E. Stayley called upon farmers to segregate GMO-free crops and announced that they would pay a premium for them. By October 1999, GM-free corn and soybeans carried a 25 to 30 percent premium. The U.S. Senate Committee on Agriculture held hearings on GM crops, and in November 1999, the first U.S. bill to mandate the labeling of GM foods was introduced in Congress.[456] According to a consumer survey conducted by Novartis, more than ninety percent of U.S. consumers supported labeling, and the FDA received a petition signed by 500,000 people demanding mandatory labeling.[457] Anti-GMO activists were also part of the anti-globalization protesters who contributed to the collapse of the WTO ministerial meeting in Seattle in December 1999.

Faced with these pressures, the Clinton administration first agreed to conduct long-term studies on the safety of GM farm products. When

---

[453] Pollack/Shaffer 2000, p. 48.

[454] Statement before the Subcommittee on International Trade, U.S. Senate Finance Committee, Washington, DC March 15, 1999. *www.state.gov/www/policy_remarks/1999 /990315_eizenstat_eu.html*

[455] Ibid.

[456] Pollack/Shaffer 2000, p. 50.

[457] "U.S. Plans Long-Term Studies on Safety of Genetically Altered Foods," New York Times, July 14, 1999.

negotiations on the Biosafety Protocol resumed in January 2000 in Montreal, the U.S. was ready to compromise. Japan, as well as the large agricultural exporters of Australia and New Zealand had by then also announced labeling requirements for GM products. Coming so shortly after the collapse of the WTO conference in Seattle, the State Department (who conducted the negotiations in Montreal) was determined to reach an agreement and went a long way to accommodate European concerns. In return, the U.S. fought and won on the principle issue that trade restrictions for safety reasons must be based on scientific evidence.[458] The U.S. however, accepted the inclusion of the precautionary principle in the Protocol, paving the way for import bans without full scientific proof. The burden of proof was effectively shifted to the exporter, who must show that their products are safe. Furthermore, it required exporters to label shipment which "may contain" bio-engineered commodities; even through Mandatory pre-shipment notification was limited to GMOs intended for release into the natural environment.[459] Finally, the Protocol diminished the chances of a WTO challenge to a GMO ban. The relationship between the Protocol and the WTO was left purposely vague: its preamble states that, "the Protocol shall not be interpreted as implying a change in the rights and obligations of a Party under any existing international agreements," and yet the next phrase states that, "the above recital is not intended to subordinate this Protocol to other international agreement." Trade lawyers noted that a WTO panel dealing with a GMO case would certainly cite the Biosafety Protocol as evidence for an international consensus that the precautionary principle applied.[460]

Just days after the Montreal conference, the European Commission published its own interpretation of the precautionary principles and stated the criteria for banning GM products and other potentially dangerous substances. Trade or sales restrictions required a cost-benefit analysis that should include social and environmental factors as well as economic inputs; they should be subject to regular reviews based on the latest scientific developments; and they should not be used to justify "unwarranted forms of protectionism." Action should be "proportionate," non-discriminatory and consistent with existing measures. This interpretation was designed to address U.S. fears that the EU would take a radical zero-risk attitude to food products as some member countries advocated.[461]

---

[458] Interview with David Aaron, U.S. deputy secretary of commerce for international trade from 1997 to 2001, on April 10, 2002 in Washington, D.C.

[459] Pollack/Shaffer 2000, p. 52; "Caution Needed," *Economist*, February 3, 2000; "Trade Rules Set on Food Genetics," Washington Post, January 30, 2000.

[460] Pollack/Shaffer p. 53

[461] "Brussels sets criteria on 'precautionary' restrictions," Financial Times, February 1, 2000.

The Commission also addressed the weaknesses its regulatory structures. On January 12, 2000, Commission president Romano Prodi presented a white paper outlining its plans for a new European Food Authority that would harmonize food regulations and restore the damaged faith of EU consumers in their food products. The paper rejected the model of the U.S. Foods and Drugs Administration (FDA), a politically independent body with full regulatory power, leaving the power to approve or ban a product with the political institutions, such as the Commission, the EU governments and the European Parliament. The U.S. was still hopeful that a central body to gather information and conduct risk assessments would help to de-politicize the European regulatory process.[462] Meanwhile, the U.S. and the EU set up under their Transatlantic Economic Partnership (TEP) a Biotechnology Consultative Forum that in June 2000 presented its recommendations for a better coordination of regulatory activities. Among other things, it proposed "content-based mandatory labeling requirements for finished products containing genetic material."[463]

The transatlantic conflict over GM foods was defused, but not resolved. The de-facto moratorium on new GM products in the EU remained in place as the Commission continued to postpone the licensing of bio-engineered crops that had been approved as safe by EU scientists, citing the need to wait for new EU-wide guidelines. Even after the European Parliament gave its final approval in February 2001 to rules on the planting of GMOs, calling for stringent risk assessment and continued crop monitoring, a dozen GM products remained stuck in the regulatory pipeline.[464] In July 2001, the Commission voted in favour of regulation that would create highly restrictive rules for GM food products. It called for a centralized approval process for authorizing GMO for food or feed, a system to trace GMOs throughout the food chain, and it required all foods derived from GMOs to be labelled such, even if they no longer contain any modified DNA or protein.[465] USTR Robert Zoellick blasted the proposal, which he claimed, "extends far beyond health protections for consumers and in fact creates onerous and impractical regulatory barriers."[466] Opposition also came from within the Commission. Trade Commissioner Lamy and Research

[462] "EU has Three Years to Fulfill its Bold Agenda for Food," Financial Times, January 13, 2000.

[463] Hanrahan 2001.

[464] "Tough new EU Law Opens Way for GM Crops," Financial Times, February 15, 2001.

[465] "EU Plans tough GM Label Rules," Financial Times, July 26, 2001.

[466] "US says bio-warfare deal is unworkable," Financial Times, July 26, 2001. U.S. experts argue that unrealistically low thresholds will result in a constant false positive test results, which would both undermine the credibility of the system and consumer confidence in food safety. It is widely believed that some of the officially GM-free crops from Brazil actually contain GMOs, but are just not tested.

Commissioner Philippe Busquin voted against the proposal. The U.S. was even more irritated when several EU member states declared that they would not lift the ban on new GMO approvals until the EU had implemented the new labelling rules, a process that could take until 2003.

Nearly five years after the EU had approved the last new genetically modified product, patience in the Bush administration was wearing off. Alan Larson, who had stayed on from the Clinton administration as undersecretary of state for economic affairs, said it was "urgent for the EU to find a way to move forward with the approval process."[467] But the chances for approvals were dim because the Commission did not dare to override EU member governments on such an emotive issue. The continued stalemate let some U.S. officials reconsider the question of a WTO challenge. The labeling requirements for GM products of the second and third generation violate the GATT principle that prohibited import barriers based on the way a certain product is made – the "product" vs. "process" issue.[468] The labeling regime "is not about ideology, but about the production process" and should therefore be challenged at the WTO, argued David Aaron. If nothing is done, these rules could easily become a world standard detrimental to U.S. interests.[469] Finally, U.S. patience wore too thin and in August 2003, the administration requested a panel within the DSB of the WTO writing, "Since October 1998, the European Communities ("EC") has applied a moratorium on the approval of products of agricultural biotechnology ("biotech products"). Pursuant to the moratorium, the EC has suspended consideration of applications for, or granting of, approval of biotech products under the EC approval system…The national marketing and import bans have restricted imports of agricultural and food products from the United States."[470]

Almost a full year later, the U.S., joined by Canada and Argentina, still wait the outcome of what will be a hard decision to reach in the DSB. Accordingly, some trade experts considered this move as a potential public-relation disaster for the U.S. and a threat to the trade organization: "…the fragile global consensus in favor of trade liberalization would be severely tested by a WTO ruling that impinged upon a subject as universal, and as emotionally charged, as the safety of food." [471] Even the *Economist*, a staunch advocate of free trade,

---

[467] "US steps up Pressure on Brussels over Modified Crops," Financial Times, December 18, 2001.

[468] This was the basis for the controversial GATT ruling outlawing the U.S. ban on Mexican tuna fished with nets that endangered dolphins. See *www.wto.org/english/thewto_e /whatis_e /tif_e/bey5_e.htm*

[469] Interview with David Aaron, U.S. deputy secretary of commerce for international trade from 1997 to 2001, on April 10, 2002 in Washington, D.C.

[470] Request for the Establishment of a Panel by the United States to the WTO DSB on August 8, 2003.

[471] Pollack/Shaffer 2000, p. 53.

warned: "If the WTO struck down an EU ban on GMOs, European governments might find it impossible to override consumer fears – however irrational – for the sake of free trade. If the WTO upheld it, that could give a green light for protectionists. Either way, the WTO's ability to keep world trade free could be fatally undermined." Despite all the political efforts to reach a compromise in this most difficult international trade issue, biotechnology has the potential to break out into a major trade war, in which all existing rules and institutions would be of little help.

5.4. U.S. Export Subsidies: Trade War as Nuclear Deterrence

The biggest (at least in terms of dollar value) transatlantic trade dispute is also the oldest and technically the most complex one. At the core of the conflict are the different tax systems in the U.S. and Europe. The U.S. has a "global approach," taxing individuals and companies for their worldwide income but granting tax credits for taxes paid in other countries. The European "territorial approach" excludes from taxation income generated outside the national borders. While the U.S. relies mostly on direct income and corporate taxes for government revenue, European countries receive the bulk of revenue from value-added taxes and other indirect levies.

In 1960, a GATT working group affirmed the distinction between the "destination principle" for indirect taxes and the "origin principle" for direct taxes. While indirect taxes can be adjusted at the border, imposing them on imports and rebating them for exports, border adjustment for direct taxes are not permissible.[472] A corporate tax exemption for exports is therefore an illegal export subsidy, but not a VAT rebate for exports.

Economists disagree on the validity of this distinction: some argue that, "a VAT amounts to a combination of a direct tax on profits, a direct tax on interest and rent paid by the corporation, and a direct tax on wages...by GATT alchemy, direct taxes can be transformed into indirect taxes and adjusted at the border."[473] Others respond, however, that VAT rebates, properly administered, do not distort comparative advantage[474] and are in fact necessary if exported goods are to be part of the same relative price structure as other goods in the importing country.[475]

The territorial approach to taxation does by itself not offer any tax relief for exports. By manipulating transfer prices within the corporation, the opportunity is there for companies to shift domestic export earnings to subsidiaries in tax

[472] Hufbauer 2002.
[473] Ibid.
[474] Grossman 1980.
[475] Brumbaugh 2002.

havens. If governments tolerate such practices, they in effect create an export subsidy. Both characteristics make the European tax system more export-friendly than the U.S. approach. For 30 years, the U.S. has tried to transplant the export advantages of the European system to its own regime. Doing that, it repeatedly ran afoul international trade agreements.

In 1962, the U.S. government actually clamped down on what it saw as tax abuse by exporters and eliminated the deferral for "foreign base company income" earned by controlled foreign corporations (CFCs) in tax haven countries. Yet this put U.S. exporters at a disadvantage compared to foreign competitors, who could benefit from foreign tax shelters. Faced with a rising trade deficit, Congress in 1971 introduced the Domestic International Sales Corporation (DISC) that permitted tax deferral for export earnings of U.S. corporations. The U.S. argued that a tax deferral was unlike a tax exemption, a view not shared by the EC who challenged the DISC at GATT in 1974. In return, the U.S. challenged the "territorial" tax laws in France, Belgium and the Netherlands that granted tax exemptions for the portion of export earnings attributed to foreign sales subsidiaries. A GATT panel ruled against all four defendants in 1976, finding that elements of both the territorial approach and DISC constituted export subsidies.

The issue became part of the Tokyo Round negotiations and addressed in the Code on Subsidies & Countervailing Duties. It preserved the distinction between direct and indirect taxes, declared that methods to avoid double taxation were no export subsidies and set the arms' length standard for transfer pricing (If parts of the same firm trade with each other, they have to charge each the same prices as if they were unrelated). The issue was seemingly settled in 1981, when the GATT Council adopted the reports of the panels but referred to the agreement reached in the Tokyo Round: "The Council adopts these reports on the understanding that with respect to these cases, and in general, economic processes (including transactions involving exported goods) located outside the territorial limits of the exporting country should not be regarded as export activities in terms of Article XVI: 4. It is further understood that Article XVI: 4 requires the arm's length pricing be observed....Furthermore, Article XVI: 4 does not prohibit the adoption of measures to avoid double taxation of foreign source income."[476] According to this passage, GATT members agreed that domestically produced goods would not count as exports under GATT if they were sold through foreign-based subsidiaries.

Based on this understanding, the U.S. repealed the DISC in 1984 and replaced it with the Foreign Sales Corporation (FSC); a vehicle that allowed U.S. based companies to reduce their tax burden on their exports by fifteen to thirty percent by selling them through an offshore corporation. The EC

---

[476] Hufbauer 2002.

questioned the validity of this construction, noting that they "did not pursue it at the time due to the opening of the Uruguay Round trade negotiations."[477] The Europeans also did not challenge the FSC during the Uruguay Round talks. The U.S. took the absence of any European action as a sign of acquiescence.

The 1994 WTO Agreement on Subsidies and Countervailing Measures (SCM) incorporated most elements of the 1979 Subsidies Code. Included in Annex I of the ASCM as an example of an export subsidy was, "the full or partial exemption, remission, or deferral specifically related to exports, of direct taxes or social welfare charges paid or payable by industrial or commercial enterprises." Footnote 59 qualifies this clause by stating that member states may take measures to avoid the double taxation of foreign-source income, but reaffirmed the arm's length principle in transfer pricing.[478] The U.S. later argued that this footnote reflected the 1981 GATT understanding and charged the EU with double-crossing them on what was clearly a political deal.

Most major U.S. corporations took advantage of the law. Thousands of FSCs, chartered mostly on Caribbean islands, handled half of U.S. exports worth some $125 billion and provided U.S. businesses with billions of dollars in tax savings. General Electric saved $150 million in 1998, Boeing $130 million. A large number of European multinationals took advantage of the FSC through their U.S. subsidiaries. The EU was aware that it had a potentially winnable case against the U.S. up its sleeves but decided to keep it there. Internally, EU experts regarded the FSC case as an insurance policy against a U.S. challenge to Airbus subsidies.[479]

Appropriately, EU Trade Commissioner Leon Brittan stunned not only the U.S., but also EU member states and many Commission officials when he announced on November 18, 1997 that the EU would a challenge the FSC at the WTO as a violation both of the ASCM and the Agreement on Agriculture. Brittan claimed that he was acting now because of the proliferation of FSC had created unfair advantages for U.S. exporters.[480] The move was widely understood as retaliation against the U.S. challenges against the EU beef and banana policies and Brittan was believed to have acted out of impulse without consulting with advisors or fellow commissioners.[481] Neither European

[477] European Commission DG Trade Press Release January 14, 2002.
[478] Langbein 2000, p. 547.
[479] Interview with Hugo Paemen, EU ambassador to the U.S. from 1993 to 1999, on April 10, 2002 in Washington, D.C.
[480] "Brittan beantragt Konsultationen," Handelsblatt, November 19, 1997.
[481] Interview with Hugo Paemen, EU ambassador to the U.S. from 1993 to 1999, on April 10, 2002 in Washington, D.C.

businesses nor member state governments liked the prospect of the WTO entering into the complex realm of tax policy.[482]

Following the required consultation process, the EU formally requested a dispute panel on July 1, 1998. A year later, the panel sided with the EU and declared the FSC a prohibited export subsidy. The report, published officially on October 8, 1999, stated that the 1981 GATT Council decision, to which the U.S. referred in its defense, was irrelevant because it had not been enshrined in the 1994 WTO Agreements. They argued that articles 3.1 and 1.1 of the ASCM provide that a subsidy exists if "government revenue that is otherwise due is foregone or not collected ... and a benefit is thereby conferred." The panel found that the FSC provisions carved out particular exceptions to various parts of U.S. tax law that would otherwise have generally resulted in taxation of the FSC export income.[483] The major weakness of the FSC was that it adopted the territorial principle to avoid taxation of foreign source income but only the export segment of foreign source income.[484] FSC tax exemption only applied if not more than fifty percent of the value of a product had come from outside the U.S.

The panel report was a bombshell. Political and business leaders in the U.S. had focused very little on the issue before that, and it was hardly at all reported in the press. Even so, the FSC was much bigger than bananas and beef combined. U.S. companies saved about $4 billion in taxes annually, and the EU considered asking for compensatory measures retroactive to 1995. This would have amounted to $26 billion in U.S. trade concessions or retaliatory tariffs. Even much scaled-down amount would have exceeded the $300 million in U.S. banana and beef sanctions.

U.S. trade officials were furious both about the decision and about the EU tactic to break the 1981 understanding not to challenge each other's tax policy. Barshefsky complained, "The panel appears to have systematically disregarded the history of this issue, the applicable WTO legal rules concerning income tax and the facts of the record before it."[485] Former Senate Majority leader Bob Dole argued, "The FSC is simply an attempt by the U.S. to allow its exporters to compete against foreign competitors that have long enjoyed far bigger tax breaks."[486] Most experts agreed that the U.S. stood on shaky legal ground. "The really amazing aspect of this story is how long it took for the WTO to rule

482 "WTO Ruling Closes Chapter in International Trade Row," Financial Times, January 14, 2002.
483 Brumbaugh 2000.
484 Hufbauer 2002.
485 USTR Press Release 99-64, June 26, 1999.
486 "Upsetting the World's Trade Balance," Financial Times, February 22, 2000.

against the FSCs," commented James Hines, research director at the University of Michigan Business School's office of tax policy research.[487]

The U.S. also lost the appeal on February 24, 2000. This left the U.S. only until October 1, 2000, five weeks before the presidential elections, to eliminate the FSC or face massive EU sanctions. Pascal Lamy, who had followed Brittan as trade commissioner in September 1999, seemed unsure about what to do with this victory. He had little interest on backing the Clinton administration into a corner or imperiling the impending votes in Congress on continued WTO membership and China's entry into the trade organization. U.S. and EU leaders were at pains to keep the "mother of all trade disputes"[488] from damaging the bilateral relations that were just showing signs of improvement.[489]

There was talk in Brussels and Washington about a grand bargain to trading FSC sanctions against the repeal of the banana and beef tariffs. Instead, the U.S. chose a different course. It also rejected proposals to counter-challenge various tax laws in EU countries that would have been cumbersome, but possible, and pledged instead to reform the law by October 1 to bring it in line with WTO rules. Treasury Secretary Lawrence Summers stated that Washington "would work closely with the Europeans, the business s community and the Congress to achieve a solution."[490]

However, this proved difficult. The U.S. government was determined to preserve the tax breaks for its corporations of which Washington regarded as legitimate in light of Europe's tax policies, and was just looking for technical changes to formally meet the WTO objections. The U.S. industry lobbied quietly, yet hard, to keep changes to a minimum.[491] On May 2, 2000, Eizenstat, who was then deputy treasury secretary, presented a new proposal that would replace the tax incentive for exports with an elective system that applied both to exports and non-export foreign sales, arguing that a similar scheme was in effect in the Netherlands. The EU rejected the offer as a "camouflage" for the original system: "If hunting elephants is prohibited by an international treaty, a national law which allows elephants to be hunted will not be brought in line with the treaty by passing a new law that says giraffes also can be hunted."[492] At first Eizenstat threatened to pass the new law unilaterally but he then decided to make another stab at finding a solution. In July, Eizenstat presented another

[487] "Europe Scores an Equalizer in WTO Clash With US," Financial Times, September 21, 1999.
[488] Stuart Eizenstat, Financial Times, February 18, 2000.
[489] "U.S. Loses Dispute on Export Sales," New York Times, February 24, 2000.
[490] "U.S. offers EU Olive Branch On Trade Row," Financial Times, February 25, 2000.
[491] "Companies Work Secretly in Attempt to Avert Trade Dispute," Financial Times, May 9, 2000.
[492] "U.S., EU Cannot Agree on Tax Law," Washington Post, May 30, 2000, and "EU rejects US Move on Tax Treatment of Exports," Financial Times, May 30, 2000.

model that went slightly beyond the May proposal. The Extraterritorial Income Exclusion (ETI) Act did away with the requirement to set up an affiliate overseas, and instead excluded from the U.S. definition of gross income certain portion of foreign source income. Eizenstat clarified, "Because this would be our general rule, there is no foregone revenue that is otherwise due – and therefore no subsidy."[493] It also formally treated exports and non-export foreign sales alike. However, the benefits of the ETI Act were conditioned on the sale of goods outside the U.S. and the use of less than fifty percent of non-US inputs.[494]

The EU objected to this and other elements of the law. "In some respects it is a backward step," said Lamy in a letter to Eizenstat, "As long as such preferential treatment for exports continues to be the objective of any U.S. proposals, it is frankly hard to see how a WTO-compatible measure can emerge."[495] This latest rejection infuriated the Clinton administration. After all, they were pushing a law through the Republican-dominated Congress in an election year just to comply with a WTO ruling for the first time in U.S. history and were getting no recognition from their trading partners.[496] Meanwhile, time was running out to get the laws passed before the October 1st deadline.

Ironically, the U.S. dilemma mirrored Europe's experience with the banana regime, where the partner had also rejected all attempts to achieve WTO-compatibility through technical maneuvers. Moreover, it was the precedence of the banana case that gave the EU the right to initiate the retaliation process immediately after October 1st. In mid-September, the U.S. approached the EU with the request to extend the compliance period by one month. U.S. officials used the threat of the carousel sanctions of which were to have been in place since June 19th as leverage in the FSC dispute. While Britain, Denmark, Sweden, the Netherlands and Finland supported a delay, Spain and France argued against it.[497]

On September 30, 2000, one day before the deadline, the U.S. and the EU reached an agreement on the subsequent procedures for the dispute settlement. The U.S. was given until November 1st to come into compliance, after which the original panel would determine the WTO-consistency of the FSC replacement law. The EU agreed to postpone any retaliation until the appeals process had been exhausted and an arbitrator had decided on the appropriate level of sanctions.[498]

---

493 U.S. Treasury Press Release LS-812, July 12, 2000

494 Hufbauer 2002.

495 "EU May Face Challenge from U.S. on Tax Systems," Financial Times, September 2, 2000.

496 Eizenstat: "The Cloud over Transatlantic Trade," Financial Times, September 8, 2000.

497 "U.S. Presses for Deal to Postpone WTO Action," Financial Times, September 15, 2000.

498 USTR Press Release 00-65, September 30, 2000.

The U.S. missed the extended deadline. After strong pressure from the White House and industry, the Senate passed the bill on November 1st but the Republican leadership in the House delayed the vote for several days.[499] By the time the House passed the ETI Act on November 14th and Clinton signed into law on November 15th, the U.S. was technically in a state of non-compliance. On November 17, 2000, the EU formally requested authorization to impose $4.04 billion in trade sanctions on the U.S. An indicative list of targets named 95 sectors and to the relief of U.S. exporters, no specific products were listed. Both sides kept the rhetoric to a minimum and the U.S. dismissed the request as a procedural move, "This is not the start of a trade war, it's part of the process by which to litigate the new legislation."[500]

The FSC dispute continued to simmer in the first months of the Bush administration, as both sides waited for the panel to decide. U.S. officials were resigned to not lose that case, yet still saw no politically feasible way out of the dilemma. In May 2001, the new USTR Robert Zoellick told a European Parliament committee that the imposition of $4 billion in sanctions "would be like using a nuclear weapon on the global trading system." He also repeated the threat to challenge European tax regimes in the WTO, "which could lead to a dispute that get outs of control." After having filed more complaints at the WTO than any other country, the USTR now had to admit "litigation is not always the solution for solving every problem."[501] Rather than go for tit-for-tat retaliation, some experts argued to take tax issues out of the realm of WTO litigation and to settle them either through political compromises in bilateral negotiations or hand responsibility to the more consensual OECD.[502]

The panel's decision took longer than expected and in August 2001 it once again sided with the EU against the U.S. It rejected the redefinition of gross income as a departure from the "normative benchmark" of the U.S. tax system, making the exemption foregone revenue. It also decided the exemption under ETI was "contingent on" exports, making it an export subsidy. The Appellate Body upheld the panel's decision in January 2002, though it narrowed its sweeping rationale in some key ways. According to at least one trade expert, "the Appellate Body returned to the main outlines of the bargain struck in the 1981 GATT Council Decision" and confirmed that "foreign source income, properly computed, could be exempt from tax" without amounting to an prohibited export subsidy.[503]

This may leave the door open for another repair of the tax law. However, political observers in Washington feared that Congress would not go along if it

---

499 "U.S. Poll Spat Fouls Trade Pact with EU," Financial Times, November 3, 2000.
500 "EU seeks sanctions of Pounds 3bn against U.S.," Financial Times, November 18, 2000.
501 "US Warns of Trade Row with EU ahead of Summit," Financial Times, May 15, 2001.
502 Langbein 2000, p. 554, and Hufbauer 2002.
503 Hufbauer 2002.

resulted in a higher tax bill for any U.S. company. The Chairman of the powerful House Ways and Means Committee, Bill Thomas (R-California) suggested to resolve the dispute by scrapping the global tax system and replacing it with a European-style territorial system that would help to simplify tax accounting for internationally active firms and provide exporters with a level playing field. Given the sharp differences over tax laws between Democrats and Republican, such a sweeping overhaul of the corporate tax system seemed difficult to achieve.[504]

A small, but respected group of politicians and economists also argued against the whole principle of providing tax breaks to some of the country's richest corporations in the name of export promotion. Columbia economist Jagdish Bhagwati called the FSC "corporate welfare,"[505] and the Democratic Congressman Peter Stark, who was cast the sole opposing vote on the House Ways and Means Committee against the reform of the FSC in September 2000, warned against subsidizing the defense industry that, "already receives more than its fair share of pork barrel spending," and pharmaceutical companies, "who sell their products to other developed countries for less than the U.S. consumer can purchase the exact same drugs."[506] Just like other export subsidies, the FSC and the ETI were a transfer of resources from U.S. taxpayers to foreign consumers, if the tax savings were passed on in form of lower prices, or to corporate profits, if they were not. According to estimates by the Congressional Research Service, FSC increased U.S. exports by 0.2 to 0.4 percent a year, and shifted economic welfare to foreign consumers by 0.1 percent. "The impact on the trade balance was probably negligible."[507] Having lost the case on substance, the U.S. now turned to challenge the EU sanctions request. While the EU request of $4.04 billion was based on the total tax savings through FSC, the U.S. argued that sanctions should be based on the "purported impact of FSC on EU trading interests." Given the EU share of world trade of about a quarter, the U.S. arrived at $956 million.[508]

On January 29, 2002 the DSB adopted the Panel and Appellate Body reports declaring that the ETI Act of 2000 violates five WTO rules (Articles 3.1(a) and 4.7 of the SCM Agreement, Articles 8 and 10.1 of the Agreement on Agriculture and Article III: 4 of the GATT 1994). At the same time, the arbitration procedure was reactivated and on August 30, 2002, the arbitrator's report authorized countermeasures at the level of US$4.043 billion if the U.S.

---

[504] "Bush: Deal can be Reached with the EU," AP January 15, 2002.

[505] "The Unwinnable War," Financial Times, January 29, 2002.

[506] Peter Stark, Statement on September 6, 2000, *www.house.gov/stark/documents/106th /dissentfsc.html*

[507] Brumbaugh 2000.

[508] USTR Press Release 02-20, February 14, 2002.

did not repeal the act and FSC.[509] Recognizing the seriousness of the countermeasures, however, the EU avoided any immediate recourse to retaliation so as to give the U.S. reasonable time to adopt the necessary changes in legislation for the repeal of FSC. By March 1, 2004, the reasonable time was finished for the EU and countermeasures began their course. As EU trade commissioner Lamy noted, "Despite waiting for more than two years, the US has not brought its legislation in line with WTO rules. We are therefore left with no choice but to impose countermeasures. The name of the game is not retaliation but compliance: countermeasures will be lifted the day the FSC is repealed."[510] A serious domestic challenge to any U.S. administration, the issue remains unresolved.

The FSC case showed the difficulty of creating a level playing field for trade in a world with different tax and regulatory systems. There were good reasons for the WTO to stay out of the dispute that threatened to turn in into an international tax court. Yet since all GATT members had signed the 1994 ASCM that addressed the issue of tax breaks for exports, the EU had every right to challenge the U.S. laws. The U.S. was vulnerable on this point because it tried to graft a tax policy favorable for exports that was rooted in a territorial system unto its global tax regime. However hard U.S. tax experts tried, this could not be reconciled with WTO principles. European tax laws did not have that problem, making a U.S. counter-challenge at the WTO a difficult undertaking.

Still, the EU need not have challenged the FSC, neither on economic nor on political grounds. It could have raised the issue of export-related taxation at various bilateral and multilateral forums and worked toward a mutually satisfactory solution. The EU Commission's decision to go to the WTO was a direct consequence of U.S. litigiousness in the banana and beef cases. The FSC complaint was another step in the escalation of a developing trade war.

If the issue had involved smaller sums, it could have created more political fallout but the enormous dimension of the potential retaliation reduced its value to the victorious party. The FSC case was more like a weapon of deterrence than of conventional warfare. Just like nuclear weapons that did not prove to be useful bargaining chips in the Cold War, the EU found no way to translate its legal successes into political leverage.[511] "It's like an atomic bomb: The day you use it, the deterrence factor is gone," noted Hugo Paemen, the former EU ambassador to the U.S. As a legal case, it did not lend itself to a political trade-

---

[509] Recourse by the European Communities to Article 4.10 of the SCM Agreement and Article 22.7 of the DSU to the WTO DSB on April 25, 2003.

[510] "FSC: EU Starts Countermeasures on US Products," Delegation of European Communities to the United States, no.34/03, March 1, 2004.

[511] Interview with Hugo Paemen, EU ambassador to the U.S. from 1993 to 1999, on April 10, 2002 in Washington, D.C.

off, and the U.S. resisted all overtures to swap its beef and banana sanctions until it had exhausted all venues of appeal.

The case did not cause the kind of damage to the transatlantic relationship that some had predicted. Given the vast potential to disrupt trade, both sides had to tread extremely carefully once Brittan had decided to pull the trigger, even when sanctions were imposed. EU officials avoided at every step triumphant grandstanding that might have played well in the domestic arena that could have upset the U.S. In Washington, trade officials contained their anger over the case, decided against any form of retaliation and focused on finding reasonable solutions.[512]

Damage control was made easier than in banana and beef because as there were no political and corporate stirrers in the background calling for tougher actions. Corporate tax law did not lend itself to emotional appeals, the dispute involved vast sums and business lobby efforts played a much less inciting role. European companies had never shown much of an interest for the FSC, and in the U.S., the big corporations feared EU retaliation at least as much as the loss of the tax breaks. In many ways, the FSC dispute resembled an epic duel: it served no real purpose, but it was kept gallant and civilized. Just like in a duel, the danger of changing the nature of the fight by inflicting a serious wound on the opponent was always present.

---

[512] Interview with Susan Esserman, deputy USTR from 1996 to 2001, on April 10, 2002 in Washington, D.C.

CHAPTER 6: TOWARD A NEW TRADE ROUND

The creation of the Word Trade Organization in 1995 was hailed as a breakthrough for the multilateral trade regime that would pave the way to further trade liberalization. But in the following years, the WTO had a hard time fulfilling these high expectations. As described in chapter 3, it succeeded to liberalize trade in information technology, telecommunications and financial services. Still, its members fought twice over its director, squabbled on the inclusion of such sensitive issues as labor standards, and finally failed to agree on the launch of a new trade round in Seattle in December 1999. Despite these apparent weaknesses, anti-globalization protesters singled out the WTO as a major force of evil in the world and attacked it, in the words of the U.S. consumer activist Ralph Nader, as an all-powerful "super-national autocratic system."[513] Success and failure at the WTO depended to a large extent on the state of transatlantic relations. Substantive disagreements, a lack of cooperation, and a weakness of leadership on both sides of the Atlantic doomed the Seattle summit. In the aftermath of Seattle, both sides helped shield the WTO from damage and finally settled their differences at the WTO summit in Doha in November 2001. This chapter will look at the role of the transatlantic relationship before and during the Seattle conference and address the question to what extent the bilateral trade disputes caused the conference to fail.

6.1. The Road to Seattle

The WTO was officially established on January 1, 1995. Instead of celebrating that date, the member states welcomed the new organization with a fight over its director-general. The Europeans nominated the former Italian trade minister and veteran trade negotiator Renato Ruggiero, who also enjoyed support from African and Middle Eastern countries. The U.S. and Latin American countries championed former Mexican president Carlos Salinas de Gotari, who had led his country into NAFTA, while the Asian states wanted South Korean trade minister Kim Chul Su. Ruggiero had the strongest support in the body but custom dictated that the director-general should be chosen by consensus. This standoff left the WTO leaderless in the first few months. Even after Salinas withdrew his candidacy when his brother Raoul was arrested on charges of conspiracy to murder a senior Mexican official, the Clinton administration refused to embrace Ruggiero, criticizing him for lack of international stature and an uncertain commitment to free trade. Only in mid-March 1995 did the U.S. drop its opposition after the EU pledged that Ruggiero would step down after a single four-year term and be followed by a non-

[513] "WTO to Meet As Protesters Rally Forces," Washington Post, November 29, 1999.

European. One U.S. official at the time commented, "The race for director-general had become a hemispheric contest which had produced a deadlock...not in the interest of the United States and the WTO."[514] Ruggiero, who enjoyed wide respect, took office on May 1, 1995.

The first major issue dividing the new organization was the inclusion of labor and environmental standards in trade agreements. Surprisingly, it was the U.S. that was pushing most ardently for these new trade issues, particularly for labor standards. At the formal signing of the Uruguay Round Agreement in Marrakesh in April 1995, the U.S. teamed up with France to place labor standards on the "built-in agenda" for the next WTO trade round. Yet they were rebuffed by developing countries that suspected behind the call for uniform labor standard a rich-country ploy to bar imports from poor nations.[515]

The debate about labor standards heated up ahead of the WTO First Ministerial Conference held in Singapore in December 1996, where the Clinton administration wanted to issue a "political declaration" linking the maintenance of an open world trade system to promotion of 'core' labor standards, including freedom of association and the prohibition of forced and child labor. Republicans in Congress rejected this plan, and most trade experts agreed that the introduction of core labor standards as a criterion for trade policy would not advance the cause of free trade nor help the workers in developing countries. It was mostly seen as a political gesture to trade unions in industrialized countries who were concerned about low-wage competition. In particular, the Clinton administration felt the need to build up support for further trade deals among skeptical Democrats by pushing the issue of labor standards. "We need to be able to give a political signal to our domestic workforce that while they may face competition from workers in low-wage countries, they will not face competition on the basis of denied workers rights," U.S. position paper wrote.[516] This view was to some extent shared by trade commissioner Brittan and was strongly supported by France, Italy and other EU members from the southern periphery. On the other hand, Germany, the Netherlands and Britain disliked the idea on ideological and political grounds. Combined with the massive opposition of most Asian nations, they worried that the issue could tear the WTO apart.

The Singapore conference was salvaged by the agreement on information technology (see chapter 3), though the countries remained far apart on the future course of trade negotiations. While the U.S. was keen on labor standards and stricter rules for public procurement, the EU proposed negotiations on the global rules for foreign investment and competition policy, in which the U.S.

---

[514] "U.S. Drops Opposition to Potential WTO Head," Washington Post, March 21/95.

[515] "Will the New World Trade Organization Work?" Washington Post, June 26, 1994.

[516] "Balancing Fair Trade and Fair Work," Financial Times, June 20/96

had little interest. Given the lack of consensus, the trade ministers settled on soft compromises and agreed to set up working groups to study trade and competition policy and trade and investment issues. Developing countries succeeded to keep labor rights off the agenda and kept the reference in the concluding declaration purposefully vague.[517]

A year later, the U.S. and the EU were still miles apart on the agenda for the next trade round. The U.S. pursued a narrow round around the "built-in agenda" left over from the Uruguay Round that could be quickly completed and provide the U.S. farm and service industry increased access to foreign markets. The EU had the opposite interest. As any deal on agriculture would require painful cuts in the EU farm support programs, Brittan wanted to create a broad-based agenda that would take the focus off agriculture and allow reciprocal concessions in other sectors.

On both sides of the Atlantic, positions were shaped by political calculations: Clinton needed to overcome opposition among his fellow Democrats, the EU Commission the tough line on key trade issues of France. During most of 1997, Clinton had tried to rally Congressional support to renew fast-track authority, widely seen as a prerequisite for successful international trade talks. Democrats had become increasingly skeptical on free trade, and insisted on the inclusion of tough labor, environmental and human-rights standards for future talks. Not only did the majority Republicans reject this, but it would have also made the conclusion of a trade round virtually impossible. In November 1997, Clinton made another push to gain passage of the bill. A majority was assured in the Senate, but not in the House, where the Republican leadership insisted on at least 70 Democratic votes to pass the bill. Clinton could win over only 45 representatives from his own party, forcing him on November 9, 1997 to abandon the effort. It was not even put to a vote.[518]

Attempts to gain fast-track authority in the following year were hampered by the approaching mid-term elections. A Republican-sponsored bill, that excluded any concessions to skeptical Democrats, went down in defeat by 243 to 180 votes on September 24, 1998.[519] Without fast-track authority, Clinton's room for maneuver to conclude a trade agreement was limited. If he made tough concessions to his partners, he would face the threat that Congress would undermine ratification by attaching amendments to the accord. Administration officials still hoped that Clinton could receive fast-track authority after the next

[517] "Uncharted, and Troubled, Waters," Financial Times, May 17, 1998 and 1996 Annual Report of the President of the United States on the Trade Agreements Program. *www.ustr.gov/html/1997tpa_part4_1.html*

[518] "Clinton's own Party Scuttles His Move on Trade Powers," Financial Times, November 10, 1997, and "President Takes Blame for 'Fast-Track' Delay," Washington Post, November 11, 1997.

[519] "Defeat for Fast Track," Financial Times, September 25, 1998.

round was launched. However, this made it even more important for Clinton that the agenda reflected U.S. economic interests.

EU trade commissioner Brittan, who had gained respect for his negotiating skills in the Uruguay Round, also saw subsequently his room for maneuver shrink. Government leaders criticized him for overstepping the negotiating mandates granted by EU ministers to conclude agreements with third countries. A finished trade pact with South Africa was vetoed by individual Southern EU members several times, leading EU trading partners to question the ability of the commission to deliver on its promises. Following the Uruguay Round Agreements, several EU countries had questioned the authority of the Commission to conclude agreements on trade in services and intellectual property that was not specifically included in Article 133 on external trade relations. The Commission asked the European Court of Justice to rule on the issue, but much to its surprise, in 1994 it decided on a conservative interpretation and ruled against the Commission. The Commission also failed in its attempt to gain an extension of its trade mandate to cover services and intellectual property at the Amsterdam summit in June 1997. As a consequence, Commission and member states now share jurisdiction over these new trade issues.[520]

This did not discourage Brittan from strongly advocating a new trade round that would encompass address all trade-related aspects of modern economic policy, particularly investment and competition issues. By drowning agriculture in a sea of other issues, Brittan hoped to create enough bargaining chips to overcome the deep-seated opposition of France and most of the Mediterranean members against a reform of the CAP. Brittan chose the term "Millennium Round" to underscore his ambitious agenda, and by early 1998, he had gained the support of the EU countries, Japan, South Korea and Australia.

When the 132 WTO members met in Geneva on May 17, 1998 for their second ministerial conference, they not only celebrated the 50th anniversary of the GATT but also hoped to bridge their differences on the new trade round. Instead, the gap appeared to grow. The U.S. demanded the opening up of the WTO operations to public scrutiny, a move other countries feared would make it harder to reach compromises on sensitive trade issues.[521] USTR Barshefsky rallied the so-called Cairns Group of agricultural exporters[522] behind a drive to force the EU to open up its farm markets. She shrugged off Brittan's call for a broad and ambitious agenda by stating that, "in today's economy we cannot

[520] Dinan 1999, p. 486; Cunningham 2000, p.37

[521] "World Trade Party-Goers Look for the Next Big Leap Forward," Financial Times, May 17, 1998.

[522] The Cairns Group includes Argentina, Australia, Brazil, Canada, Chile, Columbia, Fiji, Indonesia, Malaysia, New Zealand, Paraguay, the Philippines, South Africa, Thailand, and Uruguay.

take ten years to talk as in the Tokyo Round, or seven years as in the Uruguay Round."[523] The only firm agreement to emerge in Geneva was a promise not to introduce import duties on software and information delivered via the Internet.[524]

The U.S. had different motives for questioning Brittan's broad agenda. Washington has long been an advocate for a Multilateral Agreement on Investment (MAI), but had handed this mandate to the 29-member Organization for Economic Cooperation and Development (OECD) in Paris. This decision had aroused the suspicion of developing countries that the MAI would be set rules skewed in favor of industrialized countries. As a campaign by non-governmental organization mostly operating through the Internet succeeded to turn public opinion against the investment accord, the split between the U.S. and European countries on various elements of the pact began to widen.[525] When French Prime Minister Lionel Jospin announced in October 1998 that France would withdraw from the negotiations, the OECD countries decided to abandon the effort.[526] Given that failure, the U.S. was doubtful that the WTO would be able to achieve a deal on investment rules that was worth having.[527]

On competition policy, it was primarily the justice department and its strong-willed antitrust chief Joel Klein who warned that global negotiations would result in political compromises that would lower the tough U.S. standards and undermine enforcement of its antitrust policies. The EU dismissed these fears, arguing that a WTO agreement would not dilute existing laws but create some common basic principles of which countries should incorporate into their national laws. The more important reason for the U.S. position may have been its concern that competition rules might be used against its anti-dumping laws of which the U.S. was determined to maintain.[528] "One of the highest U.S. priorities... is maintaining strong U.S. trade laws that prevent dumping and subsidized imports from throwing Americans out of work," summarized Commerce Secretary William Daley by calling the laws, "fair and judicious."[529]

By early 1999, the U.S. had softened its opposition to a genuine new trade round. When Clinton in his State of the Union Address called for a new round of global negotiations to liberalize world trade, his administration had accepted

---

523 "WTO Vows to Tackle Farm Issues," International Herald Tribune, May 21, 1998.
524 "The Water-Treading Organization," *Economist*, May 21, 1998.
525 "Monster or Mouse," Financial Times, February 15, 1998, and "US Cool about Investment Pact," Financial Times, October 20, 1998.
526 "Retreat over OECD Pact on Investment," Financial Times, October 21, 1998.
527 "The Battle in Seattle," Financial Times, November 25, 1999.
528 "Move Afoot to Clarify WTO's Role on Competition," Financial Times, July 26, 1998; and Schott 2000, pp. 205-222
529 William Daley, "Why the U.S. Will not Dump its Defences," Financial Times, November 22, 1999.

the concept of wider talks, as long as the opening of agricultural markets remained its focus. By hosting the next WTO ministerial conference in Seattle from November 30 to December 3, 1999, the U.S. committed itself to a success. Washington was adamant not to let the drag on for years and insisted on an accelerated timetable of only three years, and suggested that specific issues that were ripe for agreement should be concluded even before the end of the round. Adding to the agenda, the U.S. proposed also talks about public procurement, corruption and electronic commerce.[530]

Hopes for forceful EU leadership faded in March 1999, when the whole European Commission decided to resign following a damaging report about corruption, mismanagement and nepotism in various departments. While its members, including Brittan, stayed on as acting commissioners until their successors were in place, their authority was seriously dented.

Meanwhile, WTO members were again at odds about filling the post of director-general. Ruggiero was scheduled to retire on May 1, 1999, and set to be replaced by a non-European. The U.S., France, Germany, Italy, Sweden and many African and Latin American states championed behind the former prime minister of New Zealand, Mike Moore, a former trade unionist who had spearheaded the dramatic market reforms in his country. Asian countries rallied behind Thai deputy premier and trade minister Supachai Panitchpakdi, and received the support of several EU governments, including Britain and the Netherlands. Washington saw in Moore the more determined free trader that also showed some sympathy for establishing core labor standards. Reflecting the Asian position, Supachai rejected the inclusion of labor issues in the WTO.

Unlike the first WTO leadership struggle the source of conflict was not a transatlantic split, though Clinton officials were frustrated that the EU could not agree on one candidate. The desire for consensus and the lack of good election procedures in the young trade organization resulted in an extended stalemate in which the two camps refused to withdraw their candidate as well as putting them to a vote.[531] It was not until July 20, nearly three months after Ruggiero's departure, that the WTO members reached a compromise: a six-year term would be split into half, with Moore taking the first three years.[532] When Moore assumed his post on September 1, 1999, he only had three months to prepare the cash-starved organization for the pivotal Seattle conference.

---

530 "US may Favor Widening Trade Talks," Financial Times, October 19, 1998; "Washington Seeks Fresh Global Trade Round by 2002," Financial Times, January 21, 1999; "Gore Opens the Fight on Farm Tariffs," International Herald Tribune, January 30, 1999.

531 "WTO Fight Raises Risk of Further Trade Wars," International Herald Tribune, April 15, 1999; Guy de Jonquières, "Trading Blows," Financial Times, May 7, 1999.

532 "WTO Ends Leadership Row as Rivals Agree to Three-Year Terms," Financial Times, July 21, 1999.

At the meeting of the WTO General Council on July 29, the big differences in expectations became obvious when countries presented their "wish-lists" for the Seattle summit. Developing countries, led by India, objected to the EU's desire for a broad agenda, arguing that poor countries were already overstretched by the implementation of the decisions taken in the Uruguay Round. The U.S. and the Cairns Group wanted to focus on reducing farm subsidies and creating scientific standards for import barriers for gene-altered crops.

Washington criticized the EU for shifting the focus away from farm subsidies, charging the Europeans with an "ABA anything but agriculture" strategy. While EU officials claimed that the Union had made progress toward a less distorting agricultural system in its Agenda 2000 reform package passed in June 1999, the U.S. was dissatisfied with the modest cuts in guaranteed prices that kept support payments enormously high and resulted in overproduction.[533] It also rejected demand by the EU, Japan, South Korea, Norway and Switzerland to recognize the "multi-functionality" of agriculture that would put equal weight to its social and environmental contribution as that of its economic role.[534] Moreover, EU officials were determined to keep biotechnology out of the realm of the WTO and deal with it only within the framework of the U.N. Biodiversity Protocol.[535]

On the issue of industrial tariffs, the U.S. wanted a sector approach, while the EU and Japan preferred "across-the-board" negotiations that would provide more opportunities for tradeoffs. The EU wanted to include the liberalization of the maritime sector, for which single-sector negotiations collapsed in 1996 because the U.S. did not want to take on its powerful maritime union and shipping industry, which benefited from heft protection.[536] In turn, the U.S. was hoping to break down the protective barriers against American audio-visual products both in France and Canada. Addressing the APEC summit in Auckland (New Zealand), Clinton demanded new rules for public procurement, accelerated tariff reduction in eight industries (lumber, fishery, toys, jewelry, chemicals, medical equipment, environmental products and power generation), continued freedom from duties and tax for e-commerce, and the issue of WTO transparency.[537]

---

[533] "The Battle in Seattle," *Economist*, November 25, 1999. According to OECD figures, the EU paid $130 billion in producer support to farmers in 1998, compared with $49 billion paid by Japan and $47 billion by the U.S. On a per-farmer basis, the EU and U.S. were about equal at $19,000 per year.

[534] "WTO Members Set to Sharpen Hatchets for Seattle Talks," Financial Times, August 6, 1999.

[535] "In Seattle, WTO Races the Clock," International Herald Tribune, December 3, 1999.

[536] "US Lets Shipping Trade Talks Gently Sink," Financial Times, February 8, 1996.

[537] "EU muss sich in Seattle auf heftige Attacken einstellen," HB, September 22, 1999.

There was movement toward a consensus on environmental issues, where the WTO itself had started to look into the environmental effects of trade.[538] The U.S. strategy was to focus on facilitating the trade in environmental technology and to stop subsidies for activities damaging to the environment. Because this included agriculture and fishery, it opened another front with the EU. Some Europeans were also unhappy with the renewed U.S. push for core labor standards. "The WTO should commit to collaborate more closely with the International Labor Organization, which has worked hard to protect human rights and to ban child labor, and with international environmental organizations," Clinton declared in a speech to the Democratic Leadership Council.[539]

The biggest debate raged over the structure of the negotiations. The Clinton administration wanted to divert from the traditional "single undertaking" strategy of one comprehensive trade agreement that would cover all areas. It feared that any progress would be held up by the continuous standoff over agriculture. Instead, U.S. trade officials advocated an "early harvest" approach to implement trade deals in specific sector as soon as agreement was reached. Clinton hoped to get the first results already in Seattle.

This strategy was not only rejected by the EU, but was also controversial in the U.S. The farm lobby feared that without the possibility of reciprocal concessions in other areas, the EU would not move much on its farm policies. Business representatives and trade experts accused the Clinton administration of putting "quick-hit" public-relations victories, helping Vice President Al Gore's presidential aspirations, ahead of substantive trade deals. "The U.S. isn't trying to develop a balanced package", argued Jeffrey Scott of the Institute for International Economics, "It's sitting back and saying to other countries 'What are you doing for us?' But it is unwilling to offer anything that would get them to accept its demands."[540] U.S. officials argued that they needed to build public support for a new round so that Congress would finally pass fast-track authority. Before that, no country would engage in serious trade negotiations.[541] The Clinton administration was also increasingly worried about the loud voices of protest to free trade in general. As Barshefsky remarked, "The single greatest threat to the multilateral trade system is the absence of public support."[542]

Faced with strong opposition to its proposals, the U.S. accepted the idea of "clustering" different trade issues, allowing some tradeoffs within these groups, although this did not resolve the fundamental differences between the big trading blocs.

---

[538] "Embracing Greenery," *Economist,* October 7, 1999.
[539] "U.S.'s WTO Focus Is Open Markets," Washington Post, October 14, 1999.
[540] "No Meeting of Minds," Financial Times, July 23, 1999.
[541] "Blunt-Spoken New Chief must Heal WTO Rifts," Financial Times, September 24, 1999.
[542] "Free Trade Under Fire," Financial Times, October 11, 1999.

As European Commission President Romano Prodi prepared to meet Clinton in Washington on October 27, 1999, the EU had internally not yet agreed on a common position on labor standards and on cultural diversity, where France insisted on a continued exception for audio-visual products from international trade rules.[543] It was not until October 21 that the new trade commissioner Pascal Lamy succeeded to forge a compromise on these two issues. It called for "a joint standing working forum" by the ILO and the WTO on trade and labor standards that was less than the working group inside the WTO demanded by the U.S. The EU also committed itself to "strongly support the protection of core labor rights" globally, but not necessarily in the WTO. On the question of cultural diversity, the compromise formula stated that the EU would make sure they maintain the possibility to preserve and develop their capacity to define and implement their cultural and audiovisual policies for the purpose of preserving their cultural diversity.[544] The agreement strengthened Prodi's hand in his meeting with Clinton. The two leaders did not make much progress on the details of the agenda but were able to agree to "cooperate closely to bridge remaining differences" until the conference.[545] Prodi commented, "I think that the U.S. and the EU will go to Seattle with a much stricter and more coordinated agenda."[546]

This prediction did not come true. At a meeting of trade ministers from 23 major WTO members and the EU in Lausanne on October 25, 1999, there was wide spread optimism that the differences can be bridged. Yet the 32-page text drafted for the meeting had 200 passages enclosed in brackets, indicating language on which had not been agreed.[547] On November 23, with only a week to go before the conference, WTO ambassadors in Geneva again failed to reach agreement on an agenda for the talks in a meeting that was described as "a complete shambles."[548] This left a huge amount of work for the four-day meeting. Furthermore, a last-minute attempt by Clinton to generate political momentum by getting more then 30 world leaders to join him in Seattle failed.

U.S. negotiators, meanwhile, seemed more interested in reaching agreement with China on the terms of its entry into the WTO (signed on November 15, 1999) than on the Seattle summit. Europeans and Americans remained far apart on the key issues. "Frankly, I fear the Atlantic alliance might be the greatest threat to getting these (WTO) talks off to a good start," warned U.S. Commerce

---

543 "Except Us," *Economist,* October 14, 1999.

544 "EU Agrees Position for Trade Talks," Financial Times, October 25, 1999.

545 Joint Declaration by President William Jefferson Clinton and European Commission President Romano Prodi, The White House, October 27, 1999. *www.eabc.org/abstracts/ clintonprodi.htm*

546 "Clinton, Prodi try to Map out Trade Agenda," Financial Times, October 28, 1999.

547 "A Seattle Primer: How not to Hold Talks," Washington Post, December 12, 1999.

548 "The Circus Comes to Town," Financial Times, November 25, 1999.

Secretary William Daley, "It would be ironic if the millennium trade talks were to blow up and become the trade crisis we have tried to avoid."[549] The prospect of massive protests by non-governmental organization was also worrisome for the governments. "NGOs are the only people who will come to Seattle prepared and knowing exactly what they want," noted John Weekes, a former Canadian ambassador to the WTO.[550]

6.2. Transatlantic Causes for the Failure of the Seattle Conference

The Seattle summit will probably be remembered as the place where anti-globalization protesters for the first time succeeded to severely disrupt an international meeting and make themselves, rather the issues discussed in the conference hall, the main focus of world public opinion. Tens of thousands of people concerned about labor standards, environmental protection, human rights, and jobs assembled in Seattle to demand that the WTO members give greater priority to their causes. Ironically their message got drowned when violent protesters usurped the bulk of media coverage.[551] Seattle police underestimated the violent tactics by the violent core that managed in the first days of the meeting to close off access to the conference hall. Once authorities got tough, declared a civil emergency and made hundreds of arrests, they were criticized of heavy-handed tactics that did not distinguish between peaceful protesters and violent provocateurs. Both the tactics of the protesters and the helplessness of the organizers set a pattern. In the following 30 months, most major international meetings of the IMF, the World Economic Forum in Davos, and the European Council were overshadowed by Seattle-style protests, culminating in the death of a demonstrator at the Group of Seven summit in Genoa, Italy, in July 2001. Only the terrorist attack on New York and Washington of September 11, 2001 broke the momentum of the movement and returned some calm to international economic conferences.

According to analysts, "the WTO meeting fell victim not to protests outside in the streets, but rather to than to more substantive disagreements inside the convention center among both developed and developing countries over the prospective agenda for new trade talks."[552] The protests were part of a pattern of Western public opinion and this made reaching a consensus on further trade liberalization much more difficult. The protest movements included both NGOs claiming to fight for the interests of developing nations and U.S. trade unions concerned about their own jobs. The Clinton administration felt it had to

549 "US-EU Rifts May Threaten Trade Round," Financial Times, October 30, 1999.
550 "The Circus Comes to Town," Financial Times, November 25, 1999.
551 Schott 2000, p. 5
552 Ibid.

respond to the demands of the unions both to build a pro-trade coalition in Congress and to advance Gore's presidential prospects. Unfortunately, this put the U.S. at odds with most of the developing countries and made it vary of any initiative to help the developing countries' interests. When Lamy announced at the eve of the conference that the EU and Japan were close to agreeing on a plan to abolish duties unconditionally on most imports from the world's 48 poorest countries, the U.S. hesitated. Even though Clinton had agreed this mostly symbolic scheme at his meeting with Prodi, the administration was concerned about union's opposition to eliminate high U.S. tariffs on textile and clothing imports.[553]

Developing countries grew even more concerned about the U.S. intentions when Clinton was seen, in an interview with the Seattle Post-Intelligencer, endorsing trade sanctions for the violation of labor standards that included, "What we ought to do first of all is to adopt the United States' position on having a working group on labor within the WTO, and then that working group should develop these core labor standards, and then they ought to be a part of every trade agreement, and ultimately I would favor a system in which sanctions would come for violating any provision of a trade agreement."[554] According to observers these comments, later retracted by the White House, hardened developing country's determination to prevent the creation of any institution that would deal with labor and trade. "Clinton has opened up a deep, deep rift with the developing countries," said Robert Litan, director of the economics program at the Brookings Institution, "It seems to be a hasty capitulation to domestic political concerns....It will make it more difficult to get agreement."[555]

In his speech to the WTO conference, Clinton made a strong pitch for free trade and defended the record of the trade organization against the street protesters. Although by focusing primarily on agriculture, Clinton was seen promoting more the U.S. priorities than the chances of the conference.[556] As the conference progressed, the old transatlantic rift over agriculture returned to the forefront as the main stumbling bloc for an agreement. Faced with heavy U.S. pressure, EU agricultural commissioner Franz Fischler made a key concession on the issue of biotechnology. He agreed to a draft declaration that called for the establishment of a working group "with a fact-finding mandate on the relationship between trade, development, health, consumer and environmental

---

[553] "Big Trading Power Try to Agree Plan to Help the Poor," Financial Times, November 30, 1999.

[554] "Clinton says he will support trade sanctions for worker abuse," Seattle Post-Intelligencer, December 1, 1999.

[555] "Clinton's Remarks on Sanctions Open Rift," Washington Post, December 3, 1999.

[556] "Clinton Defends Open Trade," Washington Post, December 2, 1999.

issues in the area of modern biotechnology."[557] This move split the EU countries. Belgium, Britain, Denmark, France and Italy issued a statement warning that a working group on such an issue would undermine negotiations about the United Nations Biosafety Protocol. This forced the Commission to withdraw its support for the draft.

Even tougher was the question of farm subsidies of which the U.S. wanted to eliminate completely. Early in the week, EU commissioner Fischler offered, "to negotiate significant reductions, but we are not prepared to accept total elimination."[558] By Thursday, EU and U.S. negotiators were able to stand united behind a text calling for "substantial and progressive" reductions in U.S. farm support in return for U.S. acknowledgement that some aid could be justified to preserve the environment and a rural way of life.[559] In the early hours of Friday, U.S. negotiators thought they had an agreement at hand. Lamy, who was negotiating for the EU at that time, had to report to the EU trade ministers, and did not return for six hours. Americans negotiators concluded that Lamy had been overruled by the ministers and effectively gave up hope for a deal. "I could see it wasn't going to happen," recalled Barshefsky, "People's positions were hardening." Mike Moore arrived at the same conclusion after consulting with negotiators from various countries. At 10.30 p.m. on Friday, Barshefsky announced that the conference would end without a result. "The complexity and novelty of the issues strained the collective capacity of delegations to make decisions. Governments were just not willing to take the leap," she concluded.[560] WTO countries agreed to resume negotiations on agriculture and services, the items of the built-in agenda, the following year in Geneva. However, few people expected single-sector talks on such complex issues to go anywhere.

There was a multitude of causes for the failure of Seattle. The summit was poorly prepared, hampered by proximity to the U.S. presidential elections, the resignation of the EU Commission and the four-month leadership vacuum at the WTO. Given that eight previous trade rounds had reduced most industrial tariffs to very low levels, new trade talks had to deal with thornier issues than its predecessors. "We've already got all the low-hanging fruit. From now on, it's going to be slow going," remarked Laura D'Andrea Tyson, former chair of Clinton's Council of Economic Advisors.[561]

Most commentators in the U.S. and abroad put most the blame on the Clinton administration. The lack of fast-track authority and the concern for

[557] "In Seattle, WTO Races the Clock," International Herald Tribune, December 3, 1999.
[558] "Clinton Defends Open Trade," Washington Post, December 2, 1999.
[559] "WTO Negotiators Reach Far Exceeded Grasp of Complexities," Washington Post, December 5, 1999.
[560] Ibid.
[561] "WTO Talks Said to Send 'Grim Message'," Washington Post, December 8, 1999.

Gore's presidential campaign made Clinton excessively sensitive to U.S. special interests, particularly within the Democratic Party, and limited his ability to offer substantial concessions to the trading partners on areas such as textiles or anti-dumping. The U.S. emphasis on labor standards, sharpened by Clinton's controversial interview, antagonized the developing countries that themselves as the losers of the Uruguay Round agreement and were therefore not keen on a new trade round. The protesters on the street caused massive delays and contributed to a tense and less conciliatory atmosphere. Commentators charged Clinton with "pandering to the demonstrators in Seattle" on the question of labor standards and thus antagonizing most developing countries.[562] EU leaders blamed the approaching U.S. presidential election as Lamy declared; "To make concessions in an election campaign is obviously not an easy thing to do, especially in the U.S."[563]

The prominent trade economist Jagdish Bhagwati argued that the failure of Seattle was part of Clinton's domestic political strategy that began with the U.S. decision to complete the accord with China just two weeks before the WTO conference. The China deal was far more important to the U.S. business community than a new trade round, but it also added to the anger of trade unions and anti-globalization protesters. "So, Clinton emerges having won the minds and cash of the business community with his China deal, and having won the hearts and cash of the unions with his destructive grandstanding at Seattle on labor rights. Not bad for the Democratic Party. The WTO and freer trade are another matter," wrote Bhagwati.[564] Clinton administration officials, however, deny that the China deal was part of a cynical political calculation. "We thought it would give a boost to the WTO," said David Aaron, undersecretary of commerce for international trade.[565]

Another target of criticism was the poor organization and particularly the role of Barshefsky, who insisted on both chairing the conference and the U.S. delegation. She was accused of an "abrasive style" that "proved ill-suited to achieving consensus."[566] Some experts argued that the U.S. could have saved the meeting and arrived at a compromise text if they had been able to "stop the clock" and continue negotiations into the weekend. The USTR had not reserved

---

[562] Reginald Dale, "Trade Hopes Die at Clinton's Hands," International Herald Tribune, December 14, 1999.

[563] "Collapse of Seattle Talks Blamed on U.S.," Financial Times, December 7, 1999.

[564] Jagdfish Baghwati, "Did Clinton Take a Dive in Seattle?" Washington Post, December 7, 1999. A similar interpretation can be found in James Shoch's book *Trading Blows*: The Clinton administration "provoked the collapse of the WTO meeting to avoid jeopardizing" the election of Al Gore and the passage of the China bill. Shoch 2001, p. 231.

[565] Interview with David Aaron, U.S.deputy secretary of commerce for intrnernational trade, on April 10, 2002 in Washington, D.C.

[566] "A Global Disaster," *Economist*, December 9, 1999.

any meeting rooms at the Seattle Convention Center for a few extra days and had to vacate the premises for a convention of optometrists.[567] Barshefsky disagreed with, "We could have stayed all night, maybe for five more days, and it wouldn't have mattered."[568]

The underlying mistake by the U.S. may have been to host the conference and to choose Seattle, a city known for left-wing activism, as its location. By putting so much of Clinton's prestige on the success of the meeting (there was even talk in Washington of naming the negotiations the "Clinton Round"), the U.S. limited its own bargaining power. As Aaron pointed out, "Everybody thought we had to have a deal, so they were not willing to compromise."[569]

U.S. trade officials acknowledged tactical and strategic mistakes in Seattle, but they put a good part of the blame on the Europeans. The whole EU premise of a broad-based round to make concessions in farm policy more palatable was mistaken, they said. "Which farmer would accept cuts in agriculture just because we agreed to talk about competition and investment? Nobody?"[570]

Moreover, the EU negotiators failed to deliver on promises they made. On two crucial issues, biotechnology and farm subsidies, they had to retract concessions after EU member states objected. "We would make progress, and then the Europeans or the Japanese would come back and start right where we began hours before," complained one U.S. trade official.[571] A major problem, they noted was the resignation of the EU Commission in March and the departure of Leon Brittan, who had fought so hard for a new trade round but insisted on an unrealistically broad agenda. His successor Lamy did not have the political clout to push through the necessary compromises needed to achieve that goal. Barshefsky noted that, "Lamy was just learning his job, he had no flexibility."[572]

U.S. officials pointed to a series of domestically painful U.S. concessions as evidence that their Seattle agenda was not driven by political opportunism. The U.S. agreed to limited negotiations to better police the implementation of anti-dumping rules. It abandoned their objective of a WTO working group on labor standards, while it continued to push for a forum that would operate outside the WTO but ultimately report to it. Washington also stepped back from its goal of

567 Schott 2000, p. 7

568 "Impasse on Trade Delivers A Stinging Blow to Clinton," New York Times, December 5, 1999.

569 Interview with David Aaron, U.S. deputy secretary of commerce for international trade, on April 10, 2002 in Washington, D.C.

570 Ibid.

571 "Impasse on Trade Delivers A Stinging Blow to Clinton," New York Times, December 5, 1999.

572 Telephone interview with Charlene Barshefsky, United States Trade Representative from 1996 to 2001, on March 19, 2002.

widening markets for GM foods, and resigned itself to miniscule steps toward more transparency. Even on farm subsidies, the U.S. felt that it moved more than its trading partners when it accepted the "multi-functionality" of agriculture in some instances.[573] Even on competition and investment, the "deal we offered Europe was better than what Europe got in Doha," where the trade round was finally launched in November 2001, said Barshefsky. The U.S. would have accepted immediate talks on these issues, but with a limited scope. In Doha, talks were agreed only with a two-year delay.[574]

The most important cause for the failure of Seattle was the breakdown of transatlantic cooperation. In previous trade meetings, it had been the Quad – the U.S., the EC, Japan and Canada – that had closely monitored the talks, prepared the necessary compromises and had "lead the process of consensus building among WTO members on launching new trade negotiations."[575] This time Quad cooperation was virtually non-existent; not even a Quad meeting was scheduled before Seattle. The effectiveness of the Quad depends primarily on the relationship between its two largest members and here the Seattle conference represented a low point in post-war history. "Agriculture aside, this is the first time in nine trade rounds that you have not had the U.S. and Europe working together," Ernest Preeg, a trade expert at the conservative Hudson Institute.[576]

One of the major causes of failure was the difficult personal relationship between Barshefsky and Sir Leon Brittan, who were effectively "not on speaking terms" according to colleagues on both sides. The two were in some ways much alike. They were both praised for their intelligence, tenacity and their hard ball bargaining skills, but criticized for also for arrogance, a lack of team spirit and weak political instincts.[577] Whatever their strengths and flaws, the mixture was explosive. "They could not be in the same room together without getting into a shouting match within three minutes," one insider, who asked not to be identified revealed, "I have never seen such an incompatibility of two personalities."

---

[573] "Trade Obstacles Unmoved, Seattle Talks End in Failure," New York Times, December 4, 1999.

[574] Telephone interview with Charlene Barshefsky, United States Trade Representative from 1996 to 2001, on March 19, 2002.

[575] Schott 2000, p. 7

[576] "U.S., on Defensive, Struggles for Accord in a Divided WTO," International Herald Tribune, December 4, 1999.

[577] On Brittan, see "Leon Brittan, Europe's Trade Warrior," *Economist*, February 4, 1999, and "High-Handed Approach Mars a Clever Operator," Financial Times, March 9, 1999. On Barshefsky, see "Objection," *Economist*, January 21, 1999, and "The First Lady of Trade," Financial Times, November 27, 1999.

Until Lamy took over from Brittan in September 1999, valuable months had been lost. Even though the bilateral atmosphere immediately improved through the change in Brussels, Lamy was forced to spend valuable time and political capital on the transatlantic trade disputes rather than on preparing for the WTO conference. In this way, bananas, beef and hush kits may have played a part in the fiasco of Seattle. Aaron suggested, "If we had closed ranks with the Europeans, we could have succeeded." The lesson from Seattle was clear: even with well over hundred WTO members, the future of the international trade regime remains in the hands of its two largest players.

6.3. From Seattle to Doha

Shocked by the failure of the Seattle conference and the highly negative media coverage, U.S. and EU leaders quickly started attempts to heal the rifts in their bilateral relationship. At a summit between Clinton and Prodi just two weeks after the WTO meeting, trade negotiators from both sides said they would try to settle some of the open issues, including the question of WTO transparency at the ambassadorial level, in order to create momentum for starting a new trade round. In a gesture toward developing countries, the U.S. and the EU also agreed that they would work toward granting tariff-free access for a wide number of goods from the world's poorest countries by the Quad that also included Japan and Canada, and help them in the implementation of the Uruguay Round Agreement.[578] Lamy also expressed optimism that a new trade round could be started before the end of 2000, but the approaching U.S. presidential elections let most experts doubt that outlook.[579] At a speech at the annual World Economic Forum in Davos in January 2000, Clinton reaffirmed his commitment to free trade though he gave only lukewarm support for a new trade round.[580] Subsequent talks between Barshefsky and Lamy showed that the U.S. and the EU were still far apart on the scope of the round. While Barshefsky demanded from the EU a "more realistic agenda" and a show of flexibility, the EU remained committed to the idea of a broad-based round involving investment and competition policy.[581] When EU trade ministers in March 2000 again refused to grant Lamy a more flexible mandate for negotiations, the start of a new trade round in 2000 was effectively doomed.[582] The endeavor would be left to the next U.S. administration.

---

[578] "U.S., Europe Hopeful on Some WTO Issues," Washington Post, December 18, 1999.
[579] Reginald Dale, "New Trade Round? Not Under Clinton," International Herald Tribune, January 18, 2000.
[580] "U.S. Heads for Post-Seattle Talks with EU," Financial Times, January 31, 2000.
[581] "Barshefsky in Plea for Trade Talks Flexibility," Financial Times, February 9, 2000.
[582] "EU Doubt on Early Trade Round," Financial Times, March 20, 2000.

The focus of European trade policy shifted to the entry of China into the WTO, an objective the EU had pursued for several years. The government in Beijing, however, always saw Washington, not Brussels, as its main negotiating partner and therefore put more effort into reaching a deal with the U.S, which it did in November 1999. The EU was unwilling to accept that agreement as a whole, as China had apparently hoped, and signaled to Beijing that it would block China's WTO membership if certain concerns were not addressed. The EU wanted China to allow foreign investors in mobile telecommunications and life insurance ventures to take controlling stakes and opposed the limit of forty-nine percent for telecom companies and fifty percent for Internet providers and life insurers, to which the U.S. had agreed. It also demanded better market access for various industrial goods that were not covered in the U.S. agreement, including glass, ceramics, cosmetics, liquor, and machinery parts.

In late January 2000, China finally sent a senior trade negotiator to Brussels.[583] The talks dragged on for four months. In the agreement reached on May 19, 2000, China made some important concessions to European commercial interests. It promised to dismantle its state procurement monopolies on imports of oil, oil products and fertilizers, and agreed to a significant reduction on a range of industrial tariffs, but not on cars. A key concession was a Chinese promise to allow foreign retailers establish wholly owned subsidiaries throughout the country. Beijing balked at allowing foreign majority shareholdings in telecom and insurance companies and just agreed to bring forward the dates by which joint ventures can be established. To match the growing presence of U.S. insurance groups, especially American International Group (AIG), China promised to grant licenses to seven European insurance companies.[584]

However, the rights for European life insurers remained a point of transatlantic controversy and for a while threatened China's WTO entry. AIG (founded in Shanghai in 1919) was the first international insurance group to aggressively eye the Chinese market. In 1992, it received the first license to sell insurance even without a Chinese partner. By the end of the decade, AIG's wholly owned subsidiary operated four branches. The U.S.-China agreement opened the insurance market to all overseas groups, but created restrictions on ownership. While the EU was willing to accept the privileged position of existing AIG operations, it opposed any expansion. AIG and the U.S. government read the U.S.-China agreements in such a way that AIG could expand its branch network without having to find a local partner and demanded from Beijing a "clarification" in that sense. Brussels warned that this right

---

[583] "China to Resume Brussels Talks On Joining WTO," Financial Times, January 12, 2000.

[584] "Deal with Brussels Clears Way for China's WTO Membership," Financial Times, May 20, 2000; "China, EU Sign Broad Trade Pact," Washington Post, May 20, 2000.

would give AIG a competitive edge over European rivals.[585] Even though China and most other WTO countries sided with the EU on the dispute, the new USTR Robert Zoellick did not give in. AIG's powerful and politically influential chairman Maurice "Hank" Greenberg lobbied hard in Washington to preserve the special status of his company in China.[586]

The dispute was not solved until mid-September 2001, just two months before the WTO summit in Doha where China's membership was to be finalized. The main accession text remained unchanged, as the U.S. insisted, but a footnote was added which referred to the right of equal treatment under the Most Favored Nation clause of the WTO. Both sides were able to claim victory, even though the compromise in essence reaffirmed the two diverging interpretations and left it to a WTO panel to settle the dispute at a later point.[587] It did, however, remove the last barrier to China's entry into the World Trade Organization, effective in 2002.

China also had a domestic hurdle in the U.S. where a long established practice demanded from the president to renew China's MFN status every year took into account China's human rights record. As a WTO member, China would become automatically entitled to MFN and could have denied U.S. companies' access to its markets if the U.S. did not grant it permanent normal trade relations (PNTR) status. While the U.S. Senate seemed willing to approve this change in law, trade unions and human right groups waged a strong campaign in the House to stop the China legislation. This time, Clinton did not risk a defeat as for the fast-track legislation and with the help of major business associations; he ran an effective lobbying campaign.[588] On May 24, 2000, the House voted in favor of PNTR, 237 to 197. The margin of victory not only exceeded the NAFTA vote in 1993 but most expectations. It also reflected the strong commercial interests riding on the Chinese market and the obvious fact that the U.S. would only hurt its own commercial interests by denying trade rights to the world's most populous and fastest growing country.[589]

The Bush administration came into office officially committed to the launch of a new trade round at the next WTO ministerial conference in Doha, Qatar, in November 2001. Its USTR Robert Zoellick had a reputation as a pragmatic free trader, and his long-standing friendship with EU trade commissioner Pascal Lamy – including a shared love for long-distance running - was seen as a good basis for braking the transatlantic logjam. Zoellick and Lamy quickly succeeded to solve the banana dispute and arrived at rules of engagements over the FSC

[585] "China Close to Finalizing WTO Entry Negotiations," Financial Times, July 21, 2000.

[586] "Insurance Chief Fights to Keep AIG's Special Status," Financial Times, September10, 2001.

[587] "WTO Set to Rubber-Stamp China Entry Terms," Financial Times, September17, 2001.

[588] Guy de Jonquières, "Against the Tide," Financial Times, May 11, 2000.

[589] "House Passes China Trade Bill," Financial Times, May 25, 2000.

case, seen as defusing that conflict. Yet European observers questioned the strength of the administration's commitment to multilateral trade liberalization, particularly following the Summit of the Americas in Quebec in April 2001 where Bush declared the establishment of a Free Trade Area of the Americas (FTAA) by 2005 as his major goal.[590] The difficult quest of the administration to gain Trade Promotion Authority (TPA), as fast-track authority had been renamed, also distracted from the preparations for Doha.[591]

The change from a Democratic to a Republican administration had removed some difficulties while adding others. The Bush White House was no longer preoccupied with including labor standards in the WTO, even though that issue came up as a major demand from some Congressional leaders who were wavering on TPA. Meanwhile, the EU had added a third objective to its already ambitious WTO agenda that included investment and competition policy as well as talks about trade and the environment. EU leaders said they did not want to change the WTO's environmental rules but rather to clarify them. In particular, they wanted to reaffirm the WTO compatibility of domestic environmental approaches such as eco-labeling or the application of the "precautionary principle" for consumer protection.[592] From the U.S. point of view, such a clarification was unnecessary because WTO panels had ruled in favor of domestic environmental legislation in virtually all disputes over environmental issues.[593] Precedence from case law, however, did not satisfy European legal experts used to codified law. Some developing countries suspected that the EU goal was "to use environmental rules as a back door to protectionism," a charge EU trade negotiators strongly denied. In return, the EU pointed to the political need to show a stronger commitment to environment and food safety to a European public unsettled by food scares and the U.S. rejection of the Kyoto protocol on climate change.[594]

Yet as the Doha conference approached, the odds for success improved. U.S. and EU negotiators continued to work together closely and WTO director-general Mike Moore, who was starting his third year in office, and WTO Council Chairman Stuart Habinson produced preparatory documents that were

---

590 "Bush Comments at Summit of Americas Working Session," Washington File, April 21, 2001. *http://usinfo.state.gov/regional/ar/summit/opening.htm*

591 The author accompanied Austrian economics and trade minister Martin Bartenstein to Washington, DC from May 1 to May 4, 2001. At meetings with political and business leaders, the hurdles for TPA dominated discussions and cast a doubt over the prospects of Doha.

592 "Playing Games with Prosperity," *Economist*, January 26, 2001.

593 In the highly publicized U.S.-Mexican GATT case over Mexican tuna fishing practices that threatened dolphins, it was the extraterritorial approach of the U.S. legislation to environmental regulations, not the environmental concern per se, which the panel declared to be in violation of the GATT. The panel's report was never adopted, however. See: *http://www.wto.org/english/thewto_e/whatis_e/tif_e/bey5_e.htm*

594 "Playing Games with Prosperity," *Economist*, January 26, 2001.

considered "balanced and objective" by most member states and that resolved most agenda disputes.[595]

Moreover, the horrific terrorist attacks on the World Trade Center in New York City and the Pentagon in Washington on September 11, 2001 galvanized efforts to launch a trade round and underlined the crucial importance of international cooperation. The attacks were also seen increasing the risks of a world recession, and experts feared that another failure at the WTO could worsen the gloom in the world economy.[596] New studies affirmed the economic gains from further trade liberalization. According to researches from Tufts University and the University of Michigan, a one-third cut in tariffs on services, agricultural and industrial products would boost global welfare by $612 billion, compared to an increase of $75 billion through the Uruguay Round. The World Bank calculated that a total elimination of trade barriers would even yield $2.8 trillion.

When representatives of the 142 WTO member countries convened in Doha on November 9, 2001, they were spared the disruptions through anti-globalization protests that had marred the Seattle summit, as the authoritarian regime in Qatar kept activists out. Inside the conference hall, many of the rifts of Seattle reappeared. The EU was trying to rally support for a broad agenda, while fending off attempts to include the "phasing out" of all agricultural export subsidies in the negotiating mandate, a measure in which France considered unacceptable. The U.S. was under pressure over demands for anti-dumping talks and access to its textile and clothing markets.[597] A first breakthrough came on the third day, when industrialized countries agreed on a declaration that intellectual property rights would not impede poor countries' access to essential medical supplies.[598] Coming on top of offers for technical help for the implementation of earlier trade agreements, this text bought the developing countries' acquiescence to key U.S. and EU demands.

On the last day of the conference, the EU found itself increasingly isolated over its rigid stance on agriculture, as even Norway and Switzerland (two non-EU countries with high levels of farm protection) were willing to accept the "phasing out" of export subsidies. The U.S. gathered support to agree to negotiations over anti-dumping rules, even though this concession was bound to cause a negative backlash in Congress. While Zoellick stood firm on developing countries' demands for an increase in textile quotas, he agreed to negotiate about a tariff reduction for apparel products.[599] On the agenda, the EU and

[595] Schott 2002.
[596] Guy de Joncquières, "Dealing in Doha," Financial Times, November 6, 2001.
[597] "WTO Logjam continues over Trade Round Agenda," Financial Times, November 12, 2001.
[598] "Deal Close on Medicine and Patents," Financial Times, November 13, 2001.
[599] "Zoellick wins Praise on Trade Concessions," Financial Times, November 16, 2001.

developing countries reached a compromise to start talks on trade and the environment immediately but to delay negotiations on investment and competition policy for two years. The Europeans gained the assurance that the Doha round would be a "single undertaking" that meant that developing countries could not block the start of investment and competition negotiations without threatening the whole round.[600]

Yet none of these compromises mattered as long as the dispute over agriculture remained unresolved. After a final all-night session, France finally accepted a compromise formula, including the controversial "phasing out" but qualified it by stating that the outcome of the round remained open. The ministerial declaration included, "Building on the work carried out to date and without prejudging the outcome of the negotiations, we commit ourselves to comprehensive negotiations aimed at...reductions of, with a view of to phasing out, all forms of export subsidies; and a substantial reduction in trade-distorting domestic support."[601] EU agricultural commissioner Franz Fischler hailed the agreement a "magnificent success" for the EU with, "We achieved what we wanted. We will decide how we reform without the Cairns Group and others forcing things upon us."[602]

The Doha declaration was shorter and in key passages less precise than the draft documents in Seattle. One EU negotiator called it a "collection of generalities."[603] Still, the conference produced exactly the kind of concessions from all sides that seemed unattainable in Seattle. The main difference with Seattle was the far better preparation, the advantage of a second attempt, when many lessons of the previous experience had been absorbed, and an international economic and political climate that sharply increased the costs of failure. "Fear was probably the biggest driving force behind the deal", wrote the *Financial Times*, "The Doha meeting succeeded because it was too important too fail."[604] Unlike in Seattle, the transatlantic axis functioned well on a technical, political and a personal level.

The evolution from Seattle to Doha underpins the hypothesis that the state of transatlantic trade relations depend less on the specific character of conflicts than on the overall strength of desire for a positive outcome. A success at the Seattle conference was not important enough for either the U.S. or the EU to make truly painful concessions. The world economy was booming, and the

---

[600] Schott 2002.

[601] WTO Ministerial declaration adopted on November 14, 2001 in Doha. *www.wto.org/english/thewto_e/minist_e/min01_e/mindecl_e.htm*

[602] "Fischler Hails Doha Meeting as 'a Magnificent Success,' Financial Times, November 16, 2001.

[603] Interview with Hugo Paemen, EU ambassador to the U.S. from 1993 to 1999, on April 10, 2002 in Washington, D.C.

[604] Guy de Jonquières, "A Deal that had to be Done," Financial Times, November 30, 2001.

international political climate relatively benign. Both the European Commission and the Clinton administration were more concerned with domestic politics than global welfare. Doha seemed almost like a throwback to the Cold War era, when huge geo-strategic interests often appeared to offset the dynamics of domestic politics. While this does not imply that the U.S. and the EU can only cooperate if they are threatened by an aggressive superpower or by international terrorism, it does indicate that narrow economic interests that hold up trade liberalization are better overcome in an atmosphere of crisis than one of complacency.

By the time of the next meeting of September 2003 in Cancun, however, this sense of urgency and awareness had faded into to a new crisis, a deepening transatlantic rift. The ambitious goals of Doha, geared to helping poor countries, soon found themselves in jeopardy over agricultural subsidies, an area of special contention for developing nations. In particular, African nations were upset by the refusal of the U.S. to discuss the dismantling of its cotton subsidies and refused to extend the negotiations into new areas. Unable to reach a decision a decision on the scope and goals of the Doha round, the summit collapsed in disarray. With both the US and the EU shifting their focuses onto internal matters (Bush on re-election, EU on enlargement), the outlook for finishing the deadline, December 31st 2004, looked certain to be missed.[605]

[605] "Raising the Barricades," *Economist*, September 18, 2003.

CHAPTER 7: THE FUTURE OF TRANSATLANTIC TRADE RELATIONS

During the Bush Jr. administration, transatlantic trade relations truly stood at the crossroads. On one hand, some of the disputes left over by the Clinton presidency were solved or at least defused (the banana issue, the hush kits and the foreign sales corporations). At the same time, the U.S. decision in early 2002 to impose tariffs on the import of a wide range of steel products, primarily those from the EU, triggered one of the most intense transatlantic trade conflict of the post-war era. In which direction will this relationship move in the coming years, and what can we learn from the experience of the previous decade?

To find some answers to this question, another look at the essentials of transatlantic trade relations becomes prudent. The United States and the European Union take generally a liberal view of the global economy. They believe in the mutual benefits of free trade that economists define primarily as access to cheaper and higher quality inputs through imports. At the same time, trade policy and the public perception of the benefits of trade is often grounded in a mercantilist approach that is intellectually easier to grasp for non-economists (including most legislators and policy-makers) and easier to sell in a democratic arena: the objective of trade is to maximize exports as an instrument for job creation and to minimize import competition for vulnerable industries.[606] Every measure that helps exports is positive, even if it involves competition-distorting subsidies, whereas allowing imports into the country at low or no tariff is a concession to the trading partners. This mercantilist philosophy even forms the basis of all trade agreements under GATT and the WTO where market access is treated as a concession that can be withdrawn when needed.[607]

The mercantilist roots of trade policy in the U.S. and the EU would matter little if they just lead to the objective of free trade but instead, they make the policy process receptive to the demands of special commercial interests for various forms of protection. The arguments of unfair competition and the preservation of jobs are quite powerful in daily politics. The proponents of such special interests often carry political weight that exceeds their economic importance because they tend to be geographically concentrated or are part of an old and well-entrenched industry that is regarded as a backbone of society –

[606] See, for example, the speech by U.S. president George W. Bush at the Port of New Orleans on January 15, 2002, where he made a pitch for trade promotion authority: "It's important to these workers that we trade. The people who are loading these ships load them because we're trading around the world. The farmers who are selling product can sell more if we trade. (...) I'm worried about jobs. And I believe if you trade more, there are more jobs available for hardworking Americans." White House Press Release *www.whitehouse.gov/news/releases/2002/01/20020115.html*

[607] See Krugman 1991 and Charnovitz 2001.

steel-making, ship-building or farming. These interests are the driving force behind most trade disputes and unless there is a well-organized counterforce with a strong interest in keeping product markets open, they have a good chance to influence and even determine trade policy in their narrow area of interest. This is a general phenomenon that can be observed in virtually every country of the world.

Protectionism helps specific industries and companies but hurts the overall economy. If the introduction of protectionist measures induces trading partners retaliate, the economic damage is even larger. In addition, the political and even strategic relationship between these partners is bound to suffer. Friendly governments therefore will try to contain and resolve these conflicts before the result in an all-out trade war of tit-for-tat retaliation. By doing so, the governments are bound to damage the interests of the group that triggered the original dispute and will therefore pay a political price. Trade negotiations are a constant balancing act between domestic and international pressures, a typical two-level game.

The higher the potential risk – military exports would talk of the "collateral damage" – of a trade dispute, the more the political leadership will try to resolve it. When it comes to broad and high-stake issues, the whole diplomatic and political machinery of governments (or supranational institutions like the EU) will strive towards a solution and will be willing to invest political capital for that task. Small issues with narrow constituencies are much more likely to be allowed to fester without even catching the attention of the highest levels of government. Special domestic interests will set the agenda as the conflict escalates and serious damage control will begin only when the conflict is already quite advanced. Conflict settlement becomes much harder at that time because both sides have committed themselves to an uncompromising stance until it eventually becomes imperative. At that moment, it will require tremendous diplomatic and political skill to find face-saving solutions in which both sides can claim some form of victory. Because the real motive for pursuing the conflict is to impress domestic constituencies, not to fulfill any national goal, such acceptable compromise formulas are usually found.

The future course of transatlantic trade relations depends on domestic issues, international relations and the institutional framework, all of which are discussed below.

7.1. The Domestic Perspective

7.1.1. Public Opinion and Trade

Throughout most of the post-war period, trade issues did not play a major role in political debates and in public opinion either in the U.S. or Western

Europe. There was a general consensus in favor of gradual trade liberalization, not totally, that was just another future vision. This has changed in the past decades, as trade barriers were drastically lowered and difficult economic changes in all industrialized countries raised concerns over foreign competition and helped to mobilize widespread opposition against free trade.

In the U.S., foreign trade became for the first time a hot political issue with the rising ride of Japanese and other Asian imports into the U.S. The debate over NAFTA helped create a coalition of labor unions and non-governmental organizations (NGOs) that while failed in their effort to stop the agreement with Mexico and Canada, remain a powerful brake on subsequent trade initiatives.

Opinion polls show a picture of an American public generally in favor of free trade but concerned about its impact on specific industries or specific issues like unemployment, the environment and human rights. Polls conducted by the Women in International Trade (WIIT) have consistently shown well over half of Americans in support of trade agreements as a way to keep prices down and domestic competitors on their toes. The same polls and others also show that half or more of U.S. voters support protectionist measures to preserve jobs, want labor standards and human rights conditions included in future trade agreements, and are skeptical of giving the president a free hand through fast-track authority.[608]

In its views on free trade and globalization, American public opinion tends to be close to the European mainstream. In Europe, the target of those who fear the economic changes brought on by free trade is usually the EU itself, not global trade. Antagonism against European integration has certainly increased since the Maastricht Treaty, but so has general support for globalization. However, there are wide national fluctuations. A 2001 survey conducted by the World Economic Forum showed that 87% of the respondents in the Netherlands saw globalization as positive for themselves and their families, while only 37% in France 36% in Spain replied similarly. With 76% positive views, the U.S. was close to Germany (77%) and Britain (73%).[609] Particularly in the U.S., the worries about free trade are mostly directed at the relations with Asia and large developing countries such as China and India, not transatlantic trade.

In both the U.S. and the EU the political elites are representatives of the central executive branches (U.S. federal government and European Commission) that are more committed to market liberalization than their domestic constituencies and the general public. U.S. presidents and EU officials "have been relatively unsuccessful in winning the war of ideas over the benefits

---

[608] For the WIIT polls, see *www.wiit.org/poll*. Other surveys showing larger opposition to free trade are cited in Shoch 2001, p. 220.

[609] World Economic Forum Survey of 25,000 citizens across 25 countries. *http://www.weforum.org/site/homepublic.nsf/Content/People+around+the+World+Increasingly+Favour+Globalization+but+Worry+about+Jobs,+Poverty+and+Environment.*

of trade and capital liberalization."[610] At the same time, the transatlantic aspects of the trade agenda enjoy the highest support and are subject to the least controversy. Notwithstanding a sudden shift in popular sentiments, there should be just enough support for free trade on both sides of the Atlantic to keep trade liberalization on track.

7.1.2. The Domestic Political Process

Trade policy has always been at the crossroad of domestic and foreign policy except during the Cold War, it was primarily in the hands of the foreign-policy establishment. The collapse of the Soviet Union allowed domestic politics to acquire a much larger role in foreign policy on both sides of the Atlantic.[611] Another complicating factor for the decision-making process has been the increase in the international role of NGOs, through which governments have little control over what gets on the international agenda, much less the eventual outcome.[612]

The political process therefore seems increasingly messy on both sides of the Atlantic. Both American and European observers usually understand and defend the intricacies of their own system, yet are baffled by the developments on the other side. Americans are frustrated with the difficult decision-making process between 15 member states, the European Parliament (whose role is still poorly understood in Washington) and the Commission. They worry about the growing influence of environmental groups, consumer advocates and other NGOs on key aspects of trade-related economic policy, particularly by pressuring the European Parliament. Meanwhile, they are astounded by the influence on foreign and trade policy of individual members of Congress with little international understanding and the power of special commercial interests.[613] The U.S. embargo against Cuba that played such a damaging role in transatlantic relations in the 1990s is their case in point: a policy proven to be ineffective and even counterproductive but kept in place against all reason by special interests and electoral politics.

While the U.S. suffers from the "privatization" of trade policy with special interests calling the tune, non-trade issues swamp the EU trade agenda as it

[610] Pollack/Shaffer 2001, p. 297.
[611] Mathew 2001.
[612] Ibid.
[613] Hugo Paemen, the former EU ambassador to the U.S. told the author that "the USTR is much more responsive to special interests than the equivalent in the Commission. The textile negotiator in the USTR comes from the textile industry and will go back there once his job is finished. This would be inconceivable in the EU. I was always farther away from specific interests than my counterparts in the USTR." (Interview with Hugo Paemen, EU ambassador to the U.S. from 1993 to 1999, on April 10, 2002 in Washington, D.C.)

experiences a "politicization" of trade policy. The proliferation of public-interest groups in Washington suggests that the U.S. policy process is exposed to similar influences as the EU bodies.[614] In both systems, legislators, civil servants and the media show little interest in "multilateral bargaining and the delicate compromises that characterize transatlantic relations," noted one British observer. "The gap between transgovernmental cooperation and domestic understanding is as wide in Europe as within the United States...the similarities between Washington and Brussels are greater than the differences."[615]

As mentioned in chapter 2, the U.S. politics of trade have been a favorite subject of political scientists since the Schattschneider study of the Smoot-Hawley tariff in 1935. As Drestler demonstrated, the slide into full protectionism did not happen because the executive branch took hold of trade policy and Congress agreed to legislate itself out of the business of making product-specific trade law.[616] The Cold War consensus that trade agreements were part of the presidency's grand international strategy frayed in the early 1970s when Congress reinserted itself into trade policy. The following three decades saw a reversal of the roles of the two parties as the free trade banner moved from the Democrats to Republicans and the need for every trade initiative to create complex and fragile coalitions across the geographical and ideological spectrum.[617] This has become increasingly difficult for both Democratic and Republican presidents, but certainly not impossible: Clinton got NAFTA, the Uruguay Round Agreement and the PNTR with China passed, Bush the renewal of fast-track authority. The need to invest plenty of time and political capital for trade initiatives might make future administrations inclined to bypass such issues. Yet the difficulty of the political process is not limited to trade and in virtually every domestic area and on many foreign-policy issues, the president is up against powerful coalitions. Compared to purely domestic issues such as tax or environmental policy, trade offers the executive still a fair amount of freedom.

In the EU, many of the same patterns can be observed. Trade policy is one of the few areas of a clear prerogative of the European Commission (despite the important role of the 133 Committee and the gray area in services and intellectual property created by the ECJ ruling of 1994). Building on a rule-

---

[614] Porter 2002 quotes the study by Baumgarner/Leech 1998, which shows that the number of U.S. associations registered in the U.S. increased from 5,843 in 1959 to 23,298 in 1995, while the share of trade and business associations dropped from 39 percent to 18 percent. Thus, the number of trade and business associations climbed from 2,278 to 4,193, the number of other groups jumped from 3,565 to 24,105.

[615] Wallace 2001, p. 30 and p. 32

[616] Destler 1995, p. 13

[617] For recent studies on the U.S. domestic trade policy process see Gibson 1999, Mundo 2000, and Shoch 2001.

based liberal system created by a series of intra-governmental treaties of which all emphasized the removal of internal economic barriers, the Commission has actually forged a powerful coalition for external trade liberalization. As European elites, justifying the philosophical underpinnings of the common market, continued to espouse the benefits of free internal trade and lower barriers, it became increasingly difficult to defend external trade barriers as a matter of principle. The neo-liberal consensus among the elites in monetary and fiscal policy (the basis for the Euro) also spilled over into foreign trade policy.[618] As free-trade members like Germany, Britain, the Netherlands and Sweden clash with the more protectionist Mediterranean countries, they are forced to make significant concessions in specific areas. With the exception of agriculture, the outcome has usually been a step toward more rather than less free trade.[619]

Negotiating EU trade policy usually involves more than a standoff between a unified Commission and some member governments. Each government is lobbied by domestic special interests and has to take electoral and often coalitional factors into account. Therefore, EU trade policy is a three-level game. The European Parliament has no direct role in commercial policy but can shape regulatory policy on environment and consumer protection that easily become the behind-the-border barriers so typical of modern trade disputes. There are also repeated rifts within the Commission, based on nationality and the area of responsibility.[620] As trade disputes shift from tariff to regulatory questions, the Commission's power becomes increasingly circumscribed.

The fragmentation of the political process both in the U.S. and the EU has not resulted in continued deadlock but rather in negotiated outcomes that take a variety of interests into account. Decisive governmental activism has become much harder, even in countries with a unified government such as Britain. Whenever the political leadership and the public see a need for action, the creaky political apparatus starts to produce results. This might make the emergence of new and often unexpected trade disputes more likely and the attainment of trade agreement more difficult, yet as long as the political leadership remains committed to transatlantic cooperation and free trade, the overall balance is unlikely to be tipped toward protectionism.

Both proponents and opponents of free trade have in recent year tried to internationalize their lobby efforts. The efforts by multinational corporations to create a transnational business lobby for trade liberalization through the TABD had less success than environmental and human rights groups, who used internet and grass-root organization skills to build cross-border coalitions

---

[618] For an analysis of the consensus behind EMU, see McNamara 1998.

[619] Hanson 1998.

[620] For example the controversial vote in favor of the GM labeling directive in July 2001.

against free trade. The failure of the MAI negotiations in 1998 and the mayhem in Seattle is evidence of their power. The attempt to integrate them into a transatlantic structure through the various non-business transatlantic dialogues has done little to bridge the gap between proponents and opponents of free trade.

7.1.3. Competition and Convergence of Economic Policy

The following section a look at an often-posed question that at first seems quite detached from trade policy: Are Europe and America growing together or drifting apart? The consequences for trade relations of diverging and converging trends are not necessarily straightforward. For instance, convergence in some areas might actually lead to more conflict if it heightens competition; divergence can facilitate trade by increasing specialization. However, the opposite can also be true.

Let us first look at trends in economic performance. A sharp increase in the productivity of either side, just like a one-sided change in overall economic philosophy, could sharply reduce the level of economic cooperation. The growing feeling of many Americans that the U.S. economy was falling behind Europe and Japan added to pressures for protectionism in the 1980s, as did non-synchronized fiscal and monetary policies between the U.S. and the major European countries. Neither of these trends is currently visible.

The U.S. economy has outperformed Europe since the mid-1990s when productivity growth rates accelerated from its sluggish pace of previous decades. From 1995 to 2001, productivity posted a 2.7 percent average annual increase, well above the 1.4 percent between 1973 (the start of the first oil crisis) and 1995, and close to the 2.9 percent rate of the 1948-1973 post-war era.[621] In about the same period, EU productivity growth slowed down to 1.3 percent from 2.2 percent in the previous two decades.[622] Combined with much stronger job creation, higher labor participation rates and longer work hours, U.S. real GDP expanded at almost twice the rate of the EU after 1995.[623] The main reason was the U.S. lead in the IT industry, the leader in productivity gains, and the better integration of the new information technology into the "old economy".

---

621 Department of Commerce and Department of Labor statistics, quoted in Baily 2002.

622 Data from Wiener Institut für Wirtschaftsforschung (WIFO) quoted in Aiginger/Landesmann 2002. The EU figures cover the period 1995-2000 and 1975-1995. The comparative U.S. figures from the WIFO study would be 2.3 percent for 1995-2000 and 1.2 percent for 1975-1995.

623 For 1995-2000, the annual growth rates are 4.1 percent for the U.S. and 2.6 percent for the EU (WIFO). Compared to the Eurozone, the difference is even more startling because of strong growth in Britain.

The dismal EU economic performance may have caused a protectionist and "dirigist" backlash in Europe. Instead, European leaders used the U.S. as their model and at the Lisbon Summit in June 2000, they agreed on ambitious goals of deregulation and structural reforms in European labor and product markets. There is still broad support for a European social market model and wide opposition to American-style capitalism. Still, the resurgence of the U.S. economy has, perhaps surprisingly, brought U.S. and Europe closer together and not pulled them further apart.

The "Lisbon spirit" is actually part of a larger convergence of transatlantic economic policy that can be traced back several decades. U.S. and European policies were not always totally synchronized, and neither were the EU countries among themselves. Since the early to mid-1980s, all countries developed their economic policies among similar lines. In monetary policy, fighting inflation had always been the primary goal of the Deutsche Bundesbank. Starting in 1980, the U.S. Federal Reserve adopted rigid anti-inflation policies and between 1983 and 1986, most major European countries subordinated their monetary policies to those of Germany. While the Fed often had more emphasis on growth and more tolerance for inflation than the Bundesbank (and later the European Central Bank), the differences were overall quite marginal.

In fiscal policy, after the binge of the early Reagan years the U.S. entered a path of budget consolidation in 1982 that accelerated in the Bush Sr. tax increases of 1990 and the Clinton tax hikes of 1993. It took over 15 years to wipe out the huge deficits but by 2000, the U.S. had a massive budget surplus. Most European countries had smaller deficits to begin with. In the 1991 Maastricht Treaty, they also committed themselves to smaller budget deficits and in the 1997 growth and stability pact to a long-term policy of balanced budgets. Even countries that did not join the Euro in the first round (i.e. Britain and Sweden) brought their budgets into surplus. However, these changes were not permanent and both the U.S. and the EU have departed, at different rates, from debt consolidation. In Europe, debate sparked in 2003 when larger nations like Germany and France refused to meet the fiscal debt requirements of the stability pact. In the U.S., the war on terrorism and the occupation in Iraq has rapidly created a budget deficit equal to about six percent of world gross savings with seven percent deterioration in the ratio of deficit relative to GDP since 2000.[624]

Deregulation started in the U.S. under the Carter administration and accelerated under the Republican presidents Reagan and Bush Sr. In Europe, the Britain's government under Margaret Thatcher took the lead in the early 1980s.

---

[624] Balls, Andrew, "Fiscal deficit in US threatens world economy, says the IMF," Financial Times, April 15, 2004.

By the end of the decade, most European governments were committed to reducing state involvement in the economy by privatization and deregulation. The most striking example is France that continued to pay lip service to its exceptionalist model of state-led capitalism, and yet became a model for privatization and deregulation in the 1990s, especially under the Socialist government of Premier Lionel Jospin from 1997 to 2002.[625]

Notwithstanding these trends of economic convergence, the U.S. and the EU still feature different models of social organization. While large parts of the European business and political elites have become adherents to a more Anglo-Saxon way of doing business, they are not ready to give up the European model as a whole. The last few years has seen American triumphalism matched by a European belief in moral, social and in the long run even economic superiority, reinforced by the accounting scandals involving large U.S. corporations like Enron and WorldCom.

How big are the differences between the two sociopolitical models, and to what extent can differences affect economic and trade relations? The debate is often shaped by extreme caricature views of the other side: An America that has "sold its soul to savage capitalism and the military-industrial complex,"[626] and a European economy, like Gulliver in Lilliput, by a horribly expensive welfare state, rigid labor protection and an overbearing economy.

True, America and Europe often approach social and economic problems from a different perspective. Immigrants escaping repressive European states founded the United States; the biggest challenge was to create some form of order in an unstructured space of potential anarchy and unregulated markets. In Europe, it was the other way around as the authoritarian nation-states created in the 17th century underwent a gradual process of political and economic liberalization. Britain and the Netherlands were the pioneers of liberalization, and still demonstrate some of the most liberal political and economic systems, though other European countries have caught up. In the U.S., the sharp increase in state activism in the 1960s has been rolled back but the state is still often gaining new functions in areas where the free market seems to fail, health care for example.

At the beginning of the 21st century, the two models are still not the same. Yet compared to the rest of the world, America and Western Europe function surprisingly similarly. Europeans often underestimate the amount of protection granted to individual workers through legislation and the courts in the U.S. Americans tend to ignore the signs of a lively and innovative business culture in all European countries that rivals its own. On the Fraser Institute Index for economic freedom, one of two popular measures for market freedom, the U.S.

[625] Cohen/Pisany-Ferry 2002.
[626] Blinken 2001, p. 39

leads Europe with 89 to 81. Still, the difference between the U.S. and the EU pales in comparison to the difference between them and the developing countries, which ranged from 51 for Africa to 72 for Latin America.[627] The transatlantic contrasts are even weaker because there is no uniform European model: the difference between Britain and Spain is certainly larger than between Britain and the U.S.

However, there are some distinct gaps. Most striking is the higher inequality in the U.S. compared to the EU. In the 1990s, America adjusted to economic change by allowing inequality to rise, Europe by accepting higher unemployment.[628] Both trends were the consequence of different degrees of wage flexibility. Inequality in the U.S. rose, however, not because poverty grew (it actually declined) but because of an unprecedented increase income and wealth on the top.

The lower inequality in European societies has important social consequences. Crime rates are lower, cities are safer, fewer people have guns at home and European governments were able to abolish the death penalty without causing a popular backlash. "American capital punishment...has become for Europeans a symbol of the weaknesses of American domestic society and law."[629]

The two societies have also different legal traditions – with the adversarial court system in the U.S. providing more safeguards for suspects and defendants, but creating a much harsher sentencing practice. In Europe, the chances of acquittal are usually smaller than in the U.S., but sentencing is often less harsh. International law, including trade law, is affected by the differences in the civil and the common and law: European legislators codify all laws, creating rules for every contingency, while Americans leave it to courts to create precedence.

These differences in domestic policies would not matter if both sides did not feel the desire to impose its norms on the rest of the world. The U.S. is particularly prone to this form of intellectual arrogance, thanks to missionary attitudes of its founding fathers. U.S. narcissism has always been coupled with incredulity over the existence of countries that do not wish to be like the United States.[630] Americans regard the founding documents of the U.S. as the greatest accomplishment in modern political thought. The constitution of 1787 created a unique and revolutionary model for the political organization that has worked without any fundamental changes until today. It succeeded to balance state rights with federal functions, individual liberties (with the glaring exception of slavery) with the common interests, integrated people with different languages,

---

[627] Freeman 2002.
[628] Blinken 2001, p. 40.
[629] Wallace 2001, p. 28.
[630] Stuermer 2001, p. 145.

religions and cultures through open immigration and a melting-pot philosophy. Most importantly, it introduced the principle of checks and balances into modern politics. While several European countries succeeded in the creation of centralized nation-states in the 19th century, they failed repeatedly in their attempts to build larger political entities. The multi-ethnic Hapsburg Empire collapsed just like multi-ethnic Yugoslavia, and the two totalitarian experiments of empire building – Nazi Germany and the Soviet Union – ended in disaster and decay.

The European Community/European Union is arguably the first new model of a large-scale political organization that has the potential to rival the United States in political and economic efficiency. Unlike the U.S., the EU decided not to abolish the sovereignty of its constituent elements but to weaken it through an increasingly dense web of functional integration based on intra-government bargaining. The Europeans have effectively redefined the concept of sovereignty. Many Americans have little understanding of it because their country abandoned the option of confederalism during the constitutional debates of 1787. But to their surprise, European multi-state integration is working and its redefined concept of sovereignty often seems to fit the modern world of global interdependence better than the American single-state approach. Flush with a new sense of self-confidence, European leaders increasingly regard the fruits of the EU decision-making process as a model for the rest of the world and an ideal basis for world standards.

This attitude creates plenty of conflict potential with the U.S. "Competing claims to superior social and economic models could well deteriorate into competing anti-European and anti-American rhetoric," warns the British liberal political scientist William Wallace, "Transatlantic relations would benefit from a process of moral disarmament, in which both sides moderate their rhetoric and their attacks on each other's failings."[631]

The feeling of European superiority is strongest in the area of environmental policy. The U.S. environmental record is better than depicted in the European press – the U.S. made catalytic converters in cars mandatory years before any European countries and has stricter standards on water purity and air quality than many EU countries. There are also huge variations in environmental rules and awareness within the EU, as most Southern countries have only recently begun to show any concern for the environment. Still, "in the last decade, Europe has become steadily greener, with German and Dutch attitudes spreading to the rest of the EU."[632] Environmental groups exercise far more influence on public attitudes and policies, particularly in EU bodies, than in the

---

631 Wallace 2001, p. 29

632 Mathews 2001.

U.S. Garbage recycling and energy conservation is increasingly becoming a characteristics of good European citizenship.

The growing concern over food safety is fueled by health scares over BSE and dioxin contaminated food, a testimony to the deficiencies of the European regulatory systems. U.S. officials like to point to the rarity of food scares in the U.S. of which they attribute to the professionalism of specialized non-political agencies like the FDA.[633] Still, the same groups and attitudes that have made Europeans more concerned for the environment also made them turn against certain farming and food processing technologies like hormone-treated beef and GMO. They prize natural and organic food products, even raw milk cheeses that are deemed unsafe by U.S. regulators. The U.S. public, in contrast, is hardly aware of the proliferation of gene-altered food products. It cares about taste and price, not the potential risks of the production process.[634]

Even on food habits, there may be more convergence than differentiation between the U.S. and Europe: McDonald's and other U.S. based fast-food chains are still gaining market share in Europe, even in France. The more European mass consumers adopt the American way of life, the larger the potential for conflict.[635] The difference in social and personal values on food safety has been the cause of several transatlantic trade disputes in the past and could become the driving force behind much stronger rifts in the future.

The trade conflict over cultural products, particularly over movies, has been relatively muted since the Uruguay Round Agreement though this could easily change in the coming years. Neither generous subsidies for European filmmakers nor restrictive quotas for U.S. movie and television products have stopped Hollywood from increasing its already dominating position in the European film industry. The U.S. market share in Europe stood at eighty percent in 1999, while European filmmakers have only a miniscule market share in the U.S.[636] European backlash against this loss of cultural self-determination is likely to trigger major tensions with the U.S. because audio-visual products have become one of the major export products of the American economy.

The other area of emotionally charged disagreement is America's habit to waste plenty of energy through gas-guzzling cars and air-conditioning. On energy consumption, the U.S. and Europe are truly worlds apart: U.S. per capita consumption of 6.2 tons of oil equivalent a year is twice as high as the 3.1 tons consumed in the EU.[637] The U.S, with five percent of the world population and

633 Jonquières 2001.
634 Echols 1998.
635 Blinken 2001, p. 40.
636 See André Lange (ed.), Statistical Yearbook 2000. Film, television, video (Strasbourg: European Audiovisual Observatory, 2000), quoted from Wagleitner 2002
637 Mathews 2001.

20 percent of global GDP, consumes a quarter of the world's energy. The U.S. dependency to cheap energy and European anger over America's profligacy affected the negotiations over a climate change convention during the Clinton years and thereafter. Despite the strong environmental credentials of vice president Al Gore, the U.S. argued for less stringent requirements for the control of greenhouse emissions during the Kyoto conference in December 1997, but ultimately signed the agreement to bring global carbon dioxide emissions 5.2 per cent below their 1990 level by 2012.[638] In the following three years, the U.S. and the EU failed repeatedly to agree on the implementation guidelines for the Kyoto protocol. The last attempt was made at the Hague summit in November 2000, when the outgoing Clinton administration attempted to convince the EU to allow trading in emissions rights and other flexible mechanisms to reach the Kyoto goals at the least cost. "These proposals made good sense, but the Europeans resented any mechanism that might enable the United States to meet its Kyoto commitments without sufficient sacrifices and changes in its profligate lifestyle...while criticism of the U.S. position on climate control has become an automatic applause line for European politicians, the inability of any European country to meet its emissions reduction commitments under the 1997 Kyoto Protocol has been completely obscured behind a cloud of anti-U.S. rhetoric."[639]

An agreement at The Hague may not have secured U.S. participation in the Kyoto process either, because the U.S. Senate had previously voted 95-0 against the convention and showed no inclination to change its mind. Even so, Europeans reacted with shock and anger when President George W. Bush in March 2001 announced the end of U.S. participation in the Kyoto process. Rather than burying the accord, the EU pressed ahead and by making many of the concessions that it denied to the U.S. at The Hague and it reached agreement with Japan and the other industrialized countries on a U.N. treaty on climate change at the Bonn summit in July 2001. The absence of the world's largest energy consumer undermines the effectiveness of the treaty and may eventually lead to trade disputes if European industry starts to complain about the one-sided obligations to reduce carbon dioxide emissions.

7.2. The International Perspective: Trade Relations and the Transatlantic Security Partnership

Even if the U.S. remains internationally engaged, there are plenty of analysts from the U.S. and Europe who doubt the continued U.S. commitment to the transatlantic security partnership established after World War II and its main

638 "Rubbing Sleep from their Eyes," *Economist*, December 11, 1997

639 Mathews 2001.

pillar the North Atlantic Treaty Organization. Given that NATO was established to fight the Soviet threat, the disappearance of the Soviet Union and Communism makes a decline in U.S. interest in NATO inevitable. There is also a general consensus that the disappearance of the common enemy costs the Western alliance some of its historical cohesion. There is, however, a lively debate among international relations experts what this change in interests and priorities on both sides means for the transatlantic partnership. While scholars from the Realist school tend to predict a growing alienation between the U.S. and Europe,[640] advocates of the liberal and functionalist schools see that the global need for cooperation and governance and the economic self-interest of both sides will keep these trends in check.[641]

The debate is critical for the argument of this study. If leaders in the U.S. and the EU no longer care much about the state of their overall relationship, trade conflicts are likely to go uncontained and unresolved. The consequence will be a breakdown or at least a significant deterioration in international economic cooperation with detrimental effects for the global economy. For the political damage-control mechanism between the U.S. and the EU to work, it requires not only an enlightened sense of economic self-interest but also an over-arching sense of transatlantic community and friendship.

To analyze the strength of the transatlantic relationship in this vital area, I will focus on three centrifugal forces: unilateralism vs. multilateralism, different issue priorities, and bipolar rivalry. I will also cover the two converging factors of cultural affinity and functional necessity.

7.2.1. Unilateralism vs. Multilateralism

The U.S. decision to abandon the Kyoto process confirmed European preconception of America on two levels: it was a policy that was damaging the environment and putting selfish interests of the U.S. ahead of the global good. Coming on the heels of the U.S. rejection of the international Landmine Treaty, the Comprehensive Test Ban Treaty (CTBT), the International Criminal Court (ICC), the rejection of Kyoto suggested that the world's only superpower was abandoning the multilateral post-war world order that it helped itself to create. A growing number of observers noted, "different approaches to foreign and security policy, with Washington relying on its sheer power to gets its way and Europe putting faith in international institutions, regimes and norms to tackle problems of common concern."[642] Several decades of European integration,

---

[640] For example, Walt 1998.

[641] See, among others, Bergsten 1999, Blinken 2001 and Wallace 2001. Daalder 2001 takes an equivocal position. The functionalist argument is often normative The U.S. and Europe should continue to cooperate in the interest of global stability.

[642] Daalder 2001, p. 553.

"allowed Europeans to acquire day-to-day experience—and hence a level of comfort—with exactly the kind of painful compromise, frustrating negotiations, and less-than-perfect outcomes that characterize multilateral problem solving in larger forums like the United Nations, the WTO, and the secretariats of major global treaties."[643] The differences in approaches to multilateral institutions between the U.S. and the EU came to a major crisis point over the war with Iraq, especially since the decision to go into war without a second UN resolution came after the U.S. unilaterally pulling out of the above mentioned international treaties and conventions. The growing transatlantic rift highlighted not only the differences on the continents threat perception, but also their views on unilateralism vs. multilateralism. The resulting failure to find agreement within the UN weakened transatlantic coordination and cooperation as Richard Lambert wrote, "In today's very different world, Washington no longer feels this sense of urgency in its relationship with Europe, and it is unrealistic to imagine that the Bush administration is going to expend much effort in building bridges."[644]

This trend could have significant consequences on trade policy, currently the most developed area of multilateral cooperation. Notwithstanding certain unilateral strands in U.S. trade policy such as the proliferation of anti-dumping suits and the cases where U.S. sanctions policy interfered with trade and capital flows, Washington has remained faithful to the multilateral trade regime, even under the Bush Jr. administration. Given the extent to which international trade rules are in line with U.S. economic interests, this is not a real surprise.

The smoldering conflict over the different approach to international policy erupted early in the Bush Jr. administration. While Clinton "frequently gave the appearance of having been forced into taking unilateralist positions against own expressed preferences,"[645] the Republican from Texas seemed to embrace unilateralism wholeheartedly and differed in that respect from his father's more internationalist outlook. The Bush administration paid some lip service to multilateralism in the immediate aftermath of September 11, but then proceeded to fight the war against terrorism virtually on its own and according to its own rules.

There are structural reasons to expect the tension between multilateral and unilateral approaches to increase in the coming years, not the least the historically unprecedented military superiority of the U.S., whose share of global defense spending is about 40 percent.[646] But one should not forget that significant elements in the U.S. political elite, particularly among Democrats,

---

643 Mathews 2001.
644 Lambert, Robert, "Misunderstanding Each Other," *Foreign Affairs*, March/April 2003, 71.
645 Daalder 2001, p. 561.
646 Paul Kennedy, "The Eagle has Landed," Financial Times, February 2, 2002.

and some of the leading international thinkers support a multilateral approach to world leadership. John Gerard Ruggie argued that, "a multilateral world order vision is singularly compatible with America's own collective self-concept...the willed formation of an international community based on 'a universal or general foundation open in principle to everyone.'"[647] And just when the furor over Bush's neglect for the interest of European interests reached its peak, Joseph Nye, the dean of the Kennedy School of Government at Harvard, argued in his latest book that "the world's only superpower can't go it alone."[648] A Democratic administration would in all likelihood embrace a good share of the European concepts of multilateralism and if it is not held back by a Republican-led Congress, it could also implement this approach.

7.2.2. Priorities

Regardless of whether the current U.S. president is a Democrat or a Republican, the U.S. and Europe have very different priorities when it comes to global issues. More disturbing than a divergent regional focus could be signs that the U.S. and Europe have very different priorities when it comes to the issues. Washington takes "a traditionalist view of international politics,"[649] focusing narrowly on security threats and "hard power" like military strength and diplomatic leadership. This tendency increased under the Bush Jr. administration, particularly after the terror attacks of September 11, 2001 that demonstrated the vulnerability of the American mainland to terrorism. Europeans have long lived with terrorism, though at a smaller scale. Still, they worry more about global challenges like climate change, environmental degradation, migration, poverty, infectious diseases, and trafficking in women and children. These problems cannot be solved with military might, but only through "soft power" instruments of persuasion, cooperation and international treaties. While drug trafficking worries both Americans and Europeans, Europeans resent the U.S. policy of focusing exclusively on drug production. While the treatment of drug addicts differs widely in the EU, there is general agreement that only a reduction in demand can solve the drug problem.

The different concerns on the two sides of the Atlantic contribute to the unilateralist-multilateralist debate. Europeans generally tend to worry about issues which international cooperation, not a show of strength. All these differences are a matter of emphasis and not necessarily of principle. U.S. policy makers, particularly Democrats, are also concerned about "new security threats" like migration and trafficking and Europeans do not close their eyes

---

[647] Ruggie 1994, p. 564.
[648] Nye 2002.
[649] Ibid., p. 555.

before the dangers of terrorism and weapons of mass destruction held by rogue states. A majority of Europeans supported the U.S. war against the Taliban regime in Afghanistan in 2001/2 in principle; the just disagreed with certain elements and measures. A key EU member, Britain, was a part of the coalition to topple Saddam Hussein in 2003, while the wide-spread opposition in most of continental Europe was echoed by broad criticism of the Bush administration's Iraq policy in the U.S. media and public opinion.

7.2.3. Rivalry

The post-Cold War era witnessed two fundamental changes in the international system: the collapse of the Soviet Union and the rise of an integrated Europe. A third trend, the economic decline of Japan, was more gradual but also contributed to the emerging sense of a new bipolar structure in the world between the U.S. and the EU (at least in the economic realm). From a Realist perspective, bipolarity is a recipe for conflict, notwithstanding all assurances of cooperation and friendship. Those political analysts who regard a currency as an instrument of national power see the Euro primarily as a challenge to the global dominance of the dollar, not as a way to facilitate business relations and economic coordination within the EU. "A United States of Europe will be larger, wealthier, and potentially more powerful than the United States of America. Overtime, Americans would probably come to regard such a European superstate as a major global rival," warned Stephen Walt.[650] President Bush echoed these concerns when he justified the Free Trade Area of the Americas (FTAA) in 2001 as a way for the Western hemisphere to "combine in a common market so we can compete in the long-term with the Far East and Europe."[651]

If worries about Europe's emergence as a global power were to dominate U.S. thinking, one would expect the U.S. to oppose previous and future moves toward European integration. The opposite is true as the U.S. was a driving force behind the first initiatives for a unified Europe, the European Payments Union (EPU), the European Coal and Steel Community (ECSC) and the EEC. Washington sometimes questioned, though never opposed, the creation of a single currency and even encouraged the establishment of a EU defense force. Most American policymakers support the full realization of a united Europe, with the express hope that it will make Europe a stronger partner for America.[652]

---

650 Walt 1998, p. 7.

651 Closing press conference of President George W. Bush at the Summit of the Americas, Quebec City, Quebec, Canada. April 22, 2001.

652 Blinken 2001, p. 44.

Some scholars see a good match between the new American 'hyper power', as the former French foreign minister Hubert Vedrine described the U.S. predominance in military, economic, cultural and technological affairs, and an integrated Europe.[653] The EU has little use of a weak and sickly U.S., while, to quote Samuel Huntington, "healthy cooperation with Europe is the prime antidote for the loneliness of U.S. superpowerdom."[654] Moreover, "the United States remains Europe's ideal ally, not least because we are an ocean away and do not threaten to dominate it," argued Walt.[655]

True, U.S. policy is not always consistent; its approach to European integration sometimes suffers from "schizophrenia on the international front. On the one hand, it claims that Europe...should assert greater international responsibility and share the 'burdens of leadership'. On the other hand, its revealed preference is to try to maintain American dominance...and to exploit national differences within Europe whenever possible."[656] At the same time, European leaders shy away from direct confrontations and open battles with the U.S. even in the economic area, thereby acknowledging the continued dominance of the world's sole superpower.[657]

Another more concrete form of transatlantic rivalry is a fight over international export markets with the aid of subsidies, diplomatic pressures and even industrial espionage, increasingly seen as just another form of strategic trade policy.[658] As noted in chapter 3, the Clinton administration changed the lackadaisical U.S. approach to export promotion and began to match European and Japanese commercial diplomacy. These efforts faded somewhat, however, when Commerce Secretary Ron Brown died in a plane crash in Bosnia in April 1996, where he led a mission to gain reconstruction contracts for U.S. companies. His successor was less outspoken und less interested in state-led export promotion. Industrial espionage by the U.S. became a hot-bottom topic in 2000, when a European Parliament report suggested that the U.S. and Britain used their global satellite surveillance system Echelon to spy on continental European firms. U.S. officials rejected these charges and argued that the only reason for spying was to counter bribery practices commonly used by European companies that are illegal in the U.S.[659] While these episodes tend to create bad feelings and strong headlines, the stable truce in the aircraft business shows that

---

[653] Walker 2000, p. 27.
[654] Quoted in Ludlow 2001, p. 169.
[655] Walt 1998, p. 10.
[656] Bergsten 1999, p. 30.
[657] Ibid., p. 23/24.
[658] Whitney/Gaisford 1996.
[659] "That's right, my continental friends, we have spied on you because you bribe", said former CIA director R. James Woolsey. "Why we Spy on Our Allies," The Wall Street Journal, March 17, 2000.

commercial rivalry is unlikely to become a major factor in transatlantic relations.[660]

Even though functionalists do not share the prediction of coming transatlantic rivalry by the Realist school, they see an urgent need for the U.S. to change its attitude toward Europe in order to avoid a future proliferation of conflicts. Washington should offer Europe "a greater – indeed an equal – voice in their relationship,"[661] as "economic relations between the United States and the European Union will…rest increasingly on a foundation of virtual equality."[662] If the U.S. persists in treating a self-confident Europe as a junior partner, the Realist scenario may come true after all, they warn.

7.2.4. Cultural Ties

Some of the most intuitive arguments in favor of a continued transatlantic relationship deal with the cultural ties between Americans and Europeans. Starting with Karl Deutsch and his "pluralistic security community"[663] generation of scholars argued that a compatibility of core values creates a feeling of solidarity and loyalty among states, which guarantees cooperation and peaceful change. More recently, Samuel Huntington identified the fault lines in the international system between a common Western bloc, including both the U.S. and Europe, and other world regions with different cultural and religious traditions.[664] The European ethnic background of most Americans, the shared religious heritage, and the strong similarities in life style, values and consumer culture make for strong bonds beyond the inter-governmental relationship.

According to Walt, "this source of transatlantic solidarity is often overstated."[665] He points to the fact that the U.S. fought in the 20th century two major wars against a European power that had previously been the biggest source of immigrants. The demographic shifts in the U.S. mean that the share of Americans with European ancestors is declining, as is the share of the population living in the Northeast, where ties to Europe are strongest. Finally, the generation that forged the transatlantic tie during World War II is passing away, and "watching 'Saving Private Ryan' is no substitute for having lived through the real thing." The same is true for Europe, where the post-war generation was used to following the U.S. lead. Among younger Europeans, anti-Americanism seems to be on the rise even if they watch Hollywood movies, munch Big Macs and wear Nike sneakers. The new anti-Americanism

[660] For a more pessimistic prognosis from a leading realist, see Calleo 2001, p. 222-223.
[661] Daalder 2001, p. 563.
[662] Bergsten, p. 20.
[663] Deutsch et al. 1957.
[664] Huntington 1996.
[665] Walt 1998, p. 7.

combines old-fashioned leftist views with a new unease about cultural and economic globalization and resentment for the "strongest power on the block."[666]

Yet, anti-Americanism does not imply that Europeans are less focused on the U.S. than before. Similarly, the U.S. has not found a substitute for Europe as a partner and friend, and perhaps never will. Ivo Daalder points out that, "the worst bilateral relationship between the United States and a European country (France) is still much better, deeper and more significant than the best bilateral relationship the United States has with any country in Asia (Japan)."[667] When the U.S. needs a truly dependable partner, it can only find it in Europe. According to Blinken, "Europeans and Americans still look to each other before they look to anyone else. Their manifest and multiple affinities far outweigh their differences."[668]

7.2.5 Necessity

The strongest argument of the functionalist school for continued transatlantic cooperation is its necessity. The argument risks being circular as just because the world would be a worse place if Europe and America do not cooperate, it does not mean that cooperation will happen. Despite this fact, it can be argued that globalization has created an urgent need for global governance that only a transatlantic alliance can provide. The vast increase in international trade and financial flows has to be controlled by global rules and institutions, lest its destructive forces trigger a global backlash. Parallel to the global economy, there are global criminal networks, global social problems and global infectious diseases, all of which do not stop at national borders. Moreover, many of the institutions for global governance are already in place and others are being discussed. This creates an institutional incentive for U.S. and European leaders to resolve existing differences and work intensively toward joint strategies to deal with global problems. Even growing disagreements on various foreign-policy issues need not disrupt functional cooperation in areas of mutual interest.

7.2.6. Outlook

Just because officials from the U.S. and Europe continue to meet and discuss joint activities, it does not mean that they will really succeed when diverging views or competing interests stand in the way. The overriding force for successful international cooperation remains fear: fear of a common threat, of a

[666] Walker 2000, p. 27.
[667] Daalder 2001, p. 564.
[668] Blinken 2001, p. 48.

crisis that can poison the overall relationship, or of a problem that is bound to get worse. The Cold War, at least until the mid-1960s, created an overriding need for common action. The true test for transatlantic cooperation is not success in dealing with urgent problems, but the ability to make progress even in the absence of urgency.

The record since 1989 is mixed. In the security area, the alliance pulled together after Iraq's invasion of Kuwait, squabbled and hesitated for four disastrous years in Croatia and Bosnia, but acted in Kosovo just in time to avoid large-scale genocide. The only example of truly successful security cooperation was the preemptive diplomatic and military intervention in Macedonia that helped to prevent a violent conflict turning into a full-fledged war. Here, the painful lessons of the previous conflicts were apparently learnt. Europe and the U.S. pulled together after the terrorist attacks on September 11, 2001, but were subsequently deeply divided over the Iraq War.

Transatlantic cooperation is a victim of its own success. Success breeds complacency, and complacency allows parochial interests to overpower the common good. "The end of the Cold War has...given Europeans and Americans alike the luxury to be irresponsible – including the luxury of allowing themselves to drift further and further apart."[669]

Because transatlantic relations have a built-in feedback, this drift is self-correcting. Once conflicts rise to a level where they truly alarm the political leadership – especially when they spill over into the political and security realm – they will act to resolve the dispute and contain the damage. The tolerance of U.S. and European leaders for conflict, both in the security and economic areas, has become so high that disputes are left to escalate while officials delay mitigating action because they are preoccupied with other problems. The consequences of such a loose feedback loop are not necessarily full-fledged conflicts, but plenty of volatility and lost opportunities for cooperation. Even in those instances where the United States and Europe decide to act in concert, they are likely to do so only late in the game.[670]

Whether conflicts can be contained and resolved depends more than anything on the personal skills of the negotiators: In 1996/7, Clinton's emissary Stuart Eizenstat almost single-handedly resolved the fight over the Cuba and Iran-Libya sanctions, while the bad chemistry between Brittan and Barshefsky did more to inflame transatlantic trade tensions than any political or structural causes. The dynamics of disputes also depends on the available instruments of arbitration and conflict-solution. In trade, the creation of the WTO dispute-

---

[669] Daalder 2001, p.565. Other scholars describe the same phenomenon with different words. Walt compares the Atlantic Alliance to "Oscar Wilde's Dorian Gray, appearing youthful and robust as it grows older – but becoming even more infirm." Walt 1998, p. 11.
[670] Daalder 2001, p.565.

settlement body in 1995 has changed the rules of conflicts and has had a particular strong effect on transatlantic trade issue. The next section will look at the role of the WTO and evaluate some of the recent suggestions for improvement.

7.3. The Institutional Perspective: The WTO and Transatlantic Trade Disputes

The creation of the WTO and particularly its dispute-settlement mechanism (DSM) is probably the biggest change in international economic governance of the last few decades. Almost alone among international organizations, the WTO has court-like powers to rule on inter-state disputes and enforce these rulings through the authorization of trade sanctions. Yet since its start in 1995, the DSM has suffered various setbacks and has, in the eyes of a number of commentators, done little to advance the cause of free trade. It has performed particularly poorly on transatlantic issues, which make up 20 percent of all WTO disputes,[671] and may have actually exacerbated existing disputes and created new ones rather than settle them.

The development of a "trade court" has been gradual. At the GATT, itself a temporary framework that only became permanent because of the failure of the International Trade Organization (ITO), trade disputes were initially resolved through diplomatic means at semiannual meetings of the contracting parties. The first panels were set up in the 1950s, and it was not until the 1980s that GATT ruling became "legally precise and juridical in nature."[672] GATT reports were widely admired and often resulted in a change of trade policy through their normative power. However, based on the consensual nature of the GATT, any party could block the adoption of report or even the setup of a panel.

This lack of "teeth" was addressed and seemingly repaired in the Dispute Settlement Understanding (DSU) of the Uruguay Round Agreement. The process was unified and streamlined and WTO members lost the power to block a panel or a ruling. As a quid pro quo for the elimination of the veto, the DSU created the Appellate Body, which gave the losing side a second chance.[673] Just like the GATT, the WTO-DSU does not have an enforcement mechanism to guarantee compliance. GATT, steeped in the mercantilist spirit, envisaged in the case of "nullification or impairment" of agreed trade concessions the rebalancing of such concessions (i.e. an increase in tariffs) by the complainant. As GATT ruling required unanimity, this instrument was effectively never used.

---

[671] Sapir 2002. 48 of 251 disputes were between the U.S. and the EU. But 184 cases, or two thirds of all cases, involved either the U.S. or the EU and third parties.
[672] Jackson 2000, p. 183.
[673] Ibid., p. 204.

Under the WTO, the same mechanism assumed a different character. Because the suspension of trade concessions could be authorized against the will of the target country, they became like a trade sanction. The DSU never mentions sanctions, and "at no point did governments make a decided move from one paradigm to the other. It just happened through the application of WTO law."[674] Moreover, the lists other remedies like compliance and compensation (through a reduction in tariffs on other products) and treats retaliation only as a last resort. Retaliation is not a new concept in trade relations, though a staple of every trade war. What the WTO did was limiting the amount of retaliation to the equivalent to the damage done by the violation of WTO rules, making tit-for-tat retaliation the rule and preventing punitive sanctions. It also ruled out retroactive compensation for past damages. The DSU thus resembles more the Geneva Conventions to regulate warfare than a court.

In two of the most high-profile cases in front of the WTO, the banana and the hormone-treated beef complaints against the EU, tit-for-tat retaliation was not sufficient to force the losing side into compliance. Instead of liberalizing trade, the WTO intervention introduced more trade barriers into the world economy. As one economist lamented, "The WTO framework is abused as a vehicle of supporting violations of, rather than enforcing adherence to, the idea of free trade."[675] This experience made a growing number of experts question the efficacy of the DSM. Some even regard the move from GATT to the WTO as a retrograde step.[676]

In the quickly expanding literature on this question, there are several strands of thinking how this problem can be resolved. One school sees the problem in the refusal by the targeted country to comply with a WTO ruling. As John Jackson, one of the fathers of the WTO, argues, "the treaty imposes an international law obligation to perform and does not give a free choice to prefer compensatory measures."[677] A key concern here is the credibility of the WTO and its rules-based system, if countries are allowed ignore their obligations or violate the rules by accepting retaliation or making other concessions. Various ways to increase the chance of compliance have been proposed. In the banana and beef cases, the U.S. targeted the punitive tariffs to inflict the largest possible political damage and Congress tried to make them even more painful through the controversial carousel rotation. Others proposals that call for modifications of current WTO practices include a dramatic reduction in the length of procedures,[678] currently take two years or more, the imposition of

---

674 Charnovitz 2001, p. 807.
675 Kohler 2002.
676 Reinhardt 1999, p. 14.
677 Jackson 2000, p. 194.
678 Telephone interview with Charlene Barshefsky, United States Trade Representative from 1996 to 2001, on March 19, 2002.

punitive sanctions with a disproportionate ratio (perhaps double sanctions) or retroactive damages, multilateral sanctions in which the defendant is penalized by all WTO members, or the withdrawal of membership rights from countries in violation of a WTO ruling, e.g. making them ineligible to invoke the WTO dispute settlement.[679] Another solution advocated by some international law experts would be to integrate international trade agreements into domestic law. This would give individuals and businesses the power to enforce the implementation of WTO rulings through the domestic court system.[680]

Most violations of multilateral trade agreements remain unsanctioned because nobody files a complaint against them. Previously, this was attributed to the high cost and uncertain outcome of complaints under GATT. Because complaints have become easier and shorter under the WTO and cannot be blocked by the target, countries have an incentive now to look for violations among trading partners and file cases even if no major commercial interests are involved. Some scholars argue such a consistent "police-patrol" approach could help to reduce trade barriers all over the world.[681] This assumes that compliance will become the rule, rather than the exception.

There may be a more systemic reason for countries not to comply with WTO rulings than just bad behavior. As the economist Wilfred Elthier argued, trade agreements are incomplete contracts; they cannot cover every conceivable future development and dispute.[682] When countries sign these disputes, they do not know how difficult and painful it will be to meet these obligations. The option not to comply with certain rulings may be necessary to make a wide-reaching trade agreement politically acceptable. For example, the EU would not have signed the SPS Agreement if it had not believed that there were some escape clauses in case of massive public concern about an imported food product.

There are plenty of such informal escape clauses in the Uruguay Round Agreement; the 22,000 pages are full of "constructive ambiguities" without which the accord would have never been signed.[683] This was also featured in the earlier concept of an "interface" or buffer mechanism to "allow different

---

[679] Charnovitz 2001, pp. 823-828.

[680] Ernst-Ulrich Petersmann, "Dispute Prevention and Dispute Settlement," in Pollack/Shaffer 2001. There a major political and legal obstacles to such a change: The European Court of Justice has in the past rejected the application of WTO agreements in its jurisprudence, for example rejecting challenges to the EU banana regime on those grounds. Similarly, the 1994 Uruguay Round Agreements Act passed by Congress prevents U.S. courts to review the WTO-consistency of federal legislation.

[681] Sevilla 2000.

[682] Elthier 2000, p. 4.

[683] Guy de Jonquières, "Rules to Fight By," Financial Times, March 25, 2000.

economic systems to trade together harmoniously."[684] While these differences in opinion and interest should certainly be adjudicated, it is in every country's interest that the accuser is constrained in its ability to punish the violator. A country does not know whether it will find itself in the role of the accuser or of the accused.[685] Some trade experts warn that even the current, limited enforcement power of the WTO is too much to bear for sovereign nations and therefore "substantially and politically unsustainable." Governments may only continue to obey WTO rulings if the powers of the organization are curbed.[686]

Others, however, conclude that limited trade sanctions authorized by the WTO are actually a satisfactory outcome of a dispute: "A complaining government can signal its outrage, placate the injured domestic constituency and move on."[687] Unlike other forms of compensation, trade sanctions are self-implementing and do not require any action by the defendant. If the complaining government does not really expect compliance, it might impose the tariffs where it serves its own political or economic interests, for example in a vulnerable import-competing sector.

The main counter-argument against this approach is the absurdity that a trade-liberalizing organization ends up restricting trade, and the "self-punishing nature of trade retaliation" of which Adam Smith already noted.[688] As the report by the Metzler Commission on international financial institutions argued, "the injured country then suffers twice – once from the restrictions on its exports, imposed by foreign governments, and again when tariffs or duties raise the domestic cost of the foreign goods selected for retaliation. To compensate for the injury done by others, we impose costs on ourselves as well as them."[689] With some trade disputes resulting in billions of retaliatory sanctions, the effect on world trade could be disastrous. While sanctions are directed against governments, they hit private individuals and companies that are not responsible for the violation of WTO rules.[690] The Metzler Report of 2000 goes on to propose, "instead of retaliation, countries guilty of illegal trade practices should pay an annual fine equal to the value of the damages assessed by the panel or provide equivalent trade liberalization."

Compensation through tariff reductions that actually contribute to free trade, or monetary compensation (like in the case of the U.S. music copyright law) is widely seen as preferable to retaliation. Bhagwati calls for much smaller

---

684 Charnovitz 2001, p. 819.
685 Elthier 2000, p. 5.
686 Barfield 2001.
687 Charnovitz 2001, p. 813.
688 Ibid., p. 815.
689 Metzler 2000, chapter 5. In line with this thinking, counties like Ecuador and Canada chose not to impose tariffs to which they were authorized. See Charnovitz 2001, p. 792.
690 Charnovitz 2001, p. 811.

compensation payments "to reflect not the value of trade affected but the gains from trade lost (only a small fraction of the sales)."[691] Because of the most-favored-nation principle of the WTO, trade concessions would have to be granted to all trading partners. Monetary compensation also favors wealthy countries over poor states, which could not afford non-compliance.[692] Moreover, they need either cooperation or an international enforcement mechanism, which does not exist. Finally, they do not change that *pacta sunt servanda* that a persistent violation of international agreements undermines the legitimacy of international law.

A large number of experts, therefore, argue to keep the most controversial trade disputes out of the WTO and to settle them with the traditional instruments of diplomacy such as negotiations, mediation and informal arbitration. The argument is two-fold: on one hand, litigation at the WTO creates an atmosphere of belligerence and makes compromise much harder to reach. While trade should be about mutual benefit, a complaint at the WTO is about winning or losing and can result in verbal and even practical escalation.

The other argument is that certain issues do not lend themselves to the WTO process because they affect complex "behind-the-border" issues with strong political or emotional constraints. Gary Hufbauer distinguishes between market-access disputes, for which the WTP is well suited, industrial policy issues (like agriculture or tax laws), of which should be settled through negotiations, and ideological conflicts like food safety, of which are probably not susceptible to any resolution.[693] Even Jackson admits that WTO members "rely too heavily on adjudication" instead of seeking negotiated solutions."[694] The corporate executives in the Transatlantic Business Dialogue appealed to the U.S. and the EU "to consider much more carefully" whether to launch dispute cases and to consider alternatives such as mediation and arbitration outside the WTO.[695]

These proposals tend to ignore the way the sole existence of the dispute-settlement body can influence such procedures. A complainant county which expects to win at the WTO is party is unlikely to accept a compromise which offers far less than the likely ruling of a WTP panel. It will be tempted to use the threat of a WTO complaint as a bargaining chip to gain more concessions than it would have received without such leverage. However, the other side knows that filing a complaint would delay the resolution of the conflict for several years and need not necessarily result in forced compliance. It might therefore choose a tough position even at the risk of a WTO case. As trade talks

[691] Jagdish Bhagwati, "The Unwinnable War," Financial Times, January 29, 2002.
[692] Jackson 2000, p. 195.
[693] Hufbauer/Neumann 2002.
[694] Guy de Jonquières, "Rules to Fight By," Financial Times, March 25, 2000.
[695] "Bad Losers Cast Gloom over WTO's Disputes Procedure," Financial Times, December 6, 2000. See also Blinken 2001, p. 46.

usually involve "saber-rattling brinkmanship,"[696] the prospect of damaging the trade organization itself is unlikely to hold the parties back.

The only way to neutralize the impact of the WTO is agreeing before the start of the talks on a "peace clause" that nobody will file any complaints. Such a clause was part of the compromise in the Uruguay Round, and will expire in 2003. It prevented high-profile trade disputes on agriculture, but did not result in a negotiated liberalization. Still, Bergsten proposes that the U.S. and the EU "should broaden their 'peace clause' on agriculture by declaring a three-year freeze on all retaliatory actions and complaints in additional sectors" – to avoid disturbances during the Doha Round.[697]

How did the WTO affect the transatlantic trade disputes of the past decade? It is clear in retrospect that the increase in conflict was caused by the new opportunity to bring old pent-up complaints from the GATT era to the new DSB. Unfortunately, the issues left over from GATT were by definition politically particularly sensitive and hard to solve. They would have tested the limits of the WTO in the best of times, but as the initial major cases for a young institution, they were particularly bad. Because compliance was so difficult for the EU and patience in the U.S. had worn so thin, the banana and beef disputes put the WTO on the path of trade retaliation, where it need not had to go. A few simple commercial cases could have established a pattern of compliance and perhaps of positive compensation through tariff cuts. The irresponsible decision by EU Commissioner Brittan to retaliate with the FSC complaint made matters worse and turned a facility of conciliation into a battlefield for "aggressive multilateralism."[698]

These were particular mistakes by decision-makers on both sides. The WTO can contribute in a systemic way to transatlantic tensions by reducing the cost of escalation. Trade conflicts before the GATT had no rules and often resulted in all-out trade wars. The GATT created a legal framework for trade policy while still leaving plenty of room for unilateral action, such as the Section 301 provisions of the U.S. trade laws. The WTO, however, regulates the timing and the amount of any retaliation, and therefore makes it seemingly less risky to hurt your trading partners with a domestically opportune policy measure. In the banana case, the EU drove U.S. negotiators berserk by exploiting every loophole and taking advantage of every delay. Such an irritation is not only annoying; it can carry heavy political costs for a government and might undermine the standing of the WTO. The Clinton administration felt it had to do something against the EU to preserve its credibility vis-à-vis Congress, even if it was not authorized by the WTO. Its decision to breach the limits of WTO

[696] Reginald Dale, "Those Self-Defeating Trade Squabbles," IHT, September 12, 2000.
[697] Bergsten 2001, p. 25.
[698] Reinhardt 1999.

rules and to press ahead with sanctions before they were authorized was a logical and understandable response to the EU delaying tactics. Given the length of WTO procedures, a country can easily be taken advantage of if it acts to responsibly.

Similarly, one can argue that the Bush Jr.'s administration decision to impose steel tariffs in the spring of 2002 was also motivated by the expectation that the EU would complain at the WTO but do nothing else. The tariffs were intended to be challenged and they were limited to three years, with the biggest effect in the first year. With a WTO case taking two years, the White House would have a good excuse in 2004 to remove the already modest tariffs and blame the WTO. However, the European Commission, prodded on by member states and anti-American public opinion, did not play along. It demanded immediate compensation and when the U.S. refused, it found a clause in the treaty that appeared to justify retaliation even before a panel authorizes any counter-measures.[699] In both cases, such dramatic steps were necessary to stop the other side from exploiting the WTO procedures. It also raised tensions and turned legal proceedings into a game of brinkmanship.

Another problem is the rigid timetables of WTO procedures that sometimes force governments into belligerent actions they would otherwise not take. This includes the publication of sanctions lists while negotiations are still under way.[700] The practice of leaking panel report before they are officially published also makes the process more political and therefore combative.

The banana and steel case suggest that the WTO would benefit from quicker dispute-settlement procedures, particularly in politically sensitive cases. A drastic reduction could affect the quality of the jurisdiction, though the EU's reaction to the U.S. steel tariffs seemed to provide for the possibility for a temporary injunction that could help to contain some conflicts. As the WTO develops a track record of compliance, countries might be more willing to accept the fact that sometimes a defendant will not comply because of massive domestic resistance. If such an outcome does not result in a barrage of charge and counter-charge, as it did on bananas, beef and later on steel, it could become easier to shift from retaliation to positive forms of compensation.

Yet all these developments depend on the political will of the WTO members, and particularly the U.S. and the EU, to make the system work. With all its faults, there is no alternative in sight. Still, the inherent contradictions of a trade organization that is built on mercantilist pillars without enforcement powers will not be so ease to overcome.

---

[699] Guy de Joncquières, "Waging a Trade War By the Book," Financial Times, April 22, 2002

[700] "Bad Losers Cast Gloom over WTO's Disputes Procedure," Financial Times, December 6, 2000.

CHAPTER 8: CONCLUSIONS

At the end of the 20th century the trade relationship between the United States and the European Union was battered, but not broken. [701] The optimism following the conclusion of the Uruguay Round and the launch of the WTO had given way to growing concerns that the increase in bilateral disputes and falling public support for free trade in the U.S. and the EU could lead to a new tide of protectionism.

These concerns are somewhat justified, but generally overstated. The surveyed literature on trade issues can remain a source of controversy and conflict between the Atlantic partners. Nothing indicates a massive breakdown of the mutually beneficial economic relationship that could result in a dangerous spiral of rising import barriers and falling trade volume similar to the 1930s.

The main thesis of this study is the inverse relationship between the importance of an issue and the intensity of conflict and the collected evidence in the subsequent chapters suggests that the self-correcting mechanisms of the larger transatlantic partnership are strong enough to keep even powerful forces of conflict generation in check. The inverse relationship could be observed throughout the whole period. The pettiness of the actual disputes was not coincidental, but a salient feature of the transatlantic relationship. Whenever there was much at stake, the political leadership managed to resolve or at least contain the conflicts.

Trade liberalization came to a standstill at the end of 1997 when the financial services agreement was signed, but none of the subsequent disputes, such as the Helms-Burton and the d'Amato bills, aircraft subsidies and hush kit bans, the EU banana regime and the ban on hormone-treated beef, and the dispute over U.S. foreign-sales corporations, led to substantial new trade barriers.

Policy-makers on both sides pursued these narrow issues for domestic reasons but underestimated the damage for the transatlantic relationship. The accumulation of trade disputes caused far more acrimony between the U.S. and Europe than it was though possible and it was a factor in the failure to launch another trade round as a successor to the Uruguay Round Agreement. Still, the actual economic damage for businesses and consumers were quite small, and the political fallout was contained through often-intensive initiative efforts of damage control. Even at their height, these disputes covered at most five percent of the overall relationship.

---

[701] The 21st century started officially on January 1, 2001, which was effectively the end of the Clinton administration and therefore coincides with the period of investigation for this dissertation. The belief that the turn of the century came a year earlier is widespread, but mistaken.

The creation of the WTO in 1995 changed the rules of the game, though not always to the better. By creating an orderly venue to pursue trade complaints, the WTO dispute-settlement mechanism actually encouraged conflict. By making tit-for-tat retaliation the instrument of choice for the winner in a dispute, it made trade restriction rather then trade expansion the main consequence of dispute settlements. Left unchecked, such a dynamics could have resulted in escalating trade wars between the U.S. and the EU. As the problem was recognized, leaders on both sides learned to become more cautious in their use of the WTO. This restrained approach was well demonstrated in the explosive case of the foreign-sales corporations, where the WTO ruling could have otherwise resulted in a massive loss of bilateral trade.

In the early years of the 21st century, the state of transatlantic trade relations is therefore like the proverbial glass that can be called half empty or half full. On one hand, the U.S. and the EU have developed the most intense, most profitable, most equal and in many ways most harmonious trade relationship in world history. Successive trade rounds have lowered tariffs to such a low level that they hardly effect business decisions. U.S. and European companies increasingly treat the two economic areas as one huge market, with all the benefits for economies of scale and diversity of products. Prodded on by business leaders, U.S. and EU negotiators chipped away from old trade and regulatory barriers and prevented the creation of new ones in the sectors of the so-called new economy. The leadership on both sides also maintained a broad public consensus in favor of maintaining and even strengthening transatlantic trade ties, which is not the case when it comes to trade between industrialized and developing countries. All this was certainly not an unqualified success, but still an impressive achievement.

The process of market integration is far from complete, however – not even the EU has yet fully created the single market pledged in the Single European Act of 1985. In the transatlantic arena, the ambitious goals of a new institutional economic framework discussed repeatedly in the 1990s never materialized. The U.S. and the EU are still far away from realizing their goal of uninhibited free trade, even in manufacturing and services. In the most sensitive areas like agriculture and audio-visual products, the two sides were still as far apart at the end of the decade as at its beginning. The domestic dynamics of trade policy did not change. When domestic constituencies pleaded for trade protection, no transatlantic coalition could match their power, whether the issue was the banana war or the imposition of steel tariff.

Anyone observing the potential of total trade liberalization between the U.S. and Europe will tend to see the glass as half empty. There is so much to be gained through the total elimination of tariffs and a removal of other barriers, with so little political and economic costs overall, that transatlantic trade looks like one big lost opportunity. This sobering conclusion would apply even if the

U.S. and the EU were not caught in any actual trade dispute. The main obstacles to free trade are in areas of non-dispute, of those thousands of small barriers and distortions which nobody complains about because they have learned to live with it or are not even aware of the unfulfilled commercial potential.[702]

Trade disputes only affect narrow slices of the trade relationship. This is the logical consequence of the inverse relationship between their intensity and their importance. As the *Economist* demonstrated, "Like an old married couple, the Americans and Europeans bicker about relatively minor issues but make sure that their broader trade relationship does not break down."[703] Once a dispute grows into a larger dimension and starts to affect major economic interests, a solution is often found. This was the case with Airbus and is still possible for the fight over the FSC. The containment disputes, however, often results in the accommodation of trade barriers, not their removal; they become part of the vast landscape of harmonious protectionism. This scenario is the most likely and is perhaps even the least bad outcome of the smoldering transatlantic dispute over food safety regulation and gene-altered crops.

Yet transatlantic trade disputes over import barriers and other trade distortions are not benign. Due to the mercantilist logic that still prevails in the GATT and the WTO, they usually result in tit-for-tat retaliation in form of additional trade barriers. In the 50 years of GATT and the WTO, trade sanctions have been rare and usually minor, though there is a danger that they could proliferate under the WTO dispute-settlement mechanism. In the words of an Austrian economist, "the general prevalence of, or the perceived likelihood of getting caught in, such disputes, might well act like a permanent trade restriction."[704] One of the most crucial questions in international trade policy will be whether the two WTO members most often involved in trade complaints will succeed either to create a culture of compliance with rulings, as they promised in the New Transatlantic Agenda of 1998,[705] or turn the negative trade sanction into a positive sanction, i.e. compensatory measures in form of tariff reductions.

It may not be so easy to change the dynamics of trade disputes. There was hope in the first year of the presidency of George W. Bush that the excellent working relationship between Lamy and Zoellick could end the trade tensions of the late Clinton era. Yet once again, domestic pressures were more powerful than enlightened statesmanship. Through the imposition of steel tariffs in the spring of 2002, the White House willingly risked a major dispute with the EU in

[702] Gary Hufbauer cite the example of E-Commerce, which is less developed in Europe because of taxes and high delivery costs – "but since the commerce never existed, it is not much missed by potential sellers." Hufbauer/Neumann 2002.

[703] "Dangerous Activities," *Economist*, May 9, 2002.

[704] Kohler 2002, p. 7.

[705] Petersmann 2001, p. 76.

order to improve its electoral chances and shore up its coalitions in Congress. These pressures are not likely to weaken. With most internationally oriented business interests generally satisfied with the status quo, they are spending less effort on trade policy, leaving more room for lobbies with a protectionist agenda.

Accordingly, the more important question on the future management of trade disputes is not whether they result in higher or lower tariffs, but whether they reduce or enhance the ability to cooperate in larger trade negotiations. If the U.S. and the EU get used to take trade complaints routinely to the WTO for settlement through emotionally detached litigation, these disputes may lose their trouble-making potential. This is easier in purely commercial issues of market access (even though they can also become emotionally charged, as the banana case showed) than in the more complex issues of industrial policy and ideology.[706] There is just no way that U.S. or EU leaders will calmly accept an adverse ruling by a WTO panel on such sensitive domestic issues as genetic engineering, farm subsidies, audio-visual products or anti-dumping. Not even negotiations on the highest level are likely to remove these types of deeply entrenched trade barriers. The best solution seems to be to let ideological disputes run their course, managing and damping their economic fallout, but not devoting extraordinary official effort to finding a swift solution.[707]

The ninth trade round under GATT launched in Doha in 2001 is therefore bound to be followed by more. In order to succeed at all, the agenda at Doha has to exclude a wide range of issues. One of the main motivations for another trade round was the U.S. push to wean the EU of its addiction to agricultural subsidies. Yet at the turn of the century, the virus has crossed the Atlantic. The 2002 farm bill brought U.S. agricultural support close to EU levels that had been significantly reduced in previous years. This development might help to defuse transatlantic tensions by making the U.S. more tolerant of EU policies. It would save the trade round from a repeat of the Seattle scenario, but it also undermines the global formula for the next trade round. As Cancun demonstrated, developing countries feel that they got a raw deal in the Uruguay Round and will insist on significant improvements in market access to the industrialized countries in their most competitive industries – agriculture and textile. In its "anything but arms" proposal, the EU has offered to open these markets to the 48 poorest countries, which are mostly in Africa, but not to the economic heavyweights in the Third World. Since the U.S. seems even more reluctant to trade liberalization in either sector, the chances for a grand deal between North and South look dim.

---

[706] See the categorization of trade disputes in Hufbauer/Neumann 2002.

[707] Ibid.

As multilateral trade agreements become increasingly difficult to reach, the hopes for further trade liberalization might shift even more on to regional trade agreements (RTA). Even so, the hopes to establish a Free Trade Area of the Americas (FTAA) by 2005 are bound to encounter the same obstacles as the Doha round: U.S. reluctance to open its textile and agricultural markets will only harden Brazilian opposition to open up its own markets to U.S. corporations. The EU, meanwhile, has already reached preferential trade deals with almost all counties in the neighborhood and does not have much to gain through special deals with Asia. If the multilateral process stalls, it will probably rekindle interest in a Transatlantic Free Trade Area (TAFTA), the project shelved in the 1990s because it interfered with WTO negotiations and was bound to fail over agriculture. Given the tremendous potential of further trade liberalization and a mutual comprehension of the domestic political constraints to total free trade, a pragmatic transatlantic deal involving the elimination of most industrial tariffs and behind-the-border barriers might be a powerful second-best solution in the absence of future multilateral agreements. As part of TAFTA, the U.S. and the EU might also create a bilateral dispute-settlement mechanism that while not quite as ambitious and judicial as the WTO, it is still more binding than informal diplomatic negotiations.

With transatlantic trade relations in a constant state of flux, it will take many years before on can judge the longer-term effects of U.S. and European trade policies during the Clinton era. The success or failure of the Doha Round, the future of the WTO and the overall transatlantic relationship will all influence the subsequent evaluation of the agreements and disputes of the 1990s. It will also be important to watch whether the disagreements over GMO and other consumer-related issues will come to dominate the agenda or remain an important side issue. On the academic front, more work is needed on the role of the WTO dispute settlement mechanism and the interaction between regionalism and multilateralism in international trade agreements. Longer-term economic trends will determine whether the transatlantic trade and investment relationship will remain the cornerstone of the global economy, or be gradually overshadowed by expanding trade relationships of both U.S. and EU with East Asia and other emerging markets.

LIST OF ABBREVIATIONS

ACP	African, Caribbean and Pacific (countries)
AIG	American International Group
BSE	Bovine Spongiform Encephalopathy
CAP	Common Agricultural Policy
CDA	Cuban Democracy Act
CJD	Creutzfeldt-Jakob Disease
CTBT	Comprehensive Test Ban Treaty
DES	Diethyl Stilboestrol
DG	Directorate-General
DSM	Dispute-Settlement Mechanism
DSU	Dispute-Settlement Understanding
EABC	European-American Business Council
EC	European Community
ECJ	European Court of Justice
ECSC	European Coal and Steel Community
EEC	European Economic Community
EMS	European Monetary System
EMU	Economic and Monetary Union
EPU	European Payment Union
ERM	Exchange-Rate Mechanism
ETI	Extraterritorial Income Exclusion (Act)
EU	European Union
FAO	Food and Agricultural Organization
FATF	Financial Action Task Force
FDA	Food and Drug Administration
FDI	Foreign Direct Investment
FSC	Foreign Sales Corporation
FTAA	Free Trade Area of the Americas
FTC	Federal Trade Commission
GATS	General Agreement on Trade in Services
GATT	General Agreement on Tariffs and Trade
GDP	Gross Domestic Product
GMO	Genetically-Modified Organism
ICAO	International Civil Aviation Organization
ICC	International Criminal Court
ILSA	Iran Libya Sanctions Act
IMF	International Monetary Fund
IT	Information Technology
ITC	International Trade Commission
ITO	International Trade Organization

LCA	Large Commercial Aircraft
LTCM	Long-Term Capital Management
MAI	Multilateral Agreement on Investments
MDD	McDonnell Douglas
MFN	Most Favored Nation
MRA	Mutual Recognition Agreement
NAFTA	North American Free Trade Area
NASA	National Aeronautics and Space Administration
NATO	North Atlantic Treaty Organization
NIC	Newly Industrialized Country
NTA	New Transatlantic Agenda
NTM	New Transatlantic Marketplace
OECD	Organization for Economic Cooperation and Development
OMB	Office of Management and Budget
OSHA	Occupational Safety and Health Administration
PNTR	Permanent Normal Trade Relations
PTT	Post, Telephone and Telegraph
RTAA	Reciprocal Trade Agreements Act
SCM	Subsidies and Countervailing Measures
SEA	Single European Act
SPS	Sanitary and Phytosanitary (agreement)
TABD	Transatlantic Business Dialogue
TACD	Transatlantic Consumer Dialogue
TAFTA	Transatlantic Free Trade Area
TALD	Transatlantic Labor Dialogue
TBR	Trade Barrier Regulation
TEP	Transatlantic Economic Partnership
TPA	Trade Promotion Authority
TRIMS	Trade-Related Investment Measures
TRIPS	Trade-Related Intellectual Property Rights
U.N.	United Nations
U.S.	United States
USTR	United States Trade Representative
VER	Voluntary Export Restraints
WGIC	Wheat Gluten Industry Council
WHO	World Health Organization
WTO	World Trade Organization

BIBLIOGRAPHY

Aiginger, Karl and Michael Landesmann. 2002. "Competitive Economic Performance: The European View." Paper presented at Conference on Transatlantic Perspectives on US-EU Economic Relations, John. F. Kennedy School of Government, Harvard University, April 11-12, 2002. www.ksg.harvard.edu/cbg/us-eu_conference

Baily, Martin Neil. 2002. "The New Economy in Europe and the United States." Paper presented at Conference on Transatlantic Perspectives on US-EU Economic Relations, John. F. Kennedy School of Government, Harvard University, April 11-12, 2002. www.ksg.harvard.edu/cbg/us-eu_conference

Baldwin, Robert E. 1985. *The Political Economy of U.S. Import Policy.* Cambridge, MA: MIT Press.

Baldwin, Robert E. and Christopher S. Magee. 2000. *Congressional Trade Votes: From NAFTA Approval to Fast-Track Defeat.* Washington, DC: Institute for International Economics.

Barfield, Claude E. 2001. *Free Trade, Sovereignty, Democracy: The Future of the World Trade Organization.* Washington, DC: American Enterprise Institute.

Baumgartner, Frank R. and Beth L. Leech. 1998. *Basic Interests: The Importance of Groups in Politics and in Political Science.* Princeton, NJ: Princeton University Press.

Bergsten, Fred C. 1999. "America and Europe: Clash of the Titans?" *Foreign Affairs* Volume 78, No.2 (March/April 1999): 20-34.

Bersten, Fred C. 2001. "America's Two-Front Economic Conflict." *Foreign Affairs* Volume 80, No. 2 (March/April 2001): 16-27.

Bignami, Francesca, and Steve Charnovitz. 2001. "Transatlantic Civil Society Dialogues." In: Mark A. Pollack and Gregory C. Shaffer. *Transatlantic Governance in the Global Economy.* Lanham, MD: Rowman & Littlefield Publishers.

Blackwill, Robert D. and Kristin Archick. 1998."U.S.-European Economic Relations and World Trade." Speech at a conference by the Council of Foreign Relations on "The Asia Crisis" Economic and Political Implications", New York, April 15, 1998. www.ciaonet.org/conf/blr01

Blinken, Anthony J. 2001. "The False Crisis over the Atlantic." *Foreign Affairs* Volume 80, No. 3 (May/June 2001): 35-48.

Borrell, Brent. 1999. "Bananas: Straightening out bent ideas of trade as aid." Paper presented at the Conference on Agriculture and the New Trade Agenda in the 2000 WTO Negotiations, October 1-2, 1999, Geneva, Switzerland. http://wbln0018.worldbank.org/Trade/DECagridoc.nsf/ConferencesGeneva/D46C8E42B2CC816E852568A3004FB32A/$FILE/borrell_banana.pdf

Brittan, Sir Leon. 1998. "EU-US Relations: Building the Transatlantic Economic Partnership." Address to the Center of European Policy Studies, 14 September 1998 www.ciaonet.org/pbei/ceps/brl01

Brumbaugh, David L. 2000. "RS20571: The Foreign Sales Corporation (FSC) Tax Benefit for Exporting and the WTO." CRS Report for Congress, Updated October 11, 2000. http://cnie.org/NLE/CRSreports/international/inter-61.cfm

Brumbaugh, David L. 2002. "Export Tax Benefits and the WTO: Foreign Sales Corporations and the Extraterritorial Replacement Provisions." CRS Report for Congress, Updated January 24, 2002. http://www.cnie.org/nle/crsreports/economics/econ-113.pdf

Burtless, Gary, Robert Z. Lawrence, Robert E. Litan and Robert J. Shapiro. 1998. *Globaphobia: Confronting Fears About Open Trade.* Washington, DC/New York, NY: Brookings Institution, Progressive Policy Institute, Twentieth Century Fund.

Busch, Marc L. 1999. *Trade Warriors: States, Firms and Strategic-Trade Policy in High-Technology Competition.* Cambridge (UK): Cambridge University Press.

Carter, Ralph G. 2001. *Contemporary Cases in U.S. Foreign Policy: From Terrorism to Trade*. Washington, DC: CQPress.

Calleo, David. 2001. *Rethinking Europe's Future.* A Century Foundation Book. Princeton, NJ: Princeton University Press.

Charnovitz, Steve. 2001. "Rethinking Trade Sanctions." *American Journal of International Law*, vol. 95/4 (October 2001): 792-832.

Clinton, Bill and Gore, Al 1992. "Position Paper" Clinton/Gore on Trade." www.ibibilio.org/pub/docs/speeches/clinton.dir/c.98.txtp

Cohen, Stephen D., Joel R. Paul, and Robert A. Blecker. 1996. *Fundamentals of U.S. Foreign Trade Policy: Economics Politics, Laws, and Issues*. Boulder, CO: Westview Press.

Conybeare, John. 1987. *Trade Wars: The Theory and Practice of International Commercial Rivalry*. New York, NY: Columbia University Press.

Cowles, Maria Green. 2001. "The Transatlantic Business Dialogue: Transforming the New Transatlantic Dialogue." In: Mark A. Pollack and Gregory C. Shaffer. *Transatlantic Governance in the Global Economy.* Lanham, MD: Rowman & Littlefield Publishers.

Cunningham, Richard, Peter Lichtenbaum and Julie Wolf. 2000. *The EU and World Trade*. London: Centre for European Reform (CER).

Daalder, Ivo H. "Are the United States and Europe Heading for Divorce?" *International Affairs* Volume 77, No. 3 (2001): 553-567.

Destler, I.M. 1995. *American Trade Politics* (3rd Edition). Washington, DC: Institute for International Economics.

Deutsch, Karl W. et al. 1957. *Political Community and the North Atlantic Area.* Princeton, NJ: Princeton University Press.

Devuyst, Youri. 2001. "Transatlantic Competition Relations." In: Mark A. Pollack and Gregory C. Shaffer. *Transatlantic Governance in the Global Economy.* Lanham, MD: Rowman & Littlefield Publishers.

Dinan, Desmond 1999. *Ever Closer Union: An Introduction to European Integration.* 2nd ed. Boulder, CO: Lynne Rienner Publishers.

Dobson, Wendy and Pierre Jacquet. 1998. *Financial Services Liberalization in the WTO.* Washington, DC: Institute for International Economics.

Dryden, Steve 1995. *Trade Warriors: USTR and the American Crusade for Free Trade.* New York/Oxford: Oxford University Press.

Duffield, John S. 2001. "Transatlantic Relations after the Cold War: Theory, Evidence and the Future." *International Studies Perspectives* (2001) 2:93-115.

Echols, Marsha, A. 1998. "Food Safety Regulation in the European Union and the United States: Different Cultures, Different Laws." *Columbia Journal of European Law*, Summer 1998. 4:5-25.

Egan, Michelle. 2001. "Mutual Recognition and Standard Setting: Public and Private Strategies for Governing Markets." In: Mark A. Pollack and Gregory C. Shaffer. *Transatlantic Governance in the Global Economy.* Lanham, MD: Rowman & Littlefield Publishers.

Eichengreen, Barry (ed.). 1998. *Transatlantic Economic Relations in the Post-Cold War Era.* New York, NY: Council of Foreign Relations.

Eizenstat, Stuart 1997. Remarks before the U.S. House of Representatives Ways and Means Trade Subcommittee of the Under Secretary for Economic, Business and Agricultural Affairs, Washington, DC, October 23, 1997. www.state.gov/www/policy_remarks/971023_eizen_house.html

Ethier, Wilfred J. 2001. "Punishments and Dispute Settlement in Trade Agreements." Copenhagen: Economic Policy Research Unit (EPRU) Working Paper Series 2001-14. www.econ.ku.dk/epru/files/wp/WEB-blaa-2001-14.pdf

Fearson, James D. 1994. "Domestic Political Audiences and the Escalation of International Disputes." *The American Political Science Review* 88/3: 577-592.

Feldstein, Martin 1997. "EMU and International Conflict" *Foreign Affairs* Volume 76 No.6 (November/December 1997).

Fischer, Thomas C. 1995. *The Europeanization of America: What Americans Need to Know about the European Union.* Durham, NC: Carolina Academic Press.

Fischer, Thomas C. 2000. *The United States, the European Union, and the "Globalization" of World Trade: Allies or Adversaries?* Westport CT: Quorum Books.

Frankel, Jeffrey A. and Orszag, Peter R. 2002. *American Economic Policy in the 1990s*. Cambridge, MA: MIT Press.

Freeman, Richard B. 2002. "Can the Egalitarian EU Compete with the Market-Driven U.S.?" Paper presented at the Conference on Transatlantic Perspectives on US-EU Economic Relations, John. F. Kennedy School of Government, Harvard University, April 11-12, 2002. www.ksg.harvard.edu/cbg/us-eu_conference

Frey, Eric. 1993. *Clintons Amerika: Präsident einer neuen Generation.* Frankfurt: Eichborn Verlag.

Frey, Eric 2002. "The Marshall Plan As a Model: Can Massive Aid Resolve International Conflicts?" Second Marshall Anniversary Lecture, University of New Orleans, March 6, 2002.

Frost, Ellen L. 1997. *Transatlantic Trade: A Strategic Agenda*. Washington, DC: Institute for International Economics.

Garten, Jeffrey E. 1992. *A Cold Peace: America, Japan, Germany, and the Struggle for Supremacy*. New York, NY: Times Books.

Garten, Jeffrey E. 1995. "Is America Abandoning Multilateral Trade?" *Foreign Affairs* Volume 74 No. 6 (November/December 1995): 50-63.

Gaster, R. and C. Prestowitz. 1994. *Shrinking the Atlantic: Europe and the American Economy*. Washington, DC: Economic Strategy Institute and North Atlantic Research Inc.

Gelb Bernard A. 2001. "RS20319: Telecommunications Services Trade and the WTO Agreement." CRS Report for Congress, Updated January 10, 2001. www.cnie.org/nle/crsreports/finance/fin-6.cfm

Gibson, Martha L. 2000. *Conflict Amid Consensus in American Trade Policy.* Washington, DC: Georgetown University Press.

Gilpin, Robert 1987. *The Political Economy of International Relations.* Princeton, NJ: Princeton University Press.

Gilpin, Robert 2000. *The Challenge of Global Capitalism: The World Economy in the 21st Century*. Princeton, NJ: Princeton University Press.

Gilpin, Robert 2001. *Global Political Economy: Understanding the International Economic Order*. Princeton, NJ: Princeton University Press.

Gomory, Ralph E., and William J. Baumol. 2000. *Global Trade and Conflicting National Interests*. Cambridge, MA: The MIT Press.

Gordon, Bernhard K. 2001 *America's Trade Follies: Turning Economic Leadership into Strategic Weakness.* London and New York: Routledge.

Grossman, Gene. 1980. "Border Tax Adjustments: Do They Distort Trade?" *Journal of International Economics*. Volume 10 No. 1 (February 1980).

Haass, Richard N. (ed). 1998. *Economic Sanctions and American Diplomacy.* Washington. DC: Council on Foreign Relations Book.

Haass, Richard N. (ed.) 1999. *Transatlantic Tensions: The United States, Europe and Problem Countries.* Washington, DC: Brookings Institution Press.

Haney, Patrick, J, Jeanne A.K. Hey and Laura Neack. 1995. *Foreign Policy Analysis: Continuity and Change in Its Second Generation.* Englewood Cliffs, NJ: Prentice Hall.

Haney, Patrick J. and Walt Vanderbush. 2001. "The Helms-Burton Act: Congress and Cuba Policy". In: Ralph G. Carter. *Contemporary Cases in U.S. Foreign Policy: From Terrorism to Trade.* Washington, DC: CQPress.

Hanrahan, Charles E. 1999. "RS20130: The U.S.-European Union Banana Dispute." Congressional Research Service (CRS), Resources, Science, and Industry Division. Updated December 9, 1999. http://cnie.org/NLE/CRSreports/Economics/econ-39.cfm

Hanrahan, Charles E. 2000. "The European Union's Ban on Hormone-Treated Meat" CRS Report for Congress, Updated December 19, 2000. http://cnie.org/NLE/CRSreports/agriculture/ag-63.cfm

Hanrahan, Charles E. 2001. "U.S. European Agricultural Trade: Food Safety and Biotechnology Issues." CRS Report for Congress, Updated January 17, 2001. http://www.cnie.org/nle/ag-51.html

Hanson, Brian T.1998. "What Happened to Fortress Europe?: External Trade Policy Liberalization in the European Union" *International Organization* Volume 52 No. 1 (Winter 1998): 55-85

Henning, C. Randall and Pier Carlo Padoan. 2000. *Transatlantic Perspectives on the Euro.* Washington, DC: Brookings Institution Press.Hilf, Meinhard. 1995. "The ECJ's Opinion 1/94 on the WTO - No Surprise, but Wise?" *European Journal of International Law* Vol. 6 No. 2 (1995): 245-259. www.ejil.org/journal/Vol6/No2/art3.html

Hindley, Brian 1999. "New Institutions for Transatlantic Trade?" *International Affairs* (London) Volume 75 No. 1: 45-60.

Hufbauer, Gary Clyde. 2002. "The FSC Case: Background and Implications". Washington, DC: Institute for International Economics, February 27, 2002. www.iie.com/paper/hufbauer0102.htm

Hufbauer, Gary Clyde and Ben Goodrich. 2002. "Time for a Grand Bargain in Steel?" Washington, DC: Institute for International Economics Policy Briefs. www.iie.com/policybriefs/news02-1.html

Hufbauer, Gary Clyde and Frederic Neumann. 2002. "Trade and Investment: An American Perspective." Paper presented at the Conference on "Transatlantic Perspectives on US-EU Economic Relations," John. F. Kennedy School of Government, Harvard University, April 11-12, 2002. www.ksg.harvard.edu/cbg/us-eu_conference

Huntington, Samuel P. 1996. *The Clash of Civilizations and the Remaking of World Order.* New York, NY: Simon & Schuster.

Mayer, Frederick. W. 1992. "Managing Domestic Differences in International Negotiations: The Strategic Use of Internal Side-Payments." *International Organization*, Volume 46, Issue 4 (Autumn 1992): 793-818.

Meltzer, Allan. 2000. Alan International Financial Institution Advisory Commission (Meltzer Commission) Report (March 2000). www.house.gov/jec/imf/meltzer.htm

Jackson, John H. 2000. "The Role and Effectiveness of the WTO Dispute Settlement Mechanism." Brookings Trade Forum 2000:179-219. http://muse.jhu.edu/demo/btf/2000.1jackson.html

Joffe, Josef. 1997. "How America Does It." *Foreign Affairs* (September/ October 1997).

Jonquières, Guy de 2001. "How can transatlantic trade disputes be avoided?" (Author's copy)

Kahler, M. 1995. *Regional Futures and Transatlantic Economic Relations*. New York: Council of Foreign Relations.

Kaplan, Edward S. 1996. *American Trade Policy, 1923-1995*. Westport, CT: Greenwood Press.

Kasteele, Adelien van de 1998. "The Banana Chain: The macroeconomics of the Banana Trade." Paper on behalf of IUF, Amsterdam, February 1998, presented at the International Banana Conference, Brussels 4-6 May 1998. http://bananas.agoranet.be/MacroEconomics.htm

Kennedy, Paul M. 1988. *The Rise and Fall of the Great Powers: Economic Change and Military Conflict from 1500 to 2000*. New York, NY: Random House.

Keohane, Robert O, and Joseph Nye. 1977. *Power and Interdependence*. Boston: Little, Brown.

Keohane, Robert O. 1980. "The Theory of Hegemonic Stability and Changes in International Economic Regimes, 1967-1977." In: O. Holsti, R. Siverson and A. George. *Changes in the International System,* Boulder, CO: Westview Press. 131-162.

Keohane, Robert. 1984. *After Hegemony: Cooperation and Discord in the World Political Economy*. Princeton, NJ: Princeton University Press.

Kerremans, Bart. 2000. "Domestic Politics and the Definition of Transatlantic Trade Relations: Is Security the Missing Link?" 41st Annual Convention of the International Studies Association, Los Angeles CA, March 14-18, 2000.www.ciaonet.org.isa/keb01

Kindleberger, Charles P. 1970. *Power and Money: The Economics of International Politics and the Politics of International Economics*. New York, NY: Basic Books.

Kindleberger, Charles P. 1975. "The Rise of Free Trade in Western Europe." *The Journal of Economic History* Volume 35 No. 1: 20-55.

Knauss, Jody and David Trubek. 2001. "The Transatlantic Labor Dialogue: Minimal Action in a Weak Structure." In: Mark A. Pollack and Gregory C. Shaffer. *Transatlantic Governance in the Global Economy.* Lanham, MD: Rowman & Littlefield Publishers.

Kohler, Wilhelm. 2002. "Issues of US-EU Trade Policy." Comment on Papers by Hufbauer/Neumann and Sapir at the Conference on "Transatlantic Perspectives on US-EU Economic Relations", John. F. Kennedy School of Government, Harvard University, April 11-12, 2002.

Krasner, Stephen. 1976. "State Power and the Structure of International Relations" *World Politics* 28: 317-347.

Krueger, Anne (ed.) 1996. *The Political Economy of American Trade Policy.* Chicago, IL: The University of Chicago Press.

Krugman, Paul. 1986. *Strategic Trade Policy and the New International Economics.* Cambridge, MA: MIT Press.

Krugman, Paul. 1996. *Pop Internationalism.* Cambridge, MA: MIT Press.

Lambert, Richard. 2003. "Misunderstanding Each Other" *Foreign Affairs* Volume
82, no.2 (March/April 2003): 62-74.

Langbein, Stanley I. 2000. "United States – Tax Treatment for 'Foreign Sales Corporations." *American Journal of International Law*, Volume 94 No.3 (July 2000): 546-555.

Lovett, William A., Alfred E. Eckes Jr., and Richard L. Brinkman. 1999. *U.S. Trade Policy: History, Theory, and the WTO.* Armonk, NY/London: M.E. Sharpe.

Ludlow, Peter. 2001."Wanted: A Global Partner" *The Washington Quarterly* Volume 24, No. 3 (Summer 2001): 163-171.

Magaziner Ira, and Mark Patinkin. 1989. *The Silent War — Inside Global Business Battles Shaping America's Future.* New York: Random House.

Mathews, Jessica T. 2001. "Estranged Partners." *Foreign Policy* (November/December)2001.www.foreignpolicy.com/issue_novdec_2001/mathews.html

McGuire, Steven 1997. *Airbus Industrie: Conflict and Cooperation in US-EC Trade Relations.* Houndsmills: MacMillan Press Ltd.

McNamara, Kathleen. R. 1998. *The Currency of Ideas: Monetary Politics in the European Union.* Ithaca, NY: Cornell University Press.

Milner, Helen. 1988. *Resisting Protectionism: Global Industries and the Politics of International Trade.* Princeton, NJ: Princeton University Press.

Moravcsik, Andrew. 1997. Taking Preferences Seriously: A Liberal Theory of International Politics. *International Organisation* Volume 51 No. 4: 513-553.

Mundo, Philip A. 1999. *National Politics in a Global Economy: The Domestic Sources of U.S. Trade Policy.* Washington, DC: Georgetown University Press.

Navaretti, Giorgio Barba, Jan I. Haaland & Anthony Venables. 2002. *Multinational Corporations & Global Production Networks: The Implications for Trade Policy.* A Centre for Economic Policy Research Report prepared for the European Commission Directorate for Trade. http://www.cepr.org.uk/pubs/fdi.htm

Neal, Larry and Daniel Barbezat. 1998. *The Economics of the European Union and the Economies of Europe.* New York, NY: Oxford University Press.

Nugent, Neil. 1994. *The Government and Politics of the European Union.* (3rd ed.) Durham, NC: Duke University Press.

Nye, Joseph S Jr. 2002. *The Paradox of American Power: Why the World's Only Superpower Can't Go It Alone.* Oxford: Oxford University Press.

Olson, Mancur 1982. *The Rise and Decline of Nations: Economic Growth, Stagflation, and Social Rigidities.* New Haven, CT: Yale University Press.

Orwell, George. 1992 (1949). *Nineteen Eighty-Four.* New York: Knopf.

Patterson, Lee Ann.1997. "Agricultural Policy Reform in the European Community: A Three-Level Game Analysis." *International Organization* Volume 51 No. 1: 135-65.

Petersmann, Ernst-Ulrich. 2001. "Dispute Prevention and Dispute Settlement in the EU-US Transatlantic Partnership." In: Mark A. Pollack and Gregory C. Shaffer. *Transatlantic Governance in the Global Economy.* Lanham, MD: Rowman & Littlefield Publishers.

Peterson, John. 2001. "Get Away from Me Closer, You're Near Me Too Far: Europe and America after the Uruguay Round." In: Mark A. Pollack and Gregory C. Shaffer. *Transatlantic Governance in the Global Economy.* Lanham, MD: Rowman & Littlefield Publishers.

Pollack, Mark. A. and Gregory C. Shaffer. 2000. "Biotechnology: The Next Transatlantic Trade War?" *The Washington Quarterly* Volume 23 no.4 (Autumn 2000): 41-54.

Pollack, Mark A. and Gregory C. Shaffer. 2001 (1). "The Challenge of Reconciling Regulatory Differences: Food Safety and GMOs in the Transatlantic Relationship." In: Mark A. Pollack and Gregory C. Shaffer. *Transatlantic Governance in the Global Economy.* Lanham, MD: Rowman & Littlefield Publishers.

Pollack, Mark A and Gregory C. Shaffer. 2001 (2). *Transatlantic Governance in the Global Economy.* Lanham, MD: Rowman & Littlefield Publishers.

Pollack, Mark A. and Gregory C. Shaffer. 2001 (3). "Who Governs?" In: Mark A. Pollack and Gregory C. Shaffer. *Transatlantic Governance in the Global Economy.* Lanham, MD: Rowman & Littlefield Publishers.

Porter, Roger B. 2002. "Government-Business Relations in the United States." Paper presented at the Conference on Transatlantic Perspectives on US-EU Economic Relations, John. F. Kennedy School of Government, Harvard University, April 11-12, 2002. www.ksg.harvard.edu/cbg/us-eu_conference

Preeg, Ernest et. al. 1996. "Policy Forum: Transatlantic Free Trade." *The Washington Quarterly* Volume 19 No.2: 105-133.

Preeg, Ernest. 1998. *From Here to Free Trade: Essays in Post-Uruguay Round Trade Strategy.* Chicago, IL: The University of Chicago Press.

Prestowitz Jr., Clyde V. 1988. *Trading Places: How We Allowed Japan to Take the Lead.* New York: Basic Books.

Putnam, Robert D 1988. "Diplomacy and Domestic Politics: The Logic of Two-Level Games". *International Organization* Volume 42: 427-460.

Reinhardt, Eric 1999. "Aggressive Multilateralism: The Determinants of GATT/WTO Dispute Initiation, 1948-1998." Paper prepared for delivery at the 1999 Annual Meeting of the International Studies Association (ISA), Washington, DC. Updated March 15, 1999.http://userwww.service.emory.edu/~erein/research/initiation.pdf

Rountree, George H. "Raging Hormones: A Discussion of the World Trade Organization's Decision in the European-Union-United States Beef Dispute." *The Georgia Journal of International and Comparative Law* Volume 3 (Summer 1999).

Ruggie, John Gerard (ed.) 1993. *Multilateralism Matters: The Theory and Practice of an Institutional Form.* New York, NY: Columbia University Press.

Ruggie, John Gerard. 1994. "Third Try at World Order? America and Multilateralism after the Cold War". *Political Science Quarterly* Volume 109 No. 4 (Autumn 1994): 553-570.

Sapir, Andre. 2002. "Old and New Issues in EC-US Trade Disputes." Paper presented at the Conference on Transatlantic Perspectives on US-EU Economic Relations, John. F. Kennedy School of Government, Harvard University, April 11-12, 2002. www.ksg.harvard.edu/cbg/us-eu_conference

Schattschneider, Elmer E. 1935. *Politics, Pressure and the Tariff.* New York, NY: Prentice-Hall.

Schelling, Thomas C. (1960) 1980. *The Strategy of Conflict.* Cambridge, MA: Harvard University Press.

Schott, Jeffrey, ed. 1998. *Restarting Fast Track.* Washington, DC: Institute for International Economics.

Schott, Jeffrey J. (ed.) 2000. *The WTO After Seattle.* Washington, DC: Institute for International Economics.

Schott, Jeffrey J. 2002. "Reflections on the Doha Ministerial". *Economic Perspectives* Volume 7 No. 1 (January 2002) http://www.iie.com/papers.schott 0102.htm

Sek, Lenore. 2001. "Trade Retaliation: The 'Carousel' Approach". CRS Report for Congress, 1/8/01. www.cnie.org/nle/crsreports/economics/econ-133.cfm

Senunas, Eric. 1997. "The 1997 GATS Agreement on Basic Telecommunications:

A Triumph For Multilateralism, or the Market?" *Intellectual Property and Technology Forum at Boston College Law School* November 14, 1997. www.bc.edu/bc_org/avp/law/st_org/iptf/articles/content/1997111401.html
Sevilla, Christina R. 1998. "Explaining Patterns of GATT/WTO Trade Complaints." Weatherhead Center for International Affairs, Working Paper No. 98/1, Harvard University. www.ciaonet.org/wps/sec01/index.html
Shaffer, Gregory C. 2001. "The Blurring of the Intergovernmental: Public-Private Partnerships behind US and EC Trade Claims." In: Mark A. Pollack and Gregory C. Shaffer. *Transatlantic Governance in the Global Economy.* Lanham, MD: Rowman & Littlefield Publishers.
Shoch, James. 2001. *Trading Blows: Party Competition and U.S. Trade Policy in a Globalizing Economy.* Chapel Hill/London: The University of North Carolina Press.
Smis, Stefaan and Kim van der Borght. 1999. "The EU-U.S. Compromise on the Helms-Burton and D'Amato Acts." *American Journal of International Law* Volume 93 No.1: 227-236.
Stuermer, Michael. 2001. "Balance from Beyond the Sea." *The Washington Quarterly* Volume 24, No. 3 (Summer 2001): 145-153
Sykes, Alan O. 1999. "Regulatory Protectionism and the Law of International Trade." *University of Chicago Law Review* Volume 6 (Winter 1999).
Thurow, Lester C. 1992. *Head to Head: The Coming Economic Battle among Japan, Europe and America.* New York, NY: Morrow.
Transatlantic Business Dialogue 1997 Priorities for the Mid Year Summit. May 13, 1997. www.tabd.org/recommendations/MYM97.pdf
Transatlantic Business Dialogue 1998 Mid Year Scorecard Report. Washington, DC, May 1998. www.tabd.org/recommendations/MYM98.pdf
Transatlantic Business Dialogue 1999 Mid Year Report. Washington, DC, May 10, 1999. www.tabd.org/recommendations/MYM99.pdf
Transatlantic Business Dialogue 2000 Mid Year Report. Washington, DC, May 23, 2000. www.tabd.org/recommendations/MYM00.pdf
Transatlantic Business Dialogue 2001 Mid Year Report. Washington, DC, May 15, 2001. www.tabd.org/recommendations/MYM01.pdf
Tsebelis, George 1990. *Nested Games: Rational Choice in Comparative Politics.* Berkeley, CA: University of California Press.
Tyson, Laura D'Andrea 1992. *Who's Bashing Whom: Trade Conflict in High-Technology Industries.* Washington, DC: Institute for International Economics.
Walker, Martin. 2000. "What Europeans Think of America." *World Policy Journal* Volume 27 No. 2 (Summer 2000). www.worldpolicy.org/journal/walker.html
Wallace, William, and Jan Zielonka. 1998. "Misunderstanding Europe." *Foreign Affairs* Volume 77 No. 6 (November/December 1998).

Wallace, William. "Europe, the Necessary Partner." *Foreign Affairs* Volume 80 No. 3 (May /June 2001): 16-34

Wagleitner, Reinhold. 2002. "The American Empire of Fun: The Foreign Politics of American Pop Culture Hegemony." Presentation at the Conference on The Westernization-Americanization of Austria in the 20th Century at the University of New Orleans, May 6-8, 2002.

Walt, Stephen, 1998. "The Ties that Fray: Why Europe and America are Approaching a Parting of the Ways." *The National Interest* No. 54 (Winter 1998-99).

Waltz, Kenneth. 1979. *Theory of International Politics.* Reading, MA: Addison-Wesley.

Whitney, Merrill, E. and James D. Gaisford. 1996. "Economic Espionage as Strategic Trade Policy." *Canadian Journal of Economics*, Volume 29, Special Issue: Part 2: 627-632.

ACKNOWLEDGEMENTS

I completed most of the research and writing for this study during my stay as the Marshall Plan Anniversary Chair in Austrian Studies at the University of New Orleans in 2001/2, which was made possible through the generous financial support of the Austrian Marshall Plan Foundation. In New Orleans, Charles Hadley, Walter "Dub" Lane, Robert Dupont, Günter Bischof and Gertraud Griessner made enormous efforts to provide me with an excellent working environment and my family with a wonderful home. Gary Hufbauer from the International Institute for Economics (IIE) and Guy de Jonquières from the Financial Times gave me valuable feedback on earlier drafts. In Vienna, Helmut Kramer supported me with along the way with lots of comments and advice, and Nicole Forbes helped me enormously to prepare the manuscript for publication. I would also like to thank my wife Katinka and my children Isabel and Gideon for supporting me during all this time with so much love and enthusiasm.

Gustav Dieckheuer / Boguslaw Fiedor (eds.)

Competition, Environment and Trade in the Globalized Economy

Frankfurt am Main, Berlin, Bern, Bruxelles, New York, Oxford, Wien, 2002.
VIII, 194 pp., num. fig. and tab.
Internationale Marktwirtschaft. General Editor: Gustav Dieckheuer. Bd. 3
ISBN 3-631-39684-8 / US-ISBN 0-8204-6001-X · pb. € 39.00*

There is an ongoing discussion about causes and consequences of economic globalization. The effects of growing international trade, worldwide integration and international policy co-ordination are widespread and thus call our attention. This book focuses on four major topics of the debate: the conditions for a country's trade on worldwide growing markets for goods and capital; environmental problems caused by international economic growth; effects of increasing international competition; national macro-policies under the influence of increasing international interdependencies.

Contents: Preparing a World Antitrust Framework – An Ordoliberal Approach · Global Information Techniques and their Economic Consequences · Regional Dimensions of National Integration · Some Theoretical and Empirical Aspects of Poland's Integration in the EU

Frankfurt am Main · Berlin · Bern · Bruxelles · New York · Oxford · Wien
Distribution: Verlag Peter Lang AG
Moosstr. 1, CH-2542 Pieterlen
Telefax 00 41 (0) 32 / 376 17 27

*The €-price includes German tax rate
Prices are subject to change without notice

Homepage http://www.peterlang.de